UNDERSTANDING FINANCIAL STATEMENTS
Fourth Edition

LYN M. FRASER

Cases prepared by Aileen Ormiston

Prentice Hall, Englewood Cliffs, New Jersey 07632

Library of Congress Cataloging-in-Publication Data

Fraser, Lyn M.
    Understanding financial statements / Lyn M. Fraser ; cases
prepared by Aileen Ormiston. — 4 ed.
        p.   cm.
    Includes index.
        1.   Financial statements.   2.   Corporate reports.   I.   Title.
    HF5681.B2F764   1995
    657'.3—dc20   94–16326
                                                                                        CIP

© 1995, 1992, 1988 1984, by Prentice-Hall, Inc.

A Simon & Shuster Company

Englewood Cliffs, New Jersey 07632

Printed in the United States of America
10 9 8 7 6 5 4 3 2 1

ISBN 0-13-103078-7

PRENTICE-HALL INTERNATIONAL (UK) LIMITED, LONDON
PRENTICE-HALL OF AUSTRALIA PTY. LIMITED, SYDNEY
PRENTICE-HALL CANADA INC., TORONTO
PRENTICE-HALL HISPANOAMERICANA, S.A., MEXICO
PRENTICE-HALL OF INDIA PRIVATE LIMITED, NEW DELHI
PRENTICE-HALL OF JAPAN, INC., TOKYO
SIMON & SHUSTER ASIA PTE. LTD., SINGAPORE
EDITORA PRENTICE-HALL DO BRASIL, LTDA., RIO DE JANEIRO

Contents

Preface

When I worked on the first edition of *Understanding Financial Statements* in the early eighties, I frequently began writing very early in the morning, like five o'clock. My eight-year-old daughter Eleanor would wander out, bewildered to see me working in—what was for her—the middle of the night. For that edition, I did the original writing by hand, had the manuscript typed, and the book was typeset from my manuscript. Eleanor is now a student at Texas A&M University, majoring in international studies, and this edition will be set from my computer disk. One thing, however, has not changed: Eleanor still thinks five o'clock is the middle of the night.

NEW FEATURES OF THE FOURTH EDITION

Revolutionary changes are currently evolving in accounting education under the auspices of the Accounting Education Change Commission, which was established by the major professional accounting groups that represent both practitioners and educators. These changes will result in a new accounting curriculum which will be more oriented to what students will encounter in practice. The focus will be on helping students learn how to think and to reason through complex, real-world situations with increased emphasis on solving unstructured problems, such as cases; and using accounting information for decision-making. The objectives of this new curriculum match well the philosophy and style of this fourth edition.

One major new feature of this edition is the inclusion of mini-cases, based on corporate annual reports. These mini-cases will aid in the practical and realistic application of the concepts and analytical techniques presented in the text. The cases provide instructors and students with the opportunity for in-depth and open-ended discussions of financial reporting and the analysis of financial statement information.

A number of instructors who have used the book as a course text or supplementary text have provided helpful comments and suggestions which I have relied on extensively in revising the book to enhance its usefulness.

This edition incorporates all new requirements and changes in accounting and reporting standards, including Statement of Financial Accounting Standards No. 115, "Accounting for Certain Investments in Debt and Equity Securities."

The footnotes throughout the book contain resource listings which form the basis of a reading list to which instructors can add references based on individual course coverage.

This fourth edition includes features of earlier editions which readers have found useful: appendices on earnings quality, the analysis of segmental data, and the understanding of bank financial statements; self-tests at the end of each chapter, study questions and problems; and a Glossary of key terms used throughout the book.

The Instructor's Manual, which is available as a supplement, contains solutions to study questions, problems, and mini-cases; a sample course project with assignment, outline, and resources; and transparency masters.

USES FOR THE FOURTH EDITION

The purpose of the book is to convey to readers the conceptual background and analytical tools necessary to understand and interpret financial statements. The presentation of material and the illustrations have evolved over several editions from the comments and suggestions of the book's readers as well as from the hours that I have spent teaching courses and making presentations to business groups on financial statement analysis. The book is designed and organized to serve a wide range of purposes which include, but are not limited to:

1. Text or supplementary text for financial statement analysis courses.
2. Supplementary text for accounting, finance, and business management classes which include financial statement analysis as a course concept.
3. Study material for short courses covering the understanding of financial statements in continuing education and executive development programs.
4. Self-study guide or text material for bank credit analysis training programs.
5. Reference book for investors, creditors, and others who make decisions based on financial statement data.
6. Background material for any reader seeking a basic understanding of financial reporting.

Reviewers of earlier editions have written that the primary strengths of the book are its readability, concise coverage, and organization. I have attempted to retain those features in the fourth edition. I hope that readers will find the material accessible, relevant, and useful.

Acknowledgments

I would like to acknowledge with considerable appreciation those who have contributed to the publication of this book.

First, I would like to thank Aileen Ormiston, now a faculty member at Mesa Community College in Arizona, who prepared the cases for the fourth edition. My collaboration with Aileen began many years ago when she was a graduate student at Texas A&M University. Aileen was enormously helpful in developing the first edition of the book, including the book's mythical company, R.E.C. Inc., and much of the text's question and problem material. She consistently manages to deal with the pressures of a book's preparation and production with balance and humor.

Several individuals have made critical comments and suggestions on the manuscript. In particular, I would like to express my thanks to: Steve D. Grossman, Texas A&M University; John Aje, University of Maryland; Peter M. Bergevin, American Graduate School of International Management; Paulette Dubofsky, Texas A&M University; Janet I. Kimbrell, Oklahoma State University; S. Scott MacDonald, Texas Tech University; and William J. Ruckstuhl, the American College.

The editorial, production, and marketing departments of Prentice Hall have provided invaluable assistance at each stage of the writing and production process. In particular, I would like to thank my senior editor, Leah Jewell, and her editorial assistant, Eileen Deguzman.

The list would be incomplete without mentioning the pets in my household—Little Bit, Picadilly Circus, Babe, and RT—who trampled, squashed, crumpled, scratched, and sat on the manuscript during its various stages of preparation.

Finally, I would like to express enormous thankfulness for the love and support of my daughter Eleanor through the four editions of this book.

Lyn M. Fraser
College Station, Texas

1

Financial Statements: An Overview

"Annual reports— the yearly report, photo album, and corporate promo in one. Some trumpet the successes of the 12 months past, real or not. Others just trumpet."
—*Business Week*, "It's Corporate America's Spring Hornblowing Festival," April 12, 1993.

MAP OR MAZE

One of the major purposes of a *map* is to help its user reach a desired destination through clarity of representation. A *maze*, however, attempts to confuse its user by purposely introducing conflicting elements and complexities that prevent reaching the desired goal. Business financial statements have the potential for being both map and maze.

As a map, financial statements form the basis for understanding the financial position of a business firm and for assessing its historical and prospective financial performance. Financial statements have the capability of making clear representations of a firm's financial health, leading to informed business decisions.

Unfortunately, there are maze-like interferences in financial statement data that hinder understanding of the valuable information they contain. The sheer quantity of information contained in financial statements can be overwhelming and intimidating. Independent auditors attest to the fairness of financial statement presentation, but many lawsuits have been filed and won against accounting firms for issuing "clean" auditor reports on companies that subsequently failed. The complexity of accounting policies underlying the preparation of financial statements can lead to confusion and variations in the quality of information presented. And these rules are constantly evolving and chang-

Figure 1.1

ing. Management discretion in a number of areas influences financial statement content and presentation in ways that affect and even impede evaluation. Changing prices can erode the usefulness of financial statement numbers. Some key information needed to evaluate a company is not available in the financial statements, some is difficult to find, and much is impossible to measure.

One of the main objectives of this book is to ensure that financial statements serve as a <u>map</u>, not a maze; that they lead to a determination of the financial health of a business enterprise which is as clear as possible for purposes of making sound business decisions about the firm.

The material in this book will convey information about how to read and evaluate business financial statements. The author will attempt to present the material in a straightforward manner so that it can be readily understood by any reader, regardless of background or perspective. The book is designed for use by those who would like to learn more about the content and interpretation of financial statements for such purposes as making investment or credit decisions about a company, evaluating a firm for current or prospective employment, advancing professionally in the current business environment, or even passing an examination or course.

The reader can expect more than a dull exposition of financial data and accounting rules. Throughout these pages we will attempt with examples, illustrations, and explanations to get behind the numbers, accounting policies, and tax laws to assess how well companies are actually performing. The chapters and appendices in the book show how to approach financial statements in order to obtain practical, useful information from their content. Although the examples in the book are based on corporate financial statements, the discussions also apply to the financial statements of small business firms that use generally accepted accounting principles.

The emphasis throughout the book is on *analysis*. We will break financial statements into parts for individual study in order that we might better understand the whole of their content as a map to intelligent decision-making.

Organization

Chapter 1 provides an overview of financial statements and presents approaches to overcoming some of the challenges, obstacles, and blind alleys that may confront the user of financial statements: 1. the volume of information, with examples of specific problems encountered in such areas as the auditor's report and the management discussion and analysis section as well as material that is sometimes provided by management but is not useful for the analyst; 2. the complexity of the accounting rules that underlie the preparation and presentation of financial statements; 3. the variations in quality of financial reporting, including management discretion in some important areas that affect analysis; 4. the impact of inflation on financial statement data; and 5. the importance of financial information that is omitted or difficult to find in conventional financial statement presentations.

Chapters 2 through 5 describe and analyze financial statements for a mythical but potentially real company: Recreational Equipment and Clothing, Incorporated (R.E.C., Inc.), which sells recreational products through retail outlets in the southwestern United States. The specifics of this particular firm should be helpful in illustrating how financial statement analysis can provide insight into a firm's strengths and weaknesses. But the principles and concepts covered throughout the book apply to any set of published financial statements, other than for specialized industries, such as financial institutions and public utilities. The interpretation of financial statements for commercial banks is covered in Appendix C.

Because no one company can provide every account and problem the user will encounter in financial statements, additional company examples are introduced throughout the text where needed to illustrate important accounting and analytical issues.

Chapters 2 through 4 discuss in detail a basic set of financial statements: the balance sheet in Chapter 2, the income (earnings) statement and statement of retained earnings (or statement of shareholders' equity) in Chapter 3, and the statement of cash flows in Chapter 4. The emphasis in each of these chapters is on what the financial statements convey about the condition and performance of a business firm as well as how the numbers have been derived.

With this material as background, Chapter 5 covers the interpretation and analysis of the financial statements discussed in Chapters 2 through 4. This process involves the calculation and interpretation of financial ratios, an examination of trends over time, a comparison of the firm's condition and performance with its competitors, and an assessment of the future potential of the company based on its historical record. The chapter also reviews additional sources of information that can enhance the analytical process.

Self-tests at the end of Chapters 1 through 5 provide an opportunity for the reader to assess comprehension (or its absence) of major topics with solutions to the self-tests listed in Appendix D. For more extensive student assignments, there are also Study Questions and Problems at the end of each chapter. A new feature of this edition is the inclusion of Mini-Cases drawn from actual company annual reports to highlight in a case-problem format many of the key issues discussed in the chapters.

Appendix A discusses and illustrates issues that relate to the quality, and thus the usefulness, of financial reporting. The Appendix contains a step-by-step checklist of key items to help the analyst assess the quality of reporting, with examples of each step provided.

Appendix B shows how to evaluate the segmental accounting data reported by diversified companies that operate in several unrelated lines of business.

Appendix C presents a guide to understanding and analyzing the financial statements of commercial banks. Given the impact of commercial banking on all aspects of financial operations in the U.S. and the spate of bank failures in recent years, it is important for a well-informed financial statement user to develop a working knowledge of bank financial statements. The financial statements of commercial banking institutions in the United States are, like their nonbank counterparts, based on generally accepted accounting principles. Because of the nature of a bank's assets and liabilities, however, the financial statements are quite different in organization, content, and appearance from other types of business organizations.

Appendix D contains solutions to self-tests for Chapters 1 through 5.

Appendix E covers the computation and definition of the key financial ratios that are used in Chapter 5 to evaluate financial statements.

Appendix F presents a Glossary of the key terms used throughout the book.

The ultimate goal of this book is to improve the reader's ability to translate financial statement numbers into a meaningful map for business decisions. It is hoped that the material covered in the chapters and the appendices will enable each reader to approach financial statements with enhanced confidence and understanding of a firm's financial, historical, current, and prospective financial condition and performance.

Usefulness

Financial statements and their accompanying notes contain a wealth of useful information regarding the financial position of a company, the success of its operations, the policies and strategies of management, and insight into its future performance. The objective of the financial statement user is to find and interpret this information in order to answer questions about the company, such as:

—Would an investment generate attractive returns?

—What is the degree of risk inherent in the investment?

—Should existing investment holdings be liquidated?

—Will cash flows be sufficient to service interest and principal payments to support the firm's borrowing needs?

—Does the company provide a good opportunity for employment, future advancement, and employee benefits?

—How well does this company compete in its operating environment?

—Is this firm a good prospect as a customer?

The financial statements and other data generated by corporate financial reporting can help the user develop answers to these questions as well as many others. The remainder of this chapter provides an approach to effective use of the information contained in a corporate annual report.[1]

---

[1] Annual reports in this book refer to the information package published primarily for shareholders and the general public. The Securities and Exchange Commission requires large, publicly held companies to file a 10-K report annually. This is generally a more detailed document and is used by regulators, analysts, and researchers. The basic set of financial statements and supplementary data is the same for both documents, and it is this basic set of information—financial statements, notes and required supplementary data—that is explained and interpreted throughout this book.

VOLUME OF INFORMATION

The user of a firm's annual report can expect to encounter a great quantity of information that encompasses the required information—financial statements, notes to the financial statements, the auditor's report, a five-year summary of key financial data, high and low stock prices, management's discussion and analysis of operations—as well as material that is included in the report at the imagination and discretion of management.

The Financial Statements

A corporate annual report contains four basic financial statements, illustrated in Exhibit 1.1 for R.E.C., Inc.

EXHIBIT 1.1 R.E.C., Inc.
Consolidated Balance Sheets at December 31, 19X9 and 19X8
(In thousands)

	19X9	19X8
Assets		
Current Assets		
Cash	$ 4,061	$ 2,382
Marketable securities (note A)	5,272	8,004
Accounts receivable, less allowance for doubtful accounts of		
$448 in 19X9 and $417 in 19X8	8,960	8,350
Inventories (note A)	47,041	36,769
Prepaid expenses	512	759
Total current assets	65,846	56,264
Property, Plant, and Equipment (notes A, C, and E)		
Land	811	811
Buildings and leasehold improvements	18,273	11,928
Equipment	21,523	13,768
	40,607	26,507
Less accumulated depreciation and amortization	11,528	7,530
Net property, plant, and equipment	29,079	18,977
Other Assets (note A)	373	668
Total Assets	$95,298	$75,909
Liabilities and Stockholders' Equity		
Current Liabilities		
Accounts Payable	$14,294	$ 7,591
Notes payable—banks (note B)	5,614	6,012
Current maturities of long-term debt (note C)	1,884	1,516
Accrued liabilities	5,669	5,313
Total current liabilities	27,461	20,432
Deferred Federal Income Taxes (notes A and D)	843	635
Long-Term Debt (note C)	21,059	16,975
Total liabilities	49,363	38,042
Stockholders' Equity		
Common stock, par value $1, authorized, 10,000,000 shares;		
issued, 4,803,000 shares in 19X9 and 4,594,000 shares in		
19X8 (note F)	4,803	4,594
Additional paid-in capital	957	910
Retained earnings	40,175	32,363
Total stockholders' equity	45,935	37,867
Total Liabilities and Stockholders' Equity	$95,298	$75,909

The accompanying notes are an integral part of these statements.

EXHIBIT 1.1   R.E.C., Inc.
(Continued)   Consolidated Statements of Earnings and Retained Earnings
for the Years Ended December 31, 19X9, 19X8, and 19X7
(in thousands except per share amounts)

	19X9	19X8	19X7
Statements of Consolidated Earnings			
Net sales	$215,600	$153,000	$140,700
Cost of goods sold (note A)	129,364	91,879	81,606
Gross profit	86,236	61,121	59,094
Selling and administrative expenses (note A)	32,664	26,382	25,498
Advertising	14,258	10,792	9,541
Lease payments (note E)	13,058	7,111	7,267
Depreciation and amortization (note A)	3,998	2,984	2,501
Repairs and maintenance	3,015	2,046	3,031
Operating profit	19,243	11,806	11,256
Other income (expense)			
Interest income	422	838	738
Interest expense	(2,585)	(2,277)	(1,274)
Earnings before income taxes	17,080	10,367	10,720
Income taxes (notes A and D)	7,686	4,457	4,824
Net earnings	$ 9,394	$ 5,910	$ 5,896
Earnings per common share (note G)	$1.96	$1.29	$1.33
Statements of Consolidated Retained Earnings			
Retained earnings at beginning of year	$ 32,363	$ 28,315	$ 24,260
Net earnings	9,394	5,910	5,896
Cash dividends (19X9—$.33 per share; 19X8 and 19X7—$.41 per share)	(1,582)	(1,862)	(1,841)
Retained earnings at end of year	$ 40,175	$ 32,363	$ 28,315

The accompanying notes are an integral part of these statements.

EXHIBIT 1.1 R.E.C., Inc.
(Continued) Consolidated Statements of Cash Flows
for the Years Ended December 31, 19X9, 19X8, and 19X7
(in thousands)

	19X9	19X8	19X7
Cash Flows from Operating Activities—Direct Method			
Cash received from customers	$214,990	$149,661	$140,252
Interest received	422	838	738
Cash paid to suppliers for inventory	(132,933)	(99,936)	(83,035)
Cash paid to employees (S & A expenses)	(32,664)	(26,382)	(25,498)
Cash paid for other operating expenses	(29,728)	(21,350)	(20,848)
Interest paid	(2,585)	(2,277)	(1,274)
Taxes paid	(7,478)	(4,321)	(4,706)
Net cash provided (used) by operating activities	$ 10,024	($ 3,767)	$ 5,629
Cash Flows from Investing Activities			
Additions to property, plant, and equipment	(14,100)	(4,773)	(3,982)
Other investing activities	295	0	0
Net cash provided (used) by investing activities	($ 13,805)	($ 4,773)	($ 3,982)
Cash flow from financing activities:			
Sales of common stock	256	183	124
Increase (decrease) in short-term borrowings (includes current maturities of long-term debt)	(30)	1,854	1,326
Additions to long-term borrowings	5,600	7,882	629
Reductions of long-term borrowings	(1,516)	(1,593)	(127)
Dividends paid	(1,582)	(1,862)	(1,841)
Net cash provided (used) by financing activities	$ 2,728	$ 6,464	$ 111
Increase (decrease) in cash and marketable securities	($ 1,053)	($ 2,076)	$ 1,758
Supplementary Schedule			
Cash Flows from Operating Activities—Indirect Method			
Net income	$ 9,394	$ 5,910	$ 5,896
Noncash revenue and expense included in net income:			
Depreciation and amortization	3,998	2,984	2,501
Deferred income taxes	208	136	118
Cash provided (used) by current assets and liabilities:			
Accounts receivable	(610)	(3,339)	(448)
Inventories	(10,272)	(7,006)	(2,331)
Prepaid expenses	247	295	(82)
Accounts payable	6,703	(1,051)	902
Accrued liabilities	356	(1,696)	(927)
Net cash provided (used) by operations	$ 10,024	($ 3,767)	$ 5,629

The accompanying notes are an integral part of these statements.

Note D—Income Taxes

A reconciliation of income tax expense computed by using the statutory Federal income tax rate and the amount of income tax expense reported in the consolidated statements of earnings is as follows:

	19X9	19X8	19X7
Federal income tax at statutory rate	$7,859,000	$4,769,000	$4,931,000
Increases (decreases)			
State income taxes	489,000	381,000	344,000
Tax credits	(465,000)	(429,000)	(228,000)
Other items, net	(197,000)	(264,000)	(223,000)
Income Tax expense reported	$7,686,000	$4,457,000	$4,824,000

Deferred tax expense applicable to major temporary differences is as follows:

	19X9	19X8	19X7
Excess of tax depreciation over book depreciation	$146,000	$98,000	84,000
Temporary differences applicable to installment sales	62,000	38,000	34,000
Total	$208,000	$136,000	$118,000

Note E—Operating Leases

The company conducts some of its operations in facilities leased under noncancellable operating leases. Certain agreements include options to purchase the property and certain agreements include renewal options with provisions for increased rental during the renewal term.

Minimum annual rental commitments as of December 31, 19X9, are as follows:

20X0	$ 14,561,000
20X1	14,082,000
20X2	13,673,000
20X3	13,450,000
20X4	13,003,000
Thereafter	107,250,000
	$176,019,000

Note F—Common Stock

The company has a stock option plan providing that options may be granted to key employees at an option price of not less than 100% of the market value of the shares at the time the options are granted. As of December 31, 19X9, the company has under option 75,640 shares (19X8—96,450 shares). All options expire 5 years from date of grant.

Note G—Earnings Per Share

Earnings per common share are based on the weighted average number of common shares outstanding during each year. For 19X9, 19X8, and 19X7 the weighted average number of common shares outstanding was 4,792,857, 4,581,395, and 4,433,083, respectively. Outstanding options are included in periods where they have a dilutive effect. Earnings per share assuming full dilution are not significantly different (less than 3%) from earnings per common share.

The first note to the financial statements provides a summary of the firm's accounting policies. If there have been changes in any accounting policies during the reporting period, these changes will be explained and the impact quantified in a financial statement note. Other notes to the financial statements present detail about particular accounts, such as:

> inventory;
>
> property, plant, and equipment;
>
> investments;
>
> long-term debt; and
>
> the equity accounts.

The notes also include information about

> any major acquisitions or divestitures that have occurred during the accounting period;
>
> officer and employee retirement, pension, and stock option plans;
>
> leasing arrangements;
>
> the term, cost, and maturity of debt;
>
> pending legal proceedings;
>
> income taxes;
>
> contingencies and commitments; and
>
> quarterly results of operations.

Certain supplementary information is required by governmental and accounting authorities—primarily the Securities and Exchange Commission (SEC) and the Financial Accounting Standards Board (FASB)—that establish accounting policies. There are, for instance, supplementary disclosure requirements relating to reserves for companies operating in the oil, gas, or other areas of the extractive industries. Firms operating in foreign countries show the effect of foreign currency translations. If a firm has several lines of business, the notes will contain a section to show revenue, expense, operating profit, and capital expenditures for each reportable segment. (The analysis of segmental data is discussed in Appendix B.)

Auditor's Report

Related to the financial statements and notes is the report of an independent auditor (Exhibit 1.3). Management has responsibility for the preparation of financial statements, including the notes, and the auditor's report attests to the fairness of the presentation.

An *unqualified* report, illustrated for R.E.C., Inc. in Exhibit 1.3, states that the financial statements present fairly, in all material respects, the financial position, the results of operations, and the cash flows for the accounting period, in conformity with generally accepted accounting principles. Some circumstances warrant other forms of the auditor's report: a *qualified* opinion is given when the overall financial statements are fairly presented "except for" certain items which are disclosed by the auditor such as a limitation in scope or uncertainties about the future resolution of material matters; an *adverse opinion* is rendered when the financial statements have not been presented fairly in accordance with generally accepted accounting principles; and a *disclaimer of opinion* means that the auditor cannot evaluate the fairness of the statements and therefore can express no opinion on them.

Exhibit 1.3   Auditor's Report
                   Board of Directors and Stockholders
                   R.E.C., Inc.

We have audited the accompanying consolidated balance sheets of R.E.C., Inc., and sub-sidiaries as of December 31, 19X9 and 19X8, and the related consolidated statements of earnings, retained earnings and cash flows for each of the three years in the period ended December 31, 19X9. These financial statements are the responsibility of the Company's management. Our responsibility is to express an opinion on these financial statements based on our audits.

We conducted our audits in accordance with generally accepted auditing standards. Those standards require that we plan and perform the audits to obtain reasonable assurance about whether the financial statements are free of material misstatement. An audit includes examining, on a test basis, evidence supporting the amounts and disclosures in the financial statements. An audit also includes assessing the accounting principles used and significant esti-mates made by management, as well as evaluating the overall financial statement presentation. We believe that our audits provide a reasonable basis for our opinion.

In our opinion, the financial statements referred to above present fairly, in all material respects, the consolidated financial position of R.E.C., Inc. and subsidiaries at December 31, 19X9 and 19X8, and the consolidated results of their operations and their cash flows for each of the three years in the period ended December 31, 19X9, in conformity with generally accepted accounting principles.

J.J. Michaels and Company
Dime Box, TX
January 27, 20X0

Although the auditor's report is independent, the analyst should be aware that the auditor is hired by the firm whose financial statements are under review. Because the auditor must sat-isfy the client, the potential for conflict of interest always exists. The analyst should also be alert to any change in auditors; a change can signal problems with a company's disclosures. Firms that change auditors are required to file Form 8-K with the Securities and Exchange Commission (available to the public from the Securities and Exchange Commission).

Malpractice suits have become increasingly common in recent years as a result of complaints that auditors protected their clients at the expense of investors. Two inter-esting examples involve Lincoln Savings and Loan Association and MiniScribe Corporation.[2]

In 1992 the accounting firm of Ernst & Young settled for $63 million a negligence suit involving Arthur Young and Company's (subsequently merged into what is now Ernst & Young) audit of the failed Lincoln Savings and Loan Association. Lincoln Savings' demise itself is the costliest thrift failure (estimated at $2.5 billion) on record. The firm's auditors, Arthur Young and Company, issued clean reports for Lincoln's 1986 and 1987 financial statements, a period in which more than half of the profits were the result of questionable transactions—approved by Arthur Young. Many of the deals involved pricing empty desert land in Arizona for amounts far above the appraised value of the land. Arthur Young and Company ultimately resigned from the account.

---

[2] Berton, Lee. "How MiniScribe Got Its Auditor's Blessing on Questionable Sales," *The Wall Street Journal*, May 14, 1992; and Thomas, P. "Auditors Say Lincoln S&L 'Sham' Deals Were Approved by Arthur Young & Co.," *The Wall Street Journal*, November 15, 1989.

In February 1992 bondholders of MiniScribe Corporation were awarded more than $550 million in damages, of which $200 million was punitive damages for negligence by the accounting firm of Coopers & Lybrand. (The suit was later settled for between $45 and $50 million.) MiniScribe, a Colorado computer disk-drive maker, needed Coopers' approval on some last-minute adjustments to its 1986 annual report in order to complete a prospectus for selling bonds. Coopers complied by issuing a clean opinion, but the financial statements actually hid financial, operating, and marketing problems that led to bankruptcy court. Records showed, for example, that MiniScribe booked as sales shipments that were subsequently returned, and shipped disk drives that customers had not ordered.

The six major accounting firms disclosed in 1993 that litigation over faulty audits had cost 12% of their total 1992 revenue. *The Wall Street Journal* reported in June 1993 that federal regulators had filed lawsuits totaling more than $1.4 billion in damages against the accounting firm of Deloitte & Touche for allegedly faulty audits of banks and savings and loans.[3]

Given the rash of lawsuits against accounting firms and the many highly publicized business failures, the American Institute of Certified Public Accountants (AICPA) has taken steps to repair the damage to public confidence in the auditing function. In addition to an extensive peer review program which has been in place since 1977, the AICPA adopted in 1993 a self-policing plan that would impose harsher punishments for faulty or fraudulent audits and that would make public the names of accountants or firms responsible for the audits.[4] The AICPA has also established a special financial reporting committee, expected to issue a report in mid-1994, that will make recommendations for changes in required disclosures, including the standard auditor's report. The committee's objective is to make financial reports more helpful to investors and financial analysts.

Other Required Information

There is additional material that is required for inclusion in an annual report that may prove helpful to the financial analyst. In 1980, the Securities and Exchange Commission adopted an *Integrated Disclosure System* which mandates a common body of information for both the 10-K report filed with the Commission and the annual report which is prepared for the company's shareholders. The basic package of information includes the audited financial statements; notes to the financial statements; the auditor's report; a five-year summary of selected financial data (net sales or operating revenue, income or loss from continuing operations, income or loss from continuing operations per common share, total assets, long-term obligations and redeemable preferred stock, and cash dividends per common share); market data (high and low sales prices) on common stock each quarter during the past two years; and a revised and expanded form of the *Management Discussion and Analysis (MD&A) of Financial Condition and Results of Operations.*

The *Management Discussion and Analysis* section, sometimes labeled "Financial Review," is of potential interest to the analyst because it contains information that cannot

---

[3] Berton, Lee. "Deloitte, RTC Suspend Talks on S&L Audits," *The Wall Street Journal*, June 18, 1993.

[4] Berton, Lee. "CPA Group Outlines Self-Policing Plan to Boost Penalties for Flawed Audits," *The Wall Street Journal*, June 9, 1993.

be found in the financial data.   The content of this section includes coverage of any favorable or unfavorable trends and significant events or uncertainties in the areas of liquidity, capital resources, and results of operations.   In particular, the analyst can expect to find a discussion of:

1. the internal and external sources of liquidity;
2. any material deficiencies in liquidity and how they will be remedied;
3. commitments for capital expenditures, the purpose of such commitments, and expected sources of funding;
4. anticipated changes in the mix and cost of financing resources;
5. unusual or infrequent transactions which affect income from continuing operations;
6. events which cause material changes in the relationship between costs and revenues (such as future labor or materials price increases or inventory adjustments); and
7. a breakdown of sales increases into price and volume components.

Alas, there are problems as well with the usefulness of the MD&A section.   One of the SEC goals in mandating this section was to make available to the public information about future events and trends that might affect future business operations.   One study to determine if the data in the MD&A section provided useful clues to future financial performance revealed that companies did a good job of describing historical events, but very few provided accurate forecasts.   Many companies provided essentially no forward-looking information at all.[5]

The Securities and Exchange Commission filed an action in April 1992 against Caterpillar, Inc. accusing the company of failing to disclose in the MD&A section of its annual report that about a quarter of its 1989 income, from its Brazilian unit, would be nonrecurring. Caterpillar negotiated a settlement with the SEC agreeing not to commit the same act in the future but not conceding it had done anything unlawful.   A spokesperson for the SEC characterized the action against Caterpillar as a message that the SEC takes the MD&A seriously.[6]

Pandora, aka "PR Fluff"

In addition to the material required for presentation, many companies add to the annual report an array of color photographs, charts, and other items to make the report and the company attractive to current and prospective investors.   Getting to what's needed through the "PR Fluff" can be a challenge.

The DuPont Company reported an earnings loss of $3.9 billion or $5.85 per share in 1992.   Finding the financial section that includes this important piece of information in

---

[5] Parva, Moses L. and Epstein, Marc J. "How Good Is MD&A As An Investment Tool?" *Journal of Accountancy*, March 1993.

[6] "A Disciplinary Message from the SEC," *Journal of Accountancy*, March 1993, p. 53. For additional reading on this subject, see Hooks, Karen L. and Moon, James E. "A Checklist for Management Discussion and Analysis," *Journal of Accountancy*, December 1991.

DuPont's 1992 income statement requires opening the striking annual report cover that shows an old man transforming into a young athlete, and then getting through 24 pages of multi-colored bar charts, photographs, and descriptions of various lines of business with clever drawings and illustrations.   It should be pointed out, which DuPont management does several places in the annual report, that the firm had huge one-time accounting changes in the 1992 fourth quarter of $4.18 billion or $7.18 per share; but the underlying fourth quarter 1992 earnings, even excluding the one-time charges, fell substantially.

The amount of "PR Fluff" sometimes varies inversely with the success of the firm's performance for a given year.   In the 1989 Annual Report of Bristol-Myers Squibb Company, the firm reported a 40% *decrease* in earnings.   (In 1989 Squibb merged with a subsidiary of Bristol-Meyers, resulting in an after-tax charge against earnings of $693 million.) The report begins using 78 pages on glossy paper, which include descriptive sections about the company and 31 full-page color photographs.   The last 23 pages of the report, on a dull-textured white paper, present the required financial statements and other financial information.   Bristol-Myers Company's 1988 Annual Report, which shows a 17 % *increase* in earnings, begins with 40 glossy pages of descriptions, 28 fewer than the 1989 report, and 15 full-page photos; the financial information in the 1988 report covers 23 pages presented on glossy paper.   The ratio of "PR Fluff" to financial data is thus 78:23 in the year of the earnings decline and 40:23 in the year of the earnings improvement.

As Federal Express' earnings declined, from a profit of $2.18 per share in 1990 to $.11 in 1991 to a loss of $2.11 in 1992, its annual report front page "Financial Highlights" devoted increasingly less space to "Operating Results" and increasingly more to "Other Operating Data," such as the weight of its packages, average revenue per package, and the aircraft fleet at the end of the year.   The 1992 Financial Highlights eliminated any reference to working capital (current assets minus current liabilities, a measure of liquidity) which had been included in prior years reports; working capital was a *negative* $211 million in 1992.   Moody's and Standard and Poor's downgraded the Company's long-term debt in 1992.

Royal Appliance Manufacturing Company, makers of Dirt Devil vacuum cleaners, reported its 39% profit decline for 1992 in a slick, clever document called "The Second Royal Report," with a subhead "One Headline Hardly Ever Tells The Story."   On the other hand, General Motors took a refreshing approach to presenting its $24 billion loss in its 1992 annual report by eliminating most of the "PR Fluff" and making a point of it in the Chairman's letter: "You will notice that this annual report is a dramatic departure from past practices.   I believe it demonstrates the Corporation's commitment to meaningful change."[7] Still more refreshing is the approach taken by Browning-Ferris Industries, a waste management firm which appropriately printed its 1992 annual report on *recycled* paper.   For the 1992 report, a year of declining profits, BFI eliminated *all* "PR Fluff," with the Chairman's letter citing the reasons: "We're taking a different approach to our Annual Report this year—it will consist of my letter to you and the accompanying financial information.   One reason for doing this is to save money.   We didn't meet our financial objectives this year at BFI, so we shouldn't go spending your money on an elaborate report telling you why."[8]

[7] General Motors Annual Report 1992, p. 3.

[8] Browning-Ferris Industries Annual Report 1992, p. 2.

Mythical Mountain

Generally accepted accounting principles—as established by the FASB and the SEC—provide a measure of uniformity, but they also allow considerable discretion in the preparation of financial statements.   One example involves the depreciation of fixed assets (also called *tangible fixed assets, long-lived assets*, and *capital assets*).   Fixed assets are those assets, such as machinery and equipment, that benefit the firm for several years and are generally shown on the balance sheet as property, plant, and equipment.   When such an asset is acquired, the cost of the asset is allocated or spread over its useful life rather than expensed in the year of purchase.   This allocation process is *depreciation*.   (The exception is land, which is not depreciated because theoretically land has an unlimited useful life.)

Assume that R.E.C. Inc. purchases an artificial ski mountain for its Houston flagship store in order to demonstrate skis and allow prospective customers to test-run skis on a simulated black diamond course.   The cost of the mountain is $50,000.   Several

Figure 1.3

choices and estimates must be made in order to determine the annual depreciation expense associated with the mountain. For example, R.E.C. Inc. management must estimate how long the mountain will last and the amount, if any, of salvage value at the end of its useful life.

Further, management must choose a method of depreciation: the *straight-line method* allocates an equal amount of expense to each year of the depreciation period, while the *accelerated method* apportions larger amounts of expense to the earlier years of the asset's depreciable life and lesser amounts to the later years.

If the $50,000 mountain is estimated to have a five-year useful life and $0 salvage value at the end of that period, annual depreciation expense would be calculated as follows for the first year.

Straight Line:

$$\frac{\text{Depreciable base (cost less salvage value)}}{\text{Depreciation period}} = \text{Depreciation expense}$$

$$\frac{\$50,000 - \$0}{5 \text{ years}} = \$10,000$$

Accelerated:[10]
Cost less accumulated depreciation $\times$ Twice the straight line rate = Depreciation expense

$$\$50,000 \times (2 \times .2) = \$20,000$$

The choices and estimates relating to the depreciation of equipment affect the amounts shown on the financial statements relating to the asset—the fixed asset account on the balance sheet is shown at historical cost less accumulated depreciation; and the annual depreciation expense is deducted on the income statement to determine net income. At the end of year 1, the accounts would be different according to the method chosen:

Straight Line:

BALANCE SHEET		INCOME STATEMENT
Fixed Assets	$50,000	Dep. Expense $10,000
Less Accum. Dep.	(10,000)	
Fixed Assets (Net)	$40,000	

Accelerated:

BALANCE SHEET		INCOME STATEMENT
Fixed Assets	$50,000	Dep. Expense $20,000
Less Accum. Dep.	(20,000)	
Fixed Assets (Net)	$30,000	

[10] The example uses the *double-declining balance method* of figuring accelerated depreciation, which is: twice the straight-line rate times the net book value (cost less accumulated depreciation) of the asset.

Depreciation for year 2 would be:

Straight Line $50,000/5 = $10,000; *Accelerated* $30,000 $\times$ .4 = $12,000

The amounts would also vary if the estimates were different regarding useful life or salvage value. For example, if R.E.C., Inc. management concludes the mountain could be sold to Denver Mountaineering Co. at the end of five years for use in testing snow shoes, the mountain would then have an expected salvage value that would enter into the calculations. This one example is compounded by all of the firm's depreciable assets and by the other accounts that are affected by accounting methods, such as the inventory account (discussed in detail in Chapter 2).

Not only are financial statements encumbered by accounting choices and estimates, but also they reflect an attempt to "match" expenses with revenues in appropriate accounting periods. If a firm sells goods on credit, there is a delay between the time the product is sold and the time the cash is collected. Published financial statements are prepared according to the "accrual" rather than the "cash" basis of accounting. This means that the revenue is recognized in the accounting period when the sale is made rather than when the cash is received. The same principle applies to expense recognition; the expense associated with the product may occur before the cash is paid out. The process of matching expense and revenue to accounting periods involves considerable estimation and judgment and, like the depreciation example, affects the outcome of the financial statement numbers.

If, for instance, the mythical $50,000 mountain needed expensive repairs because one enthusiastic customer tried snow-boarding, thereby creating a here-to-fore nonexistent back bowl in the mountain, management would have to determine whether to recognize the cost of repair in year 2 or to spread it over years 2 through 5.

Further, financial statements are prepared on certain dates at the end of accounting periods, such as a year or a quarter. Whereas the firm's life is continuous, financial data must be apportioned to particular time periods.

Because the accounting principles which underlie the preparation of financial statements are complicated, the presentation of data based on the accounting rules can be perplexing. One example of a complex accounting rule that sometimes results in confusion is that for the calculation of *earnings per share*. One typically thinks of earnings per share as the amount of net income earned for every share of common stock outstanding. But the income statement for many companies, those with complex capital structures (which include convertible securities, stock options, and warrants), will show two figures for earnings per share: primary and fully diluted. Convertible securities, stock options, and warrants represent potential "dilution" of earnings per share; that is, if they were exercised there would be more shares of stock outstanding for every dollar earned. The accounting rules require that this potential for dilution be considered in the computation of earnings per share, and the result is a dual presentation. (This topic is discussed more fully in Chapter 3.)

The earnings per share calculation is just one of a vast number of financial statement puzzles. Sorting out the consolidation of a parent and subsidiaries, the accounting for leases and pensions, or the translation of foreign operations of a U.S. company can cause nightmares for the financial analyst.

To add to the confusion, two sets of accounting rules are used by management— one for reporting purposes (preparation of financial statements for the public) and one

Figure 1.4

for tax purposes (calculation of taxes for the Internal Revenue Service). Earlier in this section there was an example of the choices associated with the depreciation of an asset. Firms typically select one depreciation method for reporting purposes and use the method for tax purposes that is specified by the tax laws (currently in use most frequently is the *Modified Accelerated Cost Recovery System*—MACRS). The objective for tax purposes is to pay the smallest amount of tax possible, while the objective for reporting purposes is to report the highest possible income but also a smooth earnings stream. Thus for reporting purposes, the firm might choose the straight-line method because it spreads the expense evenly and results in higher reported income than an accelerated method in the earlier years of an asset's life. Referring to the previous example, the following results were obtained according to the two depreciation methods for year 1:

Straight Line	Depreciation Expense $10,000
Accelerated	Depreciation Expense $20,000

Use of the straight-line method produces an expense deduction that is $10,000 less than the accelerated method; net income, therefore, would be $10,000 higher in year 1 under the straight-line method. Assume for purposes of illustration that the accelerated method allowed by the IRS also yields a depreciation expense in year 1 of $20,000. By using the straight-line method, the tax paid to the IRS under the allowed accelerated method would be less than the income tax expense reported in the published income statement because taxable income would be less than reported income.[11] Eventually this difference would reverse, because in the later years of the asset's useful life, accelerated depreciation would be less than straight line; the total amount of depreciation taken is the same under both methods. To reconcile the difference between the amounts of tax expense, there is an account on the balance sheet called deferred taxes. This account and its interpretation, discussed in Chapter 2, introduce still another challenge to the financial statement user.

QUALITY OF FINANCIAL REPORTING

It has already been pointed out that management has considerable discretion within the overall framework of generally accepted accounting principles. As a result, the potential exists for management to "manipulate" the bottom line (profit or loss) and other accounts in financial statements. Ideally, financial statements should reflect an accurate picture of a company's financial condition and performance. The information should be useful both to assess the past and predict the future. The sharper and clearer the picture presented through the financial data and the closer that picture is to financial reality, the higher is the quality of the financial statements and reported earnings.

Many opportunities exist for management to affect the quality of financial statements; some illustrations follow. (*To the reader*: Appendix A provides an analytical approach to the assessment of earnings quality with a step-by-step check list of what to look for in evaluating the quality of financial reporting.)

Accounting Policies, Estimates—Choices and Changes

In preparing financial statements, management makes choices with respect to accounting policies and makes estimations in the applications of those policies. One such choice (others will be discussed in subsequent chapters) was covered in the preceding section related to the depreciation of fixed assets. To continue the depreciation example, in choosing a depreciation method, management decides how to allocate the depreciation expense associated with a fixed asset acquisition.

Assume that the $50,000 ski mountain is more productive in the early years of its operating life, before would-be skiers dig ruts in the simulated runs. Financial reality would argue for the selection of an accelerated depreciation method, which would recognize higher depreciation expense in the early years of its useful life. An environment of

---

[11] For a firm with a 34 percent marginal tax rate, the difference would be $3,400. (Accelerated depreciation expense less straight-line depreciation expense times the marginal tax rate: ($20,000–$10,000) × .34 =$3,400.)

rising prices would also support accelerated depreciation because inflation increases the replacement cost of most assets, resulting in an understatement of depreciation based on historical cost. If, however, management wanted to show higher earnings in the early years, the straight-line method would be selected. Note the difference in depreciation expense recognized for year l:

Straight Line	**Accelerated**
INCOME STATEMENT	INCOME STATEMENT
Dep. Expense $10,000	Dep. Expense $20,000

Remember the lower the expense, the higher the reported net income. Therefore, under the straight-line method, net income would be $10,000 higher than with the accelerated method. The choice of depreciation method clearly affects the earnings stream associated with the asset, and it also affects the *quality* of the earnings figure reported. Use of accelerated depreciation would produce earnings of higher quality in this particular situation.

Management can also elect to change an accounting policy or estimate if the change can be justified as being preferable to that which was previously used. In the depreciation

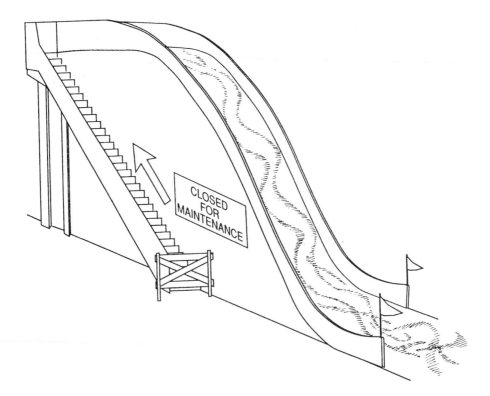

Figure 1.5

example, it was estimated that the mountain had a useful life of five years. It could be argued that competitive sporting goods stores depreciate their mountains over a ten-year rather than a five-year period. If the firm had chosen to use the straight-line method and made this accounting change (called a change in accounting estimate), depreciation expense would be decreased from $10,000 to $5,000 per year, and net income would increase by $5,000.

Before Change in Estimate	**After Change in Estimate**
INCOME STATEMENT	INCOME STATEMENT
Depreciation Expense $10,000	Depreciation Expense $5,000

When a company makes such a change, the quantitative effect of the change must be disclosed in notes to the financial statements.

Timing of Revenue and Expense Recognition

One of the generally accepted accounting principles that provides the foundation for preparing financial statements is the matching principle: expenses are matched with the generation of revenues in order to determine net income for an accounting period. Reference was made earlier to the fact that published financial statements are based on the accrual rather than the cash basis of accounting, which means that revenues are recognized when earned and expenses are recognized when incurred, regardless of when the cash inflows and outflows occur. This matching process involves judgments by management regarding the timing of expense and revenue recognition. Although accounting rules provide guidelines helpful in making the necessary and appropriate allocations, these rules are not always precise.

For example, suppose that a company learns near the end of an accounting period that a material accounts receivable is probably uncollectible. When will the account be written off as a loss—currently, or in the next accounting period when a final determination is made? Pose the same question for obsolete inventory sitting on the warehouse shelves. These are areas involving sometimes arbitrary managerial decisions. Generally, the more conservative management is in making such judgments (conservatism usually implies the choice that is least favorable to the firm) the higher the quality of earnings resulting from the matching of revenues and expenses in a given accounting period.

Discretionary Items

Many of the expenditures made by a business firm are discretionary. Management exercises control over the budget level and timing of expenditures for the repair and maintenance of machinery and equipment, marketing and advertising, research and development, and capital expansion. Policies are also flexible with respect to the replacement of plant assets, the development of new product lines, and the disposal of an operating division. Each choice regarding these discretionary items has both an immediate and a long-term impact on profitability, perhaps not in the same direction. A company might elect to defer plant maintenance in order to boost current period earnings; ultimately, the effect of such a policy could be detrimental.

The nature of a business dictates to a certain extent how discretionary dollars should be spent. For some industries, there is a direct relationship between dollars spent for advertising and market share. Through investment in advertising, Procter & Gamble has substantially increased its share of the peanut butter (Jif) and coffee (Folgers) markets from the single digits to market leadership. Kellogg and General Mills, as the result of an advertising spending war, together control 65% of the breakfast cereals market; Coke and Pepsi are prohibitive leaders for their products, jointly accounting for 70% of their markets. All of these companies invest consistently in advertising.[12] But a company can also spend too much on advertising. Royal Appliance Manufacturing's stock dropped from $31 to less than $8 a share during 1992 due in part to market reaction to excessive advertising expenditures. Royal almost doubled expenditures on advertising and promotion, increasing outlays from $40 million in 1991 to $79 million in 1992; the firm's net income declined from $33 to $20 million. Advertising and promotion expenses in 1992 accounted for more than 70% of total operating expenses.

Research and development expenditures are of critical importance to some industries, such as high technology. The introduction in 1990 by Microsoft of its new "Windows" software program threatened the entire computer industry, with Apple Computer considered especially vulnerable because "Windows" enables IBM-compatible personal computers to look and act more like Apple's user-accessible Macintosh.[13] Another directional shift in the industry is the development of networking, through which personal computer users maintain autonomy with their own PCs but also have access to sharing information through a system set up with other desktops. In order to take advantage of this important market, however, the software makers such as Microsoft and Lotus Development have to invest more heavily in consulting and custom programming services, reducing profit margins.[14] Companies sometimes have to risk tighter margins to achieve long-term benefit. The impact on Apple has been dramatic. Apple's shares lost 28% during a ten-day period in June 1993 when the firm announced that second half fiscal year earnings would be less than the previous year. Apple subsequently announced price cuts and rebates on its personal computers and a change in chief executive officer.[15]

The financial analyst should carefully scrutinize management policies with respect to these discretionary items through an examination of expenditure trends (absolute and relative amounts) and comparison with industry competitors. Such an analysis can provide insight into a company's existing strengths and weaknesses and contribute to an assessment of its ability to perform successfully in the future.

[12] Schroer, James C. "Ad Spending: Growing Market Share," *Harvard Business Review*, January–February 1990.

[13] Schwartz, John "Bill Gates' New Windows, Microsoft Might Take a Bite Out of Apple," *Newsweek*, May 21, 1990.

[14] Hammonds, K., Atchison, S., and Schwartz, E. "Software: It's a New Game," *Business Week*, June 4, 1990.

[15] Zachary, G.P. and Yamada, K. "Apple Picks Spindler as Chief for Rough Days Ahead," *The Wall Street Journal*, June 21, 1993.

Nonrecurring and Nonoperating Items

Business firms may execute financial transactions that are nonrecurring and/or nonoperating. If the analyst is seeking an earnings figure that reflects the future operating potential of the firm, such transactions—which are not part of normal ongoing business—should be reviewed and possibly eliminated from earnings. One such example would be a gain on the sale of a major plant asset, such as a building. Firms sometimes sell an asset in order to generate cash and/or profits during lean periods; Bank America Corporation sold its headquarters complex for a huge profit in order to boost earnings in a bad year.[16] Such a deal is both nonrecurring and nonoperating and should be ignored in measuring the enterprise's ability to generate future operating profits.

Exhibit 1.4 presents a checklist for earnings quality that can alert the analyst to some of the key items to consider in the assessment of earnings quality. Appendix A provides a step-by-step guide to this checklist, with a discussion and illustration of each item.

EXHIBIT 1.4 A CHECKLIST FOR EARNINGS QUALITY

I. Sales
    1. Allowance for doubtful accounts
    2. Price vs. volume changes
    3. Real vs. nominal growth

II. Cost of Goods Sold
    4. Cost flow assumption for inventory
    5. Base LIFO layer reductions
    6. Loss recognitions on write downs of inventory (see also item 13)

III. Operating Expenses
    7. Discretionary:
        Research and development
        Repair and maintenance
        Advertising and marketing
    8. Depreciation (depletion, amortization):
        Methods
        Estimates
    9. Pension accounting—Interest rate assumptions

IV. Nonoperating Revenue and Expense
    10. Gains (losses) from sales of assets
    11. Interest income
    12. Equity income
    13. Loss recognitions on write-downs of assets (see also item 6)
    14. Accounting changes
    15. Extraordinary items

V. Other issues
    16. Acquisitions and dispositions
    17. Material changes in number of shares outstanding

[16] Gray, P.B. "Bank America Agrees to Sell Headquarters," *The Wall Street Journal*, September 16, 1985.

IMPACT OF INFLATION

The *historical cost principle* of accounting is used to record transactions and to value balance sheet assets and liabilities. Inventory manufactured or purchased for sale is carried on the balance sheet at cost until a different price is established through an arms-length sales transaction. Buildings, machinery, and equipment are recorded at cost and valued on any balance sheet date at their original cost less accumulated depreciation. Land used in the business or held for investment also is valued at the original price paid, regardless of any changes in actual market value. Liabilities are measured by the amount of principal balance outstanding.

The historical cost principle forms the basis of our accounting system because it provides an objective and verifiable method of measurement. During a period of inflation, however, distortions occur in the valuation of assets and the determination of net income. Consider the example of the mountain purchased earlier in this chapter. The original purchase price was $50,000, and the equipment was expected to have a five-year useful life. At the end of year 1, using straight-line depreciation, the asset would be valued as follows:

Cost	$50,000
Less: Accum. Depreciation	(10,000)
	$40,000

Depreciation expense would be $10,000 for the year. What if, during that year, the cost to replace the mountain had increased by 10%? The replacement cost would now be 10 percent higher, $50,000 × 1.10 = $55,000, and inflation-adjusted depreciation expense, based on new replacement cost, would be $10,000 × 1.10 = $11,000. If, at the end of two years, inflation had continued at a 10 percent rate, the asset value at replacement cost would be even further from the original cost. Bear in mind that a firm will continue to purchase new assets and replace old ones. The balance sheet fixed assets category thus reflects assets purchased over many years, with dollars of varying amounts of purchasing power.

To generalize, the balance sheet fixed asset accounts for many firms are understated because prices have risen since the assets were purchased and recorded. Depreciation expense is also understated because depreciation is a cost allocation based on the under-valued historical cost of fixed assets. The effect of inflation on inventory and cost of goods sold, the other major categories of potential inflationary impact, depends on the cost flow assumption used to value inventory (see Chapter 2). During a period of inflation a LIFO[17] company would have undervalued inventory on the balance sheet and currently valued cost of goods sold expense on the income statement, while use of FIFO produces an understated cost of goods sold and currently valued inventory. During a period of inflation, the net result—of understated depreciation expense for most firms and under-stated cost of goods sold for companies that do not use LIFO—is an o*verstatement of net income* in the earnings statements of most U.S. companies.

---

[17] The LIFO method assumes that the last goods purchased are the first goods sold (last in, first out); during inflation, the higher cost goods are assumed to be sold first. Under FIFO (first in, first out), the first goods or older, lower cost goods are assumed to be sold first.

The impact of inflation is uneven. For capital intensive industries with outdated plant and equipment—such as steel, autos, and paper—the toll taken by inflation has been tremendous. Some industries—such as electronics, instruments, and computers—have been virtually unscathed by inflation.

The accounting rule-makers wrestled for many years with the challenge of how to account for inflation. Reliance on historical cost results in statements that are objective and verifiable but, in some cases, not meaningful. If the relevant accounts are adjusted for inflation, however, there is controversy over how the adjustments should be made. The *general price level* approach (also called the *constant dollar* approach) adjusts each account by applying the change in a general price index, such as the CPI or GNP deflator, to the historical cost of the asset. The *current cost* approach considers the specific price change of each asset. Since the general price level method is still based on historical cost, it is considered to be more objective, and it is also less costly and easier to apply because one index is used for all assets. However, current cost is probably more relevant and useful for analysts, but it is also a more subjective and costly approach, requiring estimates of current value.

In October 1979 the Financial Accounting Standards Board issued for a five-year trial period Statement of Financial Accounting Standards No. 33, "Financial Reporting and Changing Prices." This statement required large ($1 billion of total assets or $125 million of inventories and gross property, plant, and equipment) publicly traded companies to disclose supplementary schedules to account for the impact of inflation on key balance sheet items and related income statement expenses. The data were supplementary to the primary financial statements and unaudited. In late 1986, the FASB issued Statement of Financial Accounting Standards No. 89 which said that companies were no longer required to provide the supplementary disclosures mandated by FASB Statement No. 33. Firms may choose to provide the data voluntarily. Reasons given by the FASB for dropping the requirements were that research studies indicated the information was not widely used and the costs to provide the data outweighed the benefits.

It should also be noted that the rate of inflation slowed, thus lessening the impact of inflation on earnings relative to the 1970s and reducing the pressure for inflation accounting disclosures. The financial statement user should continue to be aware, however, that any inflation distorts asset valuations and income recognition.

The analyst should also be concerned with the price component of sales growth. Consider the following sales information for Food Way, Incorporated:

	19X9	19X8	19X7	19X6	19X5	19X5-19X9
Sales (in millions of dollars)	19,650	19,642	18,585	17,633	16,580	
Percent change	.04	5.69	5.40	6.35		18.50

In "nominal terms," as reported in the primary financial statements, sales increased in each year during the period and by 18.5% for the entire period. Now consider the same sales data, adjusted for the effects of general inflation as measured by the average

Consumer Price Index (19X5, 19X6, 19X7, and 19X8 sales are expressed in 19X9 dollars):[18]

	19X9	19X8	19X7	19X6	19X5	19X5-19X9
Sales—Adjusted for general inflation (in millions of dollars)	19,650	20,343	20,067	19,652	19,611	
Percentage change	(3.41)	1.38	2.11	.21		.20

There was essentially no growth—only .2%—in real terms from 19X5 to 19X9; and there was actually a decline between 19X8 and 19X9. These adjustments enable the analyst to compare nominal with real increases in sales.

Inflation also produces purchasing power gains and losses. When a firm has debt outstanding and the purchasing power of the dollar decreases in value as a result of inflation, the debt will be repaid in "cheaper" dollars—a purchasing power gain. On the other hand, holding cash and accounts receivable during inflation results in purchasing power losses because these items lose value during inflation. Firms in a net monetary[19] liability position (more monetary liabilities than monetary assets) experience purchasing power gains during inflation, while a net monetary asset position results in a purchasing power loss.

MISSING AND HARD-TO-FIND INFORMATION

Some of the facts needed to evaluate a company are not available in the financial statements. These include such intangibles as employee relations with management, the morale and efficiency of employees, the reputation of the firm with its customers, its prestige in the community, the effectiveness of management, provisions for managment succession, and potential exposure to changes in regulations—such as environmental or food and drug enforcement. These qualities impact the firm's operating success directly and indirectly but are difficult to quantify.

[18] Adjustments are made using the average Consumer Price Index.

19X9	19X8	19X7	19X6	19X5
322.2	311.1	298.4	289.1	272.4

The proceedure involves the following:

$$\frac{19X9\ \text{CPI}}{19X8\ \text{CPI}} \times 19X8\ \text{Sales} \qquad \frac{322.2}{311.1} \times 19,642 = 20,343$$

$$\frac{19X9\ \text{CPI}}{19X7\ \text{CPI}} \times 19X7\ \text{Sales} \qquad \frac{322.2}{298.4} \times 18,585 = 20,067$$

$$\frac{19X9\ \text{CPI}}{19X6\ \text{CPI}} \times 19X6\ \text{Sales} \qquad \frac{322.2}{289.1} \times 17,633 = 19,652$$

$$\frac{19X9\ \text{CPI}}{19X5\ \text{CPI}} \times 19X5\ \text{Sales} \qquad \frac{322.2}{272.4} \times 16,580 = 19,611$$

[19] Monetary assets and liabilities include items such as cash, accounts receivable, and almost all liabilities other than deferred income or contracts to provide future goods and services that are stated in terms of current value and do not have to be adjusted for inflation.

Publicity in the media, which affects public perception of a firm, can also impact its financial performance. When the publicity is negative, companies often try to counter the damage as soon as possible. General Motors Corporation management moved aggressively to offset the news of an enormous negligence verdict on GM's pre-1988 pickups, asserting that "it will have no effect on sales or customer loyalty."[20] After a series of racial discrimination suits were filed against Denny's Inc. in 1993, the restaurant chain prepared television commercials to convey the message, "You are welcome," and Denny's parent changed its name to Flagstar from TW Holdings. The firm also agreed with the NAACP to establish a program to enhance opportunities for minorities.[21] An article about crop damage caused by a DuPont fungicide, Benlate DF, was followed one week later by a full-page national newspaper ad that stated DuPont has complete confidence in its research exonerating the fungicide and issued a challenge to parties filing lawsuits against the company. Further, DuPont offered to pay to have the fungicide returned and tested; if it was found to cause damage, DuPont would pay for crop damage and if not, the plaintiff would withdraw its suit.[22]

Some relevant facts are available in the financial statements but may be difficult for an average user to find. For example, the amount of long-term debt a firm has outstanding is disclosed on the face of the balance sheet in the noncurrent liability section. But "long-term" could apply to debt due in 12.5 months or 2 years or 15 years. To determine when cash resources will be required to meet debt principal payments, the user must find and analyze the note to the financial statements on long-term debt with its listing of principal, interest and maturity of a firm's long-term debt instruments.

All U.S. companies—large, small, public, private, financial, and nonfinancial—are now required by Financial Accounting Standards Board Statement No. 107, "Disclosures about Fair Value of Financial Instruments," to disclose the market value of financial instruments—including receivables, payables, forward contracts, options, guaranties, and equity instruments. Firms are allowed to show this information either on the face of the balance sheet or in financial statement notes.

Many firms have begun using complicated financing schemes—leases, product financing arrangements, sales of receivables with recourse, limited partnerships, joint ventures—which do not have to be recorded on balance sheets. Called *off balance sheet financing*, these techniques, in essence, enable firms to borrow money without recording the debt as a liability on the balance sheet. Companies using these techniques must meet supplementary requirements specified in Statement of Financial Accounting Standards No. 105, "Disclosure of Information about Financial Instruments with Off Balance Sheet Risk and Financial Instruments with Concentrations of Credit Risk," which require disclosure of information about the extent, nature, and terms of off balance sheet financial arrangements.[23]

[20] Adler, Alan L. "GM Fights to Counter Publicity," *Fort Worth Star-Telegram*, February 2, 1993.

[21] "Denny's Parent, NAACP To Push Minorities Plan," *The Wall Street Journal*, June 2, 1992; and Denny's TV Ad Seeks to Mend Bias Image, *The Wall Street Journal*, June 21, 1993.

[22] Burton, Thomas M. "DuPont Questioned on Data Showing Fungicide's Effect," *The Wall Street Journal*, June 11, 1993; and *The Wall Street Journal*, June 18, 1993, p. C22.

[23] For additional reading about these disclosures, see Carlson, Ronald E. and Mooney, Kate, "Implications of FASB Statement No. 105," *Journal of Accountancy*, March 1991.

Figure 1.6

Another important form of supplementary information is that reported by diversified companies which operate in several unrelated lines of business. These conglomerates report financial information for the consolidated entity on the face of their financial statements. For a breakdown of financial data by individual operating segments, the analyst must use information in notes to the financial statement. The analysis of segmental data is discussed in Appendix B.

There are many other examples of material that must be extracted from notes, supplementary schedules, or the management discussion and analysis section in order to interpret the financial statement. The facts are there, but finding them may involve a search. The remaining material in this book is directed to help the reader find and to use effectively the information in financial statements and supplementary data.

SELF-TEST   SOLUTIONS ARE PROVIDED IN APPENDIX D

___ 1. What are the basic financial statements provided in an annual report?
   (a) Balance sheet and income statement.
   (b) Statement of financial earnings and statement of shareholders' equity.
   (c) Balance sheet, income statement, and statement of cash flows.
   (d) Balance sheet, income statement, statement of cash flows, and statement of retained earnings or statement of shareholders' equity.

___ 2. What is the function of the statement of cash flows?
   (a) To provide information about cash receipts and payments during an accounting period.
   (b) To provide information about the operating, investing, and financing activities for an accounting period.
   (c) To reconcile the beginning and ending balance of all equity accounts.
   (d) Both (a) and (b).

___ 3. What items are included in the notes to the financial statements?
   (a) Summary of accounting policies.
   (b) Changes in accounting policies, if any.
   (c) Detail about particular accounts.
   (d) All of the above.

____ **4.** What does an "unqualified" auditor's report indicate?
   (a) The financial statements unfairly and inaccurately present the company's financial position for the accounting period.
   (b) The financial statements present fairly the financial position, the results of operations, and the changes in cash flows for the company.
   (c) There are certain factors that might impair the firm's ability to continue as a going concern.
   (d) Certain managers within the firm are unqualified and as such, are not fairly or adequately representing the interests of the shareholders.

____ **5.** Who hires the auditor?
   (a) The firm which is audited.
   (b) The auditor's accounting firm.
   (c) The Financial Accounting Standards Board.
   (d) The Securities and Exchange Commission.

____ **6.** What subject(s) should the management discussion and analysis section discuss?
   (a) Liquidity.
   (b) Commitments for capital expenditures.
   (c) A breakdown of sales increases into price and volume components.
   (d) All of the above.

____ **7.** What is the allocation of the cost of fixed assets called?
   (a) Fixed cost allocation.
   (b) Depreciation.
   (c) Salvage value.
   (d) Matching revenues and expenses.

____ **8.** Why could depreciation expense be considered a discretionary item?
   (a) Management must estimate the useful life of the asset.
   (b) A salvage value must be estimated.
   (c) Management must select a method of depreciation.
   (d) All of the above.

____ **9.** What do the choices and estimates relating to depreciation affect?
   (a) Gross fixed assets on the balance sheet and depreciation expense on the income statement.
   (b) Accumulated depreciation on the income statement and depreciation expense on the balance sheet.
   (c) Net fixed assets on the balance sheet and depreciation expense on the income statement.
   (d) Only net fixed assets on the balance sheet.

____ **10.** Which of the following statements is true?
   (a) Published financial statements are prepared according to the cash basis of accounting.
   (b) Published financial statements are prepared according to the accrual basis of accounting.

(c) Published financial statements may be prepared according to either the accrual or cash basis of accounting.

(d) Published financial statements must be prepared according to both the accrual and cash basis.

____ 11. Why do some firms present two figures for earnings per share—primary and fully diluted?

(a) The auditor may feel that as a result of poor management, future earnings potential has been diluted and therefore the firm should adjust current earnings per share to reflect this.

(b) The financial statements contain many accounting changes which affect income in the current year but not future earnings potential or cash flow. Therefore, net income is adjusted for these items and referred to as fully diluted.

(c) The firm has a complex capital structure with convertible securities, stock options, and warrants, which may represent potential "dilution" of earnings per share.

(d) The firm expects to issue more stock within the next year which will lower earnings per share.

____ 12. Which balance sheet account is used to reconcile the differences that arise because of temporary differences in tax actually paid to the IRS and income tax expense reported in the income statement?

(a) Taxes payable.

(b) Deferred taxes.

(c) Taxes receivable.

(d) Tax adjustment liability.

____ 13. Why might the use of accelerated depreciation rather than straight-line depreciation produce earnings of higher quality?

(a) Accelerated depreciation more accurately reflects financial reality because higher depreciation expense would be taken in the early years of an asset's productive period.

(b) During inflationary periods, rising prices increase replacement costs of most assets, resulting in an understatement of depreciation based on historical cost.

(c) Both (a) and (b).

(d) None of the above.

____ 14. Which of the following are methods by which management can manipulate earnings and possibly lower the quality of reported earnings?

(a) Changing an accounting policy to increase earnings.

(b) Refusing to take a loss on inventory in an accounting period when the inventory is known to be obsolete.

(c) Decreasing discretionary expenses.

(d) All of the above.

____ 15. Which of these statements is true during periods of inflation?

(a) Depreciation expense tends to be understated.

(b) Depreciation expense tends to be overstated.

    (c) The firm should change the method they use to account for depreciation.

    (d) Gross fixed assets are overstated.

___ **16.** What can the analyst accomplish by adjusting reported sales with the average Consumer Price Index?

    (a) Determine whether management has manipulated earnings.

    (b) Determine whether depreciation and cost of goods sold are understated.

    (c) Compare real and nominal sales growth.

    (d) All of the above.

___ **17.** Which section or pieces of information can be ignored when analyzing financial statements?

    (a) Auditor s report.

    (b) Management discussion and analysis.

    (c) The statement of cash flows.

    (d) None of the above.

18. Where would you find the following information?

___   **(1)** An attestation to the fairness of financial statements.

___   **(2)** Summary of significant accounting policies.

___   **(3)** Cash flow from operating, financing and investing activities.

___   **(4)** A qualified opinion.

___   **(5)** Information about principal, interest, and maturity of long-term debt.

___   **(6)** Financial position on a particular date.

___   **(7)** Discussion of the company's results of operations.

___   **(8)** Description of pension plans.

___   **(9)** Anticipated commitments for capital expenditures.

___   **(10)** Reconciliation of beginning and ending balance or retained earnings.

        (a) Financial statements.

        (b) Notes to the financial statements.

        (c) Auditor's report.

        (d) Management discussion and analysis.

STUDY QUESTIONS AND PROBLEMS

1.1 What is the difference between an annual report and a 10-K report?

1.2 What are the particular items an analyst should review and study in an annual report, and what material should be avoided?

1.3 What causes an auditor's report to be "qualified"? "adverse"?

1.4 Why is depreciation expense not a precise measure of the annual outflow associated with capital assets?

1.5 What is meant by keeping "two sets of books," and what is the significance to the financial statement analyst?

1.6 How has inflation caused distortion of financial statements?

1.7 What are the intangible factors important in evaluating a company's financial position and performance but not available in the annual report?

1.8 Timber Products recently purchased new machinery at a cost of $450,000. Management estimates that the equipment will have a useful life of 15 years and no salvage value at the end of the period. If the straight-line depreciation method is used for financial reporting, calculate:

(a) Annual depreciation expense.

(b) Accumulated depreciation at the end of year 1 and year 2.

(c) The balance sheet account: fixed assests (net), at the end of year 1 and year 2.

Assume depreciation expense for tax purposes in year 1 is $45,000 and that the firm's tax rate is 30 percent.

(a) By how much will depreciation expense reported for tax purposes in year 1 exceed depreciation expense reported in the financial statements in year 1?

(b) What is the differnece between taxes actually paid in year 1 and tax expense reported in the financial statements in year 1?

1.9 The three-year summary of Kogo's reported sales is shown below:

19X9	19X8	19X7
$11,200	$10,900	$9,070

The average CPI for the period was:

19X9	389.2
19X8	362.4
19X7	346.1

(a) Make the necessary calculations to adjust Kogo's 19X7 and 19X8 sales for the effects of general inflation.

(b) Compare "nominal" and "real" sales growth for the periods 19X8–19X9 and 19X7–19X8.

1.10 R-M Corp.—An earnings quality problem.

C. Stern, chief financial officer of R-M Corp., has just reviewed the current year's third-quarter financial results with company president R. Macon. R-M Corp. sets an annual target for earnings growth of 12 percent. It now appears likely that the company will fall short of that goal and achieve only a 9 percent increase in earnings. This would have a potentially detrimental impact of the firm's stock price. President Macon has directed C. Stern to develop alternative plans to stimulate earnings during the last quarter in order to reach the 12 percent target.

C. Stern has approached you, a recent finance graduate of a well known southwestern business school, to make recommendations for meeting the firm's earnings growth objective during the current year.

Discuss techniques which could be used to increase earnings. Differentiate between those which would

(a) Increase earnings but lower quality of reported earnings.

(b) Increase earnings and also have a positive "real" impact on the firm's financial position.

CHAMBERS DEVELOPMENT COMPANY, INC.
MINI-CASE

Chambers Development Company is a provider of integrated solid waste management services in the United States. The following excerpts are provided from the Chambers Development Company's 1989 and 1991 annual reports.

1989—MANAGEMENT'S DISCUSSION AND ANALYSIS

Financial Overview

The company continued its record of strong performance and growth in 1989 as net sales increased 32.7% over the prior year, following a 133.1% increase in 1988 over 1987. Net income in 1989 was $27.1 million, up from $20.7 million in 1988 and $10 million in 1987. Similar achievements were reflected in the company's fully diluted earnings per share, which increased from $ .44 in 1987 to $ .86 in 1988 to $1.03 in 1989. Additionally, the company has enhanced its financial position in recent years with a number of debt and equity transactions.

Results of Operations

Net sales increased to $181.9 million in 1989, up from $137 million in 1988 and $58.8 million in 1987. Waste services continued to represent an increasing percentage of the company's net sales, providing 65.0%, 87.1% and 89.7% of total net sales in 1987, 1988 and 1989, respectively. Net sales from the waste services segment reached a record level of $163.1 million in 1989, an increase of 36.7% over 1988, following a 212.2% increase in 1988 over 1987. Security services sales rebounded from a 14.0% decrease from 1987 to 1988, to increase by 6.3% to $18.8 million in 1989.

The increases in waste services net sales reflect a number of positive factors. The largest single factor in 1988 was the commencement of operations at two transfer stations in Morris County, New Jersey. These transfer stations opened in January 1988, and produced $44.9 million in net sales during the year. Full year operations under the company's waste disposal contracts entered into in late 1987 relating to Passaic, Essex and Union Counties in New Jersey, together with transportation revenues from Union and Essex Counties, constituted an additional $22.3 million of the 1988 increase in net sales. To a lesser degree, acquisitions, other new contracts, and price increases under existing commercial and residential contracts and at the company's landfills also contributed to the increase.

During 1989, volume growth accounted for a 16.8% increase in waste services net sales over the prior year, with price increases and acquisitions accounting for 10.9% and 9.0%, respectively. The company's contract to transport waste from Essex County, New Jersey, which began in December, 1988, was the largest contributor to the volume growth. Net sales from the disposal contract with Passaic County, New Jersey also contributed to the volume increase. Combined net sales generated from both the Morris County transfer stations and the New Jersey contracts described above totaled $86.7 million in 1989. These contracts, although of limited duration, should provide the company with significant sales for the next several years. The company was informed, however, that the planned waste-to-energy facility in Essex County may commence operation in late 1990; when that facility opens, the company's contracts in Essex County are expected to terminate. Other factors contributing to the Company's internal growth were new collection, transportation, and disposal service contracts with commercial and municipal entities and increased utilization of the company's landfill capacities.

The increase in waste services net sales in 1989 due to acquisitions reflects 14 new collection, hauling, and recycling businesses. The company's corporate development activities continue to focus on prudent expansion into new market territories, the improvement of market share in existing areas, and the enhancement of complementary landfill and hauling activities. The impact of price increases on waste services net sales in 1989 primarily reflects the passing through to the customer of higher disposal costs (as discussed more fully below) and scheduled contractual price increases.

In a significant event affecting future net sales, during 1989, the company and Morris County, New Jersey executed an agreement concerning the settlement of the proceedings before the New Jersey Office of Administrative Law establishing rates for the company's services at its two transfer stations in Morris County. Under the terms of the agreement, the company will provide a rate reduction from $122 to $118 per ton of municipal solid waste beginning in 1990; the rate will be increased to $125 per ton in 1991 and $132 per ton in 1992. Under the settlement, which is subject to certain regulatory approvals, the company will continue to operate the transfer stations through 1994, an extension of two years over the original contract, unless the County's planned resource recovery facility has commenced operations. The extension of these operations allows the company to recover certain costs associated with the transfer stations over an extended life. If the regulatory approvals are not received, the company will be entitled to resume the rate establishment proceedings.

The increase in security services sales in 1989 is due primarily to the acquisition of seven security services companies during the year and the company's emphasis on an improved marketing program. The acquisitions accounted for an 18.4% increase in security net sales, which more than offset the 9.6% decrease due to the decline in nuclear security services. Nuclear security net sales decreased from 1987 to 1988 and again in 1989 due to a reduction in services provided to Duquesne Light Company resulting from the winding down of construction, and final completion during 1988, at its Beaver Valley Nuclear Power Station #2.

Operating expenses increased 28.9% in 1989 over 1988, following a 167.8% increase over 1987. The increases in both 1988 and 1989 primarily resulted from operations at the two transfer stations in Morris County, New Jersey. Operating expenses at these transfer stations exceed those at most of the company's facilities, largely due to higher disposal costs paid to third parties. Additionally, increased volume in 1989 from the Passaic and Union County disposal contracts and the temporary disposal of certain waste at third party landfills contributed to the overall increase in operating expenses. The company believes that disposal cost increases are likely to continue in future years, largely attributable to the increasing scarcity of landfill airspace, the higher costs associated with environmental compliance, and landfill closure and post-closure requirements. The company believes that these increased costs can be recovered through increased prices and a continued strategy of developing and operating regional sanitary landfills.

Selling, general, and administrative expenses as a percentage of net sales decreased to 11.7% in 1989 from 13.1% in 1988 and 17.0% in 1987, due largely to the increase in net sales associated with the New Jersey waste disposal and transportation operations, which required proportionately lower levels of indirect and overhead costs. Additionally, volume and price increases permitted certain fixed components of selling, general and administrative expenses to be spread over an expanded revenue base.

Depreciation and amortization expense has remained relatively constant as a percentage of sales; while increasing in dollar amount by 42.7% in 1989 and 121.4% in 1988. Due to continuing changes in environmental regulations, the costs to develop environmentally safe landfills have risen dramatically. These increased costs are reflected in the company's significant investment in the construction and expansion of its sanitary landfills and the resulting depreciation.

As a result of the factors discussed above, earnings from operations increased by $13 million, or 51.3%, from 1988 to 1989, and by $12.4 million, or 96.0%, from 1987 to 1988.

Interest expense, primarily attributable to the waste services segment, increased 54.9% from $0.5 million in 1987 to $0.7 million in 1988, and increased 86.0% to $1.3 million in 1989. The increase in 1989 was due to the issuance of the 6 3/4% Debentures. The level of interest expense for each year was substantially less than actual interest charges as a result of interest capitalization related to the company's development of its sanitary landfills. The increase in total interest charges as a result of higher levels of long-term obligations reflects the company's acquisition strategy and expansion into new geographical areas, the upgrading and additional purchases of equipment used in collection, hauling and recycling services, and the substantial investment in developing existing and newly acquired landfills.

Liquidity and Capital Resources

The company continually evaluates the cash flows necessary to develop existing and proposed sanitary landfills, to acquire additional solid waste and security businesses, and to fund property, equipment and associated needs for internal expansion. Based on its evaluation, in April 1989, the company completed a public offering of 2,750,000 shares of its Class A Common Stock, which provided $64.9 million in net proceeds to the company. Part of the proceeds were used to retire $35 million in outstanding indebtedness under the company's revolving credit agreement. The balance was added to working capital to be used for general corporate purposes and capital expenditures, including acquisitions.

On September 28, 1989, the company issued $110 million of 6 3/4% Debentures which are convertible into shares of Class A Common Stock at a conversion price of $42.25 per share.

During 1989, the net proceeds of the financing activities described above and the net cash provided by operations totaled $220.2 million, which more than offset the $145.8

million utilized for net capital expenditures, acquisitions of businesses and other investing activities. During 1989, the company expended $62.8 million for the continuing development of its sanitary landfills and $10 million to obtain hauling, collection and recycling vehicles and equipment.

The company currently anticipates expending $120 to $140 million in 1990 for the development of its existing and proposed sanitary landfills and in connection with the acquisition of solid waste and security businesses and other property and equipment. The company's anticipated capital expenditures for landfill development and related environmental matters, are however, for several reasons, extremely difficult to quantify. A number of uncertainties are inherent in the waste management industry, including such matters as changing laws and regulations which may require upgrading or corrective actions at landfills, competitive bidding processes for major contracts, possible delays or difficulties in permitting existing and proposed facilities, potential local opposition to siting of waste disposal facilities, and difficulties in predicting the outcome of acquisition negotiations.

With continuing changes in environmental regulations, the costs to develop environmentally safe landfills have increased dramatically and are expected to continue increasing as more states enact or revise such regulations. The company, like others in the industry, cannot predict with certainty whether particular proposed projects will result in revenue-producing operations, despite substantial expenditures in developing such projects. The permitting process for landfills is often lengthy and subject to intense public and regulatory scrutiny, thereby placing a premium on financial flexibility to enable the company to develop those projects which become viable.

In order to maintain that flexibility, the company is continually evaluating its anticipated cash flow needs. In both 1988 and 1989, the company completed several substantial debt and equity financings in both public and private markets, as discussed in the preceding paragraphs, to enable it to continue its growth. The company's long range capital requirements are expected to be met by a combination of debt and equity placements, together with utilization of existing credit facilities and cash provided by operating activities.

1991—REPORT OF INDEPENDENT AUDITORS

To the Board of Directors and Stockholders of Chambers Development Company, Inc.:

We have audited the accompanying consolidated balance sheets of Chambers Development Company, Inc. and subsidiaries as of December 31, 1991 and 1990, and the related consolidated statements of operations, stockholders' equity and cash flows for each of the three years in the period ended December 31, 1991. These financial statements are the responsibility of the Company's management. Our responsibility is to express an opinion on these financial statements based on our audits.

We conducted our audits in accordance with generally accepted auditing standards. Those standards require that we plan and perform the audit to obtain reasonable assurance about whether the financial statements are free of material misstatement. An audit includes examining, on a test basis, evidence supporting the amounts and disclosures in the financial statements. An audit also includes assessing the accounting principles used and significant estimates made by management, as well as evaluating the overall financial statement presentation. We believe that our audits provide a reasonable basis for our opinion.

In our opinion, such consolidated financial statements present fairly, in all material respects, the financial position of Chambers Development Company, Inc. and subsidiaries as of December 31, 1991 and 1990 and the results of their operations and their cash flows for each of the three years in the period ended December 31, 1991 in conformity with generally accepted accounting principles.

As discussed in Note B to the consolidated financial statements, the accompanying consolidated financial statements for 1990 and 1989 have been restated.

As discussed in Note P to the consolidated financial statements, certain actions have been brought under federal and state securities laws against the Company, certain of its present and former officers and directors, and others alleging, among other things, misrepresentation by the Company of its earnings and financial condition. The outcome of these actions is not presently determinable. Accordingly, no provision for any liability that may result from these actions has been made in the accompanying consolidated financial statements.

Deloitte & Touche

Pittsburgh, Pennsylvania
December 23, 1992

1991—INTRODUCTION TO ANNUAL REPORT

On February 5, 1992, Chambers Development Company, Inc. (the "Company"), originally announced its financial results for the year ended December 31, 1991. On March 17, 1992, the Company announced a change in its accounting method with respect to capitalization of certain costs and expenses which resulted in a revision of previously-announced financial results for the year ended December 31, 1991. On April 15, 1992, the Company dismissed its then current auditors, Grant Thornton, and retained Deloitte & Touche to audit its consolidated financial statements for the year ended December 31, 1991 and in July, 1992, engaged Deloitte & Touche to audit the Company's consolidated financial statements for the years ended December 31, 1990 and 1989. On October 20, 1992, the Company announced a restatement of its previously reported financial results for 1991 and prior years, and a reduction of $362 million in both earnings originally reported since its inception and retained earnings at December 31, 1991. Deloitte & Touche has now completed its audits of the Company's consolidated financial statements for the years ended December 31, 1991, 1990 and 1989, thus enabling the Company to file this report on Form 10-K with the Securities and Exchange Commission.

As a result of certain of the events referred to in the preceding paragraph, the Company was not in compliance with certain covenants of its various long-term borrowing agreements. The Company has obtained interim waivers of the defaults and is negotiating with the lenders for a comprehensive amendment of the agreements. While the

Company is making every effort to negotiate a longer term transaction, and management of the Company believes that a satisfactory agreement will be reached, there is no assurance that such a resolution will be achieved. In the absence of such an agreement, or in the alternate, a restructuring or refinancing of its principal borrowing agreements, the liquidity and business of the Company would be materially adversely affected. The Company has also become a defendant in litigation arising out of certain of the events described in the preceding paragraph. An unfavorable result in that litigation could have a material adverse effect on the Company.

1991—SUMMARY OF RESTATEMENT

A summary of the cumulative effect on retained earnings through December 31, 1991 and 1990 of these revisions is as follows (in millions):

	1991	1990
Reduction in property and equipment	$362	$230
Reduction in intangible assets	43	26
Reduction in deferred costs	28	22
Reduction in provision for income taxes	(76)	(45)
Other, principally increase in accrued closure and postclosure costs	5	7
Cumulative reduction in retained earnings	$362	$240

Details of the Restatement

Certain of the aforementioned capitalized amounts were originally recorded as assets on the basis that they resulted from, or were indirectly related to, permitting and construction activities at the Company's landfills. In particular, the Company had capitalized certain operating costs which were incurred between 1988 and 1991 when various Pennsylvania sites, due to repermitting and construction activities, had their operations substantially reduced in terms of service capacity to the Company's collection and hauling operations and the Company's long-term disposal agreements with third parties. During the period of repermitting, the Company was required, pursuant to the 1988 Pennsylvania regulations, to cease or substantially alter its operations at existing Pennsylvania facilities to implement new construction standards, to add additional monitoring for methane gas, and to implement the new leachate treatment and disposal provisions. These actions also required costly nonrecurring expenditures in the Company's collection and hauling operations, as certain of the vehicles and waste streams of the Company were redirected and rerouted to alternate landfill sites, both Company-owned and external. It is the view of the Company that, but for the repermitting and construction activities on the Pennsylvania sites which were necessary to continue the operations of such sites into future periods, the operating costs and expenses would not have been incurred.

The Pennsylvania sites have now been fully repermitted and are operational, and the Company does not anticipate the incurrence of similar costs in the future.

Other amounts originally capitalized or deferred that have been retroactively charged to costs and expenses included interest on the aforementioned amounts capitalized as property, that have been restated as charges to costs and expenses, as well as interest on property during periods when it was ready for its intended use, although not placed in service at utilization levels consistent with full design capacity.

The retroactive charges to costs and expenses also include compensation and related costs of certain regional and corporate office personnel, including engineering, legal, executive and development personnel, whose activities pertained, in part, to the permitting and construction of landfills and to the development of new businesses. During the audits recently completed, the Company determined that there were not sufficient contemporaneously prepared documents that would enable the Company to determine accurately the amounts appropriate to capitalize or defer. If adequate records were available to support the capitalization or deferral of the costs that were related to construction and other activities of these personnel, the amounts so supported would have been included on the consolidated balance sheets in accordance with generally accepted accounting principles.

REQUIRED:

1. Why is the Management Discussion and Analysis section of the annual report useful to the financial analyst? What types of information can be found in this section?

2. Using the excerpts from the 1989 Management Discussion and Analysis section of the Chambers Development Company annual report, evaluate the presentation provided. Has the company discussed the types of information that should be found in this section? Based on this section only, what is your assessment of the prospects for this company?

3. Is the opinion in the 1991 auditor's report unqualified, qualified, adverse or a disclaimer of opinion? Explain.

4. Based on the material provided from the 1991 annual report, discuss the quality of financial reporting for Chambers Development Company. Which items might concern a prospective investor?

2

The Balance Sheet

Old accountants never die; they just lose their balance.

—Anonymous

A balance sheet, also called the statement of condition or statement of financial position, provides a wealth of valuable information about a business firm, particularly when examined over a period of several years and evaluated in relation to the other financial statements. A prerequisite to learning what the balance sheet can teach us, however, is a fundamental understanding of the accounts in the statement and the relationship of each account to the financial statements as a whole.

Consider, for example, the balance sheet *inventory* account. Inventory is an important component of liquidity analysis, which considers the ability of a firm to meet cash needs as they arise. (Liquidity analysis is discussed in Chapter 5.) Any measure of liquidity that includes inventory as a component would meaningless without a general understanding of how the balance sheet inventory amount is derived. This chapter will cover such issues as what inventories are, how the inventory balance is affected by accounting policies, why companies choose and sometimes change methods of inventory valuation, where to find disclosures regarding inventory accounting, and how this one account contributes to the overall measurement of a company's financial condition and operating performance. This step-by-step study of inventories and other balance sheet accounts will provide the background necessary to analyze and interpret balance sheet information.

FINANCIAL CONDITION

The balance sheet shows the financial condition or financial position of a company *on a particular date*. The statement is a summary of what the firm *owns* (*assets*) and what the firm *owes* to outsiders (*liabilities*) and to internal owners (*stockholders equity*). By definition, the account balances on a balance sheet must balance; that is, the total of all assets must equal the sum of liabilities and stockholders' equity. The balancing equation is expressed:

Assets = Liabilities + Stockholders' equity.

EXHIBIT 2.1 R.E.C., Inc.
Consolidated Balance Sheets at December 31, 19X9 and 19X8
(In thousands)

	19X9	19X8
Assets		
Current Assets		
Cash	$ 4,061	$ 2,382
Marketable securities (note A)	5,272	8,004
Accounts receivable, less allowance for doubtful accounts of		
$448 in 19X9 and $417 in 19X8	8,960	8,350
Inventories (note A)	47,041	36,769
Prepaid expenses	512	759
Total current assets	65,846	56,264
Property, Plant and Equipment (notes A, C, and E)		
Land	811	811
Buildings and leasehold improvements	18,273	11,928
Equipment	21,523	13,768
	40,607	26,507
Less accumulated depreciation and amortization	11,528	7,530
Net property, plant, and equipment	29,079	18,977
Other Assets (note A)	373	668
Total Assets	$95,298	$75,909
Liabilities and Stockholders' Equity		
Current Liabilities		
Accounts payable	$14,294	$7,591
Notes payable—banks (note B)	5,614	6,012
Current maturities of long-term debt (note C)	1,884	1,516
Accrued liabilities	5,669	5,313
Total current liabilities	27,461	20,432
Deferred Federal Income Taxes (notes A and D)	843	635
Long-Term Debt (note C)	21,059	16,975
Total liabilities	49,363	38,042
Stockholders' Equity		
Common stock, par value $1, authorized, 10,000,000 shares;		
issued, 4,803,000 shares in 19X9 and 4,594,000 shares in		
19X8 (note F)	4,803	4,594
Additional paid-in capital	957	910
Retained earnings	40,175	32,363
Total stockholders' equity	45,935	37,867
Total Liabilities and Stockholders' Equity	$95,298	$75,909

The accompanying notes are an integral part of these statements.

This chapter covers account by account the Consolidated Balance Sheet of Recreational Equipment and Clothing, Inc. (R.E.C., Inc.), Exhibit 2.1. This firm sells recreational products through retail outlets, some owned and some leased, in cities throughout the southwestern U.S. While the accounts on a balance sheet may vary somewhat by firm and by industry, those described here are common to most companies.

Consolidation

Note first that the statements are "Consolidated" for R.E.C., Inc. and subsidiaries. When a parent company owns more than 50% of the voting stock of a subsidiary, the financial statements are combined for the companies despite the fact they are separate legal entities. The statements are consolidated because the companies are *in substance* one company, given the proportion of control by the parent. In the case of R.E.C., Inc., the subsidiaries are wholly owned, which means that the parent controls 100% of the voting shares of the subsidiaries. When less than 100% ownership exists, there are accounts in the consolidated balance sheet and income statement to reflect the minority interest in net assets and income. (This topic is discussed more fully in Chapter 3.)

Balance Sheet Date

The balance sheet is prepared at a point in time at the end of an accounting period, a year or a quarter. Most companies, like R.E.C., Inc., use the calendar year with the accounting period ending on December 31. Interim statements are prepared for each quarter, ending March 31, June 30, and September 30. Some companies adopt a *fiscal year* ending on a date other than December 31.

The fact that the balance sheet is prepared on a particular date is significant. For example, cash is the first account listed on the balance sheet and represents the amount of cash on hand on December 31; the amount could be materially different on December 30 or January 2.

Comparative Data

Financial statements for only one accounting period are of limited value because there would be no reference point for determining changes in a company's financial record over time. As part of an integrated disclosure system required by the Securities and Exchange Commission, the information presented in annual reports to shareholders includes two-year audited balance sheets and three-year audited statements of income and cash flows. The balance sheet for R.E.C., Inc. thus shows the condition of the company at December 31, 19X9 and 19X8.

ASSETS

EXHIBIT 2.2 R.E.C., Inc.
Consolidated Balance Sheets at December 31, 19X9 and 19X8
(In thousands)

	19X9	19X8
Assets		
Current Assets		
Cash	$ 4,061	$ 2,382
Marketable securities (note A)	5,272	8,004
Accounts receivable, less allowance for doubtful accounts of		
$448 in 19X9 and $417 in 19X8	8,960	8,350
Inventories (note A)	47,041	36,769
Prepaid expenses	512	759
Total current assets	65,846	56,264
Property, Plant, and Equipment (notes A, C, and E)		
Land	811	811
Buildings and leasehold improvements	18,273	11,928
Equipment	21,523	13,768
	40,607	26,507
Less accumulated depreciation and amortization	11,528	7,530
Net property, plant, and equipment	29,079	18,977
Other Assets (note A)	373	668
Total Assets	$95,298	$75,909

Current Assets

Assets are segregated on a balance sheet according to how they are utilized (Exhibit 2.2).
Current assets include cash or those assets expected to be converted into cash within one
year or one operating cycle, whichever is longer. The *operating cycle* is the time required
to purchase or manufacture inventory, sell the product, and collect the cash. For most
companies the operating cycle is less than one year, but in some industries—such as
tobacco and wine—it is longer. The designation "current" refers essentially to those
assets that are continually used up and replenished in the ongoing operations of the business. The term *working capital* or *net working capital* is used to designate the amount by
which current assets exceed current liabilities (current assets less current liabilities).

Cash and Marketable Securities

These two accounts, shown separately for R.E.C., Inc. in Exhibit 2.2, are often combined
as "cash and cash equivalents." The cash account is exactly that, cash in any form—cash
awaiting deposit or in a bank account. Marketable securities are cash substitutes, cash
that is not needed immediately in the business and is temporarily invested to earn a return.
These investments are in instruments with short-term maturities (less than one year) to
minimize the risk of interest rate fluctuations. They must be relatively riskless securities

and highly liquid so that funds can be readily withdrawn as needed. Instruments used for such purposes include U.S. Treasury bills, certificates, notes, and bonds; negotiable certificates of deposit at financial institutions; and commercial paper (unsecured promissory notes of large business firms).

Under an accounting rule issued in 1993, the valuation of marketable securities on the balance sheet as well as other investments in debt and equity securities depends on the intent of the investment. Statement of Financial Accounting Standards No. 115, "Accounting for Certain Investments in Debt and Equity Securities,"[1] effective for fiscal years beginning after December 15, 1993, requires the separation of investment securities into three categories:

1. *Held to maturity* applies to those debt securities which the firm has the positive intent and ability to hold to maturity; these securities are reported at amortized *cost*.

2. *Trading securities* are debt and equity securities which are held for resale. These securities are reported at *fair value* with unrealized gains and losses included in earnings.

3. *Securities available for sale* are debt and equity securities that are not classified as one of the other two categories, either held to maturity or trading securities. Securities available for sale are reported at *fair value* with unrealized gains and losses excluded from earnings and reported as a separate component of stockholders' equity.

FASB Statement No. 115 does not apply to investments in consolidated subsidiaries nor to investments in equity securities accounted for under the equity method (discussed in Chapter 3).

This accounting requirement will most significantly affect financial institutions and insurance companies, both of which trade heavily in securities as part of their operating activities. The kinds of securities held by companies such as R.E.C., Inc. under the category "marketable securities" or "cash equivalents" are selected for ready conversion into cash, and they have market values that are equal to or very close to cost. Should values be different from cost, however, then the company would have to determine which category of investment applies. For example, if these kinds of securities were considered to be "available for sale," they would be marked to current value and

---

[1] Some terms that may be helpful to the reader are: *Debt securities* are securities representing a creditor relationship, including U.S. Treasury securities, municipal securities, corporate bonds, convertible debt, and commercial paper. *Equity securities* represent an ownership interest in an entity, including common and preferred stock. *Fair value* is the amount at which a financial instrument could be exchanged in a current transaction between willing parties; if a quoted market price is available, the fair value is the number of trading units multiplied by the market price. *Amortized cost* refers to the fact that bonds (a debt security) may sell at a premium or discount because the stated rate of interest on the bonds is different from market rate of interest; the premium or discount is "amortized" over the life of the bonds so that at maturity the cost equals the face amount.

For more information about FASB Statement No. 115, see Parks, J.T. FASB 115: "It's Back to the Future for Market Value Accounting," *Journal of Accountancy*, September 1993.

unrealized gains and losses would be carried as a component of stockholders' equity in the balance sheet.

Accounts Receivable

Accounts receivable are customer balances outstanding on credit sales and are reported on the balance sheet at their net realizable value, that is, the actual amount of the account less an *allowance for doubtful accounts*. Management must estimate—based on such factors as past experience, knowledge of customer quality, the state of the economy, the firm's collection policies—the dollar amount of accounts they expect will be uncollectible during an accounting period. Actual losses are written off against the allowance account, which is adjusted at the end of each accounting period.

The allowance for doubtful accounts can be important in assessing earnings quality. If, for instance, a company expands sales by lowering its credit standards, there should be a corresponding percentage increase in the allowance account. This account estimate will affect both the valuation of accounts receivable on the balance sheet and the recognition of bad-debt expense on the income statement. The analyst should be alert to changes in the allowance account—both relative to the level of sales and to the amount of accounts receivable outstanding—and to the justification for any variations from past practices.

The allowance account for R.E.C., Inc. represents approximately 5% of total customer accounts receivable. To obtain the exact percentage, the amount of the allowance account must be added to the net accounts receivable balance shown on the face of the statement:

	19X9		19X8	
Allowance for doubtful accounts	$\dfrac{448}{8960 + 448}$	$= 4.8\%$	$\dfrac{417}{8350 + 417}$	$= 4.8\%$
Accounts receivable (net) + Allowance				

An analysis of accounts receivable and their quality is covered in Chapter 5.

Inventories

Inventories are items held for sale or used in the manufacture of products that will be sold. A retail company, such as R.E.C., Inc., lists only one type of inventory on the balance sheet: merchandise inventories purchased for resale to the public. A manufacturing firm, in contrast, would carry three different types of inventories: raw materials or supplies, work-in process, and finished goods. For most firms, inventories are the firm's major revenue producer. Exceptions would be service-oriented companies which carry little or no inventory. Exhibit 2.3 illustrates the proportion of industries at the manufacturing, wholesale, and retail levels. For these industries—drugs, household appliances, and sporting goods—the percentage of inventories to total assets ranges from 24% to 39% at the manufacturing stage to about 47% to 64% for retail firms. The balance sheet for R.E.C., Inc. reveals that inventories comprise slightly under 50% of total assets.

	19X9	19X8
Inventories/Total Assets	47,041/95,298 = 49.4%	36,769/75,909 = 48.4%

Exhibit 2.3 Inventories as a Percentage of Total Assets

	%
Manufacturing	
Drugs and Medicine	23.6
Household Electric Appliances	29.8
Sporting and Athletic Goods	39.4
Wholesale	
Drugs	40.2
Electrical Appliances	43.5
Sporting and Recreational Goods	49.4
Retail	
Drugs	47.1
Household Appliances	50.7
Sporting Goods and Bicycles	63.6

Source: Robert Morris Associates, *Annual Statement Studies*, Philadelphia, PA, 1992.

Given the relative magnitude of inventory, the accounting method chosen to value inventory and the associated measurement of cost of goods sold have a considerable impact on a company's financial position and operating results. Understanding the fundamentals of inventory accounting and the effect various methods have on a company's financial statements are essential to the user of financial statement information.

Inventory Accounting Methods

The method chosen by a company to account for inventory determines the value of inventory on the balance sheet and the amount of expense recognized for cost of goods sold on the income statement. The significance of inventory accounting is underlined by the presence of inflation and by the implications for tax payments and cash flow. Inventory valuation is based on an *assumption* regarding the flow of goods and has nothing to do with the *actual* order in which products are sold. The cost-flow assumption is made in order to *match* the cost of products sold during an accounting period to the revenue generated from the sales and to assign a dollar value to the inventory remaining for sale at the end of the accounting period.

The three cost-flow assumptions most frequently used by U.S. companies are *FIFO* (first in, first out), *LIFO* (last in, last out), and *average cost*. As the terms imply, the FIFO method assumes the first units purchased are the first units sold during an accounting period; LIFO assumes that the items bought last are sold first; and the average cost method uses an average purchase price to determine the cost of products sold. A simple example should highlight the differences in the three methods.

A new company in its first year of operation purchases five products for sale in the order and at the prices shown:

Item	Purchase Price
#1	$5
#2	$7
#3	$8
#4	$9
#5	$11

The company sells three of these items, all at the end of the year. The cost flow assumptions are:

Accounting Method	Goods Sold	Goods Remaining in Inventory
FIFO	#1,#2,#3	#4,#5
LIFO	#5,#4,#3	#2,#1
Average Cost	(Total Cost/5) X 3	(Total Cost/5) X 2

The resulting effect on the income statement and balance sheet would be:

Accounting Method	Cost of Goods Sold (Income Statement)	Inventory Valuation (Balance Sheet)
FIFO	$20	$20
LIFO	$28	$12
Average Cost	$24	$16

It can be clearly seen that during a period of inflation, with product prices increasing, the LIFO method produces the highest cost of goods sold expense ($28) and the lowest ending valuation of inventory ($12). Further, cost of goods sold under the LIFO method most closely approximates the current cost of inventory items since they are the most recent purchases. However, inventories on the balance sheet are undervalued with respect to replacement cost because they reflect the older costs when prices were lower. If a firm uses LIFO to value inventory, no restatement is required to adjust cost of goods sold for inflation because LIFO matches current costs to current sales. Inventory on the balance sheet, however, would have to be revalued upward to account for inflation. FIFO has the opposite effect; during a period of rising prices, balance sheet inventory is valued at current cost, but cost of goods sold on the income statement is understated.

In an annual survey of accounting practices followed by 600 industrial and merchandising corporations in the U.S. in the early 1970s, 146 companies surveyed reported using LIFO to account for all or part of inventory. By the early 1990s, this number had increased to 361.[2] Why have so many companies switched to LIFO? The answer is taxes.

Referring to the example, note that when prices are rising, LIFO produces the largest cost of goods sold expense. The greater the expense deduction, the lower the taxable income. Use of LIFO thus reduces a company's tax bill during inflation. Unlike the case for some accounting rules—when a firm is allowed to use one method for tax and another method for reporting purposes—companies that elect LIFO to figure taxable income must also use LIFO for reported income. The many companies that have switched to LIFO from other methods are apparently willing to trade lower reported earnings for the positive cash benefits resulting from LIFO's beneficial tax effect. There is evidence, however, that the trend toward LIFO is reversing and that the number of firms electing FIFO is gradually increasing. Reasons could include both a lower inflation rate and the desire to report higher earnings.

---

[2] *Accounting Trends and Techniques*, American Institute of Certified Public Accountants, 1971 and 1992.

In the previous example, LIFO produced lower earnings than FIFO or average cost, but there can be exceptions. Obviously, in a *period of falling prices* the results would reverse. Also, some firms experience price movements that are counter to the general trend e.g., the high technology industry, where prices on many products have declined, is a case in point. Another interesting phenomenon—a *base LIFO layer liquidation*—occurs with use of LIFO when the firm sells more goods than purchased during an accounting period. Continuing the previous example, the valuation of inventory at the end of year 1 was as follows:

Accounting Method	Items Inventory	Valuation
FIFO	#4,#5	$20
LIFO	#1,#2	$12
Average Cost	(Total Cost/5) X 2	$16

Suppose that during its second year of operation, the company bought two more items: #6 for $12 and #7 for $14. Further assume that the firm sold those newly purchased items plus the two items remaining in stock at the end of year 1. Cost of goods sold under the three assumptions would be:

Accounting Method	Old + New Inventory	Cost of Goods Sold
FIFO	$20 + $26	$46
LIFO	$12 + $26	$38
Average Cost	$16 + $26	$42

In this situation the lowest cost of goods sold expense results from using LIFO because the older, less expensive items were sold. Usually companies maintain a base layer of LIFO inventory that remains fairly constant. Goods are bought during the year and sales are made from the more recent purchases (for purposes of cost allocation). It is only when stocks of inventory are substantially reduced that the base layer is affected, and LIFO earnings are higher. Base LIFO layer liquidations occur when companies are shrinking rather than increasing inventories. There is an actual reduction of inventory levels, but the earnings boost stems from the cost-flow assumption: that the older and lower priced products are those being sold. The effects of LIFO reductions, which are disclosed in notes to the financial statements, can be substantial.[3]

Because the inventory cost-flow assumption has a significant impact on financial statements—the amount of inventory reported on the balance sheet and the cost of goods sold expense in the income statement—it is important to know where to find its disclosure. The method used to value inventory will be shown either on the face of the balance sheet with the inventory account or, more commonly, in the note to the financial statements relating to inventory. R.E.C., Inc. has the following explanation in Note A: Inventories are carried at the lower of cost (LIFO) or market. This statement indicates that the LIFO method is used to determine cost. The fact that inventories are valued at the lower of cost or market reflects the accounting convention of conservatism. If the actual market value of inventory falls below

[3] To avoid the LIFO liquidation problem, some firms use the dollar-value LIFO method, which is applied to goods in designated pools and which measures inventory changes in cost dollars, using a price index, rather than physical units.

cost, as determined by the cost-flow assumption (LIFO for R.E.C., Inc.), then inventory will be written down to market price. Notice that the phrase is *lower* of cost or market. The carrying value of inventory would never be written up to market value; only down.

The inventory note for R.E.C., Inc. also provides information regarding the value of inventory had FIFO been used, since the FIFO valuation would be higher than that recorded on the balance sheet and more closely approximates current value: "If the first in, first out (FIFO) method of inventory accounting had been used, inventories would have been approximately $2,681,000 and $2,096,000 higher than reported at December 31, 19X9 and 19X8."

Prepaid Expenses

Certain expenses, such as insurance, rent, property taxes, and utilities are sometimes paid in advance. They are included in current assets if they will expire within one year or one operating cycle, whichever is longer. Generally, prepayments are not material to the balance sheet as a whole. For R.E.C., Inc. prepaid expenses represent less than 1% of total current assets in 19X9.

Property, Plant, and Equipment

This category encompasses a company's *fixed assets* (also called tangible, long-lived, and capital assets)—those assets not consumed in annual business operations. These assets produce economic benefits for more than one year, and they are considered "tangible" because they have a physical substance. Fixed assets other than land (which theoretically has an unlimited life span) are "depreciated" over the period of time they benefit the firm. Depreciation is the method of allocating the cost of long-lived assets. The original cost, less any estimated residual value at the end of the asset's life, is spread over the expected life of the asset. Cost is also considered to encompass any expenditures made to ready the asset for operating use. On any balance sheet date property, plant, and equipment are shown at *book value,* which is the difference between original cost and any accumulated depreciation to date.

Management has considerable discretion with respect to fixed assets, as was explained in Chapter 1. Depreciation involves estimates of the economic time period served by the asset and any salvage value expected to be recoverable at the end of this period. Further, the amount of depreciation expense recognized each period is determined by the depreciation method chosen. While the total amount is the same regardless of method, the rate of depreciation varies. The straight-line method spreads the expense evenly by periods, and the accelerated method yields higher depreciation expense in the early years of an asset's useful life. Another depreciation choice is the the unit-of-production method, which bases depreciation expense for a given period on actual use. According to *Accounting Trends and Techniques* most companies use the straight-line method for financial reporting:[4]

Straight line	558
Accelerated	106
Unit-of-Production	50

[4] *Accounting Trends and Techniques*, American Institute of Certified Public Accountants, 1992.

Refer now to the property, plant, and equipment section of the R.E.C., Inc. balance sheet. First note that there are three categories listed separately: land, buildings and leasehold improvements, and equipment. *Land*, as designated in the fixed asset section, refers to property used in the business; this would be land on which there are corporate offices and retail stores. Any land held for investment would be segregated from property used in the business. (For R.E.C., Inc. see the "Other Assets" section.)

R.E.C., Inc. owns some of its retail outlets, while others are leased. *Buildings* would include those stores owned by the company as well as its corporate offices. *Leasehold improvements* are additions or improvements made to leased structures. Because leasehold improvements revert to the property owner when the lease term expires, they are amortized by the lessee over the economic life of the improvement or the life of the lease, whichever is shorter.[5]

Equipment represents the original cost, including delivery and installation charges, of the machinery and equipment used in business operations. Included are a variety of items such as the centralized computer system; equipment and furnishings for offices, stores, and warehouses; and delivery trucks. The final two lines under the property, plant, and equipment section for R.E.C., Inc. show the amount of accumulated depreciation and amortization (for all items except land) and the amount of net property, plant, and equipment after the deduction of accumulated depreciation and amortization.

The relative proportion of fixed assets in a company's asset structure will largely be determined by the nature of the business. A firm that manufactures products would likely to be more heavily invested in capital equipment than a retailer or wholesaler. Exhibit 2.4 shows the relative percentage of net fixed assets to total assets for the same three industries identified in Exhibit 2.3. Fixed assets are most prominent at the manufacturing level; retailers are next, probably because retailers require stores and buildings in which to sell products; and the wholesale segment requires the least investment in fixed assets.

Exhibit 2.4   Net Fixed Assets as a Percent of Total Assets

	%
Manufacturing	
Drugs and Medicine	28.2
Household Electric Appliances	19.1
Sporting and Athletic Goods	17.2
Wholesale	
Drugs	9.8
Electrical Appliances	9.3
Sporting and Recreational Goods	11.8
Retail	
Drugs	14.6
Household Appliances	19.3
Sporting Goods and Bicycles	14.2

Source: Robert Morris Associates, *Annual Statement Studies*, Philadelphia, Pa., 1992.

[5] *Amortization* is the term used to designate the cost allocation for assets other than buildings, machinery, and equipment–such as leasehold improvements and intangible assets, discussed later in the chapter.

For R.E.C., Inc., net fixed assets have increased in proportion to total assets from 25% to 30% between 19X8 and 19X9

	19X9	19X8
Net property, plant, and equipment	$\dfrac{29,079}{95,298} = 30.5\%$	$\dfrac{18,977}{75,909} = 25.0\%$
Total assets		

Chapter 5 covers the financial ratios used to measure the efficiency managing these assets.

Other Assets

Other assets on a firm's balance sheet can include a multitude of other noncurrent items such as property held for sale, start-up costs in connection with a new business, the cash surrender value of life insurance policies, and long-term advance payments. For R.E.C., Inc. other assets represent minor holdings of property not used in business operations (as explained in Note A to the financial statements).

Additional categories of noncurrent assets frequently encountered (but not present for R.E.C., Inc.) are long-term investments[6] and intangible assets such as goodwill recognized in business combination, patents, trademarks, copyrights, brand names, and franchises. Of the intangible assets, *goodwill* is the most important for analytical purposes because of its potential materiality on the balance sheet of firms heavily involved in acquisitions activity. Goodwill arises when one company acquires another company (in a business combination accounted for as a purchase) for a price in excess of the fair market value of the net identifiable assets (identifiable assets less liabilities assumed) acquired. This excess price is recorded on the books of the acquiring company as goodwill. The cost of goodwill is amortized over its estimated life, a period not to exceed 40 years. Information about goodwill is disclosed in notes to the financial statements, such as the following: "Other assets include the excess purchase price over net tangible assets of businesses acquired of $243,246,000 at June 30, 1992 and $252,287,000 at June 30, 1991. These amounts are net of accumulated amortization of $32,928,000 and $26,545,000."[7]

---

[6] Reporting requirements for investments in debt and equity securities must follow the provisions of FASB Statement No. 115, presented earlier in the chapter. A more extensive discussion of investments in unconsolidated subsidiaries is provided in Chapter 3. As noted earlier , FASB Statement No. 115 does not apply to investments in consolidated subsidiaries nor to investments in equity securities accounted for by the equity method.

[7] Tandy Corporation, 1992 Annual Report, p. 23.

LIABILITIES

EXHIBIT 2.5 R.E.C., Inc.
Consolidated Balance Sheets at December 31, 19X9 and 19X8
(In thousands)

	19X9	19X8
Liabilities and Stockholders' Equity		
Current Liabilities		
Accounts payable	$14,294	$ 7,591
Notes payable—banks (note B)	5,614	6,012
Current maturities of long-term debt (note C)	1,884	1,516
Accrued liabilities	5,669	5,313
Total current liabilities	27,461	20,432
Deferred Federal Income Taxes (notes A and D)	843	635
Long-Term Debt (note C)	21,059	16,975
Total liabilities	49,363	38,042
Stockholders' Equity		
Common stock, par value $1, authorized, 10,000,000 shares; issued, 4,803,000 shares in 19X9 and 4,594,000 shares in 19X8 (note F)	4,803	4,594
Additional paid-in capital	957	910
Retained earnings	40,175	32,363
Total stockholders' equity	45,935	37,867
Total Liabilties and Stockholders' Equity	$95,298	$75,909

The accompanying notes are an integral part of these statements.

Current Liabilities

Liabilities represent claims against assets, and current liabilities are those that must be satisfied in one year or one operating cycle, whichever is longer. Current liabilities include accounts and notes payable, the current portion of long-term debt, accrued liabilities, and deferred taxes.

Accounts Payable

Accounts payable are short-term obligations that arise from credit extended by suppliers for the purchase of goods and services. For example, when R.E.C., Inc. buys products on credit from a wholesaler for eventual sale to its own customers, the transaction creates an account payable.

This account is eliminated when the bill is satisfied. Ongoing business operations result in the spontaneous generation of accounts payable, which increase or decrease depending on the credit policies available to the firm from its suppliers, economic conditions, and the cyclical nature of the firm's own business operations. Note that R.E.C., Inc. has almost doubled the amount of accounts payable between 19X8 and 19X9 (Exhibit 2.5). Part of the balance sheet analysis should include an exploration of the causes for this increase. To jump ahead briefly, the reader might also note that the income statement reveals a significant sales increase in 19X9. Perhaps the increase in accounts payable is at least partially explained by this sales growth.

Notes Payable

Notes payable are short-term obligations in the form of promissory notes to suppliers or financial institutions. For R.E.C., Inc. these notes (explained in Note B to the financial statements) are payable to a bank and reflect the amount extended under a *line of credit.* A line of credit permits borrowing from a financial institution up to a maximum amount. The total amount that can be borrowed under R.E.C., Inc.'s line of credit is $10,000,000, of which about half ($5,614,000) was outstanding debt at the end of 19X9.

Current Maturities of Long-Term Debt

When a firm has bonds, mortgages, or other forms of long-term debt outstanding, the portion of the principal that will be repaid during the upcoming year is classified as a current liability. The currently maturing debt for R.E.C., Inc. occurs as the result of several long-term obligations, described in Note C to the financial statements. The note lists the amount of long-term debt outstanding, less the portion due currently, and also provides the schedule of current maturities for the next five years.

Accrued Liabilities

Like most large corporations, R.E.C., Inc. uses the accrual rather than the cash basis of accounting: revenue is recognized when it is earned, and expenses are recorded when they are incurred, regardless of when the cash is received or paid. Accrued liabilities result from the recognition of an expense in the accounting records prior to the actual payment of cash. Thus, they are liabilities because there will be an eventual cash outflow to satisfy the obligations.

Assume that a company has a $100,000 note outstanding, with 12% annual interest due in semi-annual installments on March 31 and September 30. For a balance sheet prepared on December 31, interest will be accrued for three months (October, November, and December):

$$\$100,000 \times .12 = \$12,000 \text{ annual interest;}$$
$$\$12,000/12 \quad = \$1,000 \text{ monthly interest;}$$
$$\$1,000 \times 3 \quad = \$3,000 \text{ accrued interest for three months.}$$

The December 31 balance sheet would include an accrued liability of $3,000. Accruals also arise from salaries, rent, insurance, taxes, and other expenses.

Deferred Federal Income Taxes

Deferred taxes are the result of temporary differences in the recognition of revenue and expense for taxable income relative to reported income. The accounting principles for recording and reporting deferred taxes are specified in Statement of Financial Accounting Standards No. 109, "Accounting for Income Taxes," which superseded Statement of

Financial Accounting Standards No. 96 and is effective for fiscal years beginning after December 15, 1992. Most large companies use one set of rules for calculating income tax expense paid to the IRS and another set for figuring income reported in the financial statements. The objective is to take advantage of all available tax deferrals in order to reduce actual tax payments, while showing the highest possible amount of reported net income. There are many areas in which firms are permitted to use different procedures for tax and reporting purposes. One such example, based on depreciation methods, was discussed in Chapter 1. Most firms use an accelerated method (the Modified Accelerated Cost Recovery System) to figure taxable income and the straight-line method for reporting purposes. The effect is to recognize more depreciation expense in the early years of an asset's useful life for tax calculations.

While depreciation methods are the most common source, other temporary differences arise from the methods used to account for installment sales, long-term contracts, leases, warranties and service contracts, pensions and other employee benefits, and subsidiary investment earnings. They are called *temporary differences* because, in theory, the total amount of expense and revenue recognized will eventually be the same for tax and reporting purposes. There are also *permanent differences* in income tax accounting. Municipal bond revenue, for example, is recognized as income for reporting purposes but not for tax purposes; life insurance premiums on officers are recognized as expense for financial reporting purposes but are not deductible for income tax purposes. These permanent differences do not affect deferred taxes because a tax will never be paid on the income.

The deferred tax account reconciles the temporary differences in expense and revenue recognition for any accounting period. Under FASB Statement No. 109,[8] business firms recognize deferred tax liabilities for all temporary differences, that is , when the item causes financial income to exceed taxable income with an expectation that the difference will be offset in future accounting periods. Deferred tax assets are reported for deductible temporary differences and operating loss and tax credit carryforwards. A deductible temporary difference is one which causes taxable income to exceed financial income, with the expectation that the difference will be offset in the future. Measurement of tax liabilities and assets is based on provisions of the enacted tax law; effects of future anticipated changes in tax law are not considered. A *valuation allowance* is used to reduce deferred tax assets to expected realizable amounts when it is determined that it is more likely than not that some of the deferred tax assets will not be realized.

To illustrate the accounting for deferred taxes, assume that a company has a total annual revenue of $500,000; expenses other than depreciation are $250,000; depreciation expense is $100,000 for tax accounting and $50,000 for financial reporting (eventually this difference would reverse and the reported depreciation expense in later years would be greater than the tax depreciation expense). The income for tax and reporting purposes would be computed two ways, assuming a 34% tax rate:

---

[8] For more reading about FASB 109, its application and implementation, see Read, W.J. and Bartsch, A.J., "Accounting for Deferred Taxes Under FASB 109"; and Gregory, G.J., Petree, T.R., and Vitray, R.J., "FASB 109: Planning for Implementation and Beyond," *Journal of Accountancy*, December 1992.

	Tax	Reporting
Revenue	$500,000	$500,000
Expenses	(350,000)	(300,000)
Earnings before tax	$150,000	$200,000
Tax expense (x.34)	(51,000)	(68,000)
Net income	$ 99,000	$132,000

Taxes actually paid ($51,000) are less than the tax expense ($68,000) reported in the financial statements. To reconcile the $17,000 difference between the expense recorded and the cash outflow, there is a deferred tax liability of $17,000:

Reported tax expense	$68,000
Cash paid for taxes	51,000
Deferred tax liability	$17,000

Companies that invest heavily in capital assets are able to continue to defer taxes and thereby build the deferred tax liability account over time because, for tax purposes, accelerated depreciation is used for the newly purchased assets. In reality, the deferred tax account does not disappear because new layers of fixed assets are added, year after year with new tax deferrals, creating new and larger temporary differences.

Deferred taxes are classified as current or noncurrent on the balance sheet, corresponding to the classification of related assets and liabilities underlying the temporary difference. For example, a deferred tax asset arising from accounting for 90-day warranties would be considered current. On the other hand, a temporary difference based on 5-year warranties would be noncurrent; depreciation accounting would also result in a noncurrent deferred tax because of the noncurrent classification of the underlying plant and equipment account. A deferred tax asset or liability that is not related to an asset or liability for financial reporting, including deferred tax assets related to carryforwards, are classified according to anticipated reversal or benefit. At the end of the accounting period the firm will report one net current amount and one net noncurrent amount unless the liabilities and assets are attributable to different tax-paying components of the enterprise or to different tax jurisdictions. Thus, the deferred tax account can conceivably appear on the balance sheet as a current asset, current liability, noncurrent asset, or noncurrent liability.

R.E.C., Inc. reports Deferred Federal Income Taxes as a noncurrent liability. The temporary differences are based on depreciation methods and long-term installment sales.

Long-Term Debt

Obligtations with maturities beyond one year are designated on the balance sheet as noncurrent liabilities. This category can include bonded indebtedness, long-term notes payable, mortgages, obligations under leases, pension liabilities, and long-term warranties. In note C to the financial statements, R.E.C., Inc. specifies the nature, maturity, and interest rate of each long-term obligation.

Other Liabilities

Other liability accounts (not present for R.E.C., Inc.), such as pension and lease obligations, can appear under the liability section of the balance sheet.[9] Statement of Financial Accounting Standards No. 106, "Employers' Accounting for Postretirement Benefits Other Than Pensions," adopted by the Financial Accounting Standards Board in 1990, has had a significant impact on many corporate balance sheets. This statement requires companies to disclose as a balance sheet liability the obligation to pay medical bills of retired employees and spouses—in accordance with the accrual method of accounting—by accruing promised future benefits as a form of deferred compensation. Most companies previously deducted medical expenses in the year paid. This accounting rule also impacts profitability for many firms by substantially increasing the recognition of annual postretirement benefit expense. Statement of Financial Accounting Standards No. 112, "Employers' Accounting for Postemployment Benefits," established accounting standards for benefits provided to former or inactive employees, their dependents, and beneficiaries, and is effective for fiscal years beginning after December 15, 1993.

Adopting new accounting requirements has a major impact on the financial statements of some companies. DuPont, for example, reported charges to earnings in 1992 of about $5 billion for adopting the accounting requirements relating to deferred taxes and postretirement benefits: "In the fourth quarter of 1992, the company adopted Statement of Financial Accounting Standards (SFAS) No. 106, 'Employers' Accounting for Post Retirement Benefits Other Than Pensions"; and SFAS No. 109 'Accounting for Income Taxes,' both retroactive to January 1, 1992. The company recorded charges to net income of $3,788 million ($5.63 per share) and $1,045 million ($1.55 per share), respectively, as of January 1, 1992 for the effects of transition to these two new standards."[10]

STOCKHOLDERS' EQUITY

The ownership interests in the company are represented in the final section of the balance sheet, stockholders' equity or shareholders' equity. Ownership equity is the residual interest in assets that remain after deducting liabilities. The owners bear the greatest risk because their claims are subordinate to creditors in the event of liquidation; but owners also benefit from the rewards of a successful enterprise. The relationship between the amount of debt and equity in a firm's capital structure and the concept of financial leverage, by which shareholder returns are magnified, will be explored in Chapter 5.

Common Stock

R.E.C., Inc. has only common stock shares outstanding. Common stockholders do not ordinarily receive a fixed return but do have voting privileges in proportion to ownership interest. Dividends on common stock are declared at the discretion of a company's board

---

[9] The disclosures relating to pension obligations are covered in Appendix A. Lease accounting is discussed in Chapter 3.

[10] DuPont 1992 Annual Report, p. 26.

of directors. Further, common *stock holders* can benefit from stock ownership through potential price appreciation (or the reverse can occur if the share price declines).

The amount listed under the common stock account is based on the *par* or *stated value* of the shares issued. The par or stated value usually bears no relationship to actual market price but rather is a floor price below which the stock cannot be sold initially. At year-end 19X9, R.E.C. Inc. had 4,803,000 shares outstanding of $1 par value stock, rendering a total of $4,803,000 in the common stock account.

Additional Paid-In Capital

This account reflects the amount by which the original sales price of the stock shares exceeded par value. If, for example, a company sold 1,000 shares of $1 par value stock for $3 per share, the common stock account would be $1,000, and additional paid-in capital would total $2,000.

Reference to the additional paid-in capital account for R.E.C., Inc. reveals that the firm's common stock initially sold at a price slightly higher than the $1 par value. The additional paid-in capital account is not affected by the price changes resulting from stock trading subsequent to its original issue.[11]

Retained Earnings

The retained earnings account is the sum of every dollar a company has earned since its inception, less any payments made to shareholders in the form of cash or stock dividends. Retained earnings do not represent a pile of unused cash stashed away in corporate vaults; retained earnings are funds a company has elected to reinvest in the operations of the business rather than pay out to stockholders in dividends. Retained earnings should not be confused with cash or other financial resources currently or prospectively available to satisfy financial obligations. Rather, the retained earnings account is the measurement of all undistributed earnings.

Other Equity Accounts

In addition to the stockholders' equity accounts shown on the R.E.C., Inc. balance sheet, there are other accounts that can appear in the equity section. These include preferred stock, foreign currency translation effects, treasury stock, and the accumulation of unrealized gains or losses on investments in debt and equity securities that are classified as "available for sale." Exhibit 2.6 illustrates these additional items for General Corporation.

---

[11] The paid-in capital account can be affected by treasury stock transactions, preferred stock, retirement of stock, stock dividends and warrants, and the conversion of debt into stock.

Exhibit 2.6 General Corporation, Stockholders' Equity at December 31
(In Thousands)

	19X9	19X8
Preferred stock, $1 par value, 1,000,000 shares authorized, 100,000 shares issued	$ 100,000	$ 100,000
Common stock, $1 par value, 250,000,000 shares authorized, 85,645,000 shares issued	85,645	85,645
Additional paid-in capital		92,984
105,650		
Retained earnings	2,039,782	1,917,851
Foreign currency translation effects	2,279	(1,198)
Common stock, in treasury, at cost, 22,456,000 and 7,250,000 shares, respectively	(734,132)	(267,153)
Net unrealized gains (losses) on marketable securities	(4,033)	8,035
Total stockholders' equity	$1,582,525	$1,948,830

Preferred stock usually carries a fixed annual dividend payment but no voting rights.

The *foreign currency translation effects* reported in stockholders' equity are the result of disclosures specified in FASB Statement No. 52, "Foreign Currency Translation." When U.S. firms operate abroad, the foreign financial statements must be translated into U.S. dollars at the end of the accounting period. Because the value of the dollar changes in relation to foreign currencies, there are gains and losses that can result from the translation process. These exchange gains and losses, which fluctuate from period to period, are "accumulated" in the stockholders' equity section in most cases.[12] General Corporation has a net foreign currency translation gain in 19X9 and a loss in 19X8.

Firms often repurchase shares of their own stock for a variety of reasons: to meet requirements for employee stock option and retirement plans, to build shareholdings for potential merger needs, to increase earnings per share by reducing the number of shares outstanding, to prevent takeover attempts by reducing the number of shareholders, and as an investment use of excess cash holdings. If the repurchased shares are not retired, they are designated as *treasury stock* and are shown as an offsetting account in the stockholders' equity section of the balance sheet. General Corporation held 22,456,000 shares in treasury at year-end 19X9 and 7,250,000 in 19X8. The cost of the shares is shown as a reduction of stockholders' equity.[13]

According to the provisions of FASB Statement No. 115, discussed earlier, unrealized gains and losses on investments in debt and equity securities classified as "available for sale" are shown as a component of stockholders' equity. General Corporation reported net unrealized losses in 19X9 and gains in 19X8.

---

[12] Exceptions are when the U.S. company designates the U.S. dollar as the "functional" currency for the foreign entity–such is the case, for example, when the foreign operations are simply an extension of the parent company's operations. Under this circumstance, the foreign translation gains and losses are included in the calculation of net income on the income statement.

[13] The two methods used to account for treasury stock transactions are the *cost method* (deducting the cost of the purchased shares from equity) and the *par value method* (deducting the par or stated value of the shares from equity). Most companies use the cost method.

Other Balance Sheet Items

Corporate balance sheets are not limited to the accounts described in this chapter for R.E.C., Inc. and for other companies. The reader of annual reports will encounter additional accounts and will also find many of the same accounts listed under a variety of different titles. Those discussed in this chapter, however, should be generally sufficient for understanding the basics of most balance sheet presentations in a set of published financial statements. The balance sheet will be discussed throughout the book because of the inter-relationship among the financial statements and because of its important role in the analysis of financial data.

SELF-TEST   SOLUTIONS ARE PROVIDED IN APPENDIX D

____ **1.** What does the balance sheet summarize for a business ?
  (a) Operating results for a period.
  (b) Financial position at a point in time.
  (c) Financing and investment activities for a period.
  (d) Profit or loss at a point in time.

____ **2.** What is the balancing equation for the balance sheet?
  (a) Assets = Liabilities + Stockholders' Equity.
  (b) Assets + Stockholders' Equity = Liability.
  (c) Assets + Liabilities = Stockholders' Equity.
  (d) Revenues - Expenses = Net Income.

____ **3.** Why do annual reports include more than one year of the balance sheet and statements of income and cash flows?
  (a) The SEC requires only one year's data.
  (b) Financial statements for only one year would have no reference point for determining changes in a company's financial record over time.
  (c) The income statement is for a period of time, while the balance sheet is for a particular date.
  (d) The information is required as part of an integrated disclosure system adopted by shareholders.

____ **4.** What does the cash account include?
  (a) Cash awaiting deposit.
  (b) Cash in bank accounts.
  (c) Both (a) and (b).
  (d) None of the above.

____ **5.** Which of the following would be classified as marketable securities in the current asset section of the balance sheet?
  (a) Commercial paper, U.S. Treasury bills, land held for investment.
  (b) Commercial paper, U.S. Treasury bills, negotiable certificates of deposit.
  (c) Commercial paper, land held for investment, bonds with maturities in ten years.
  (d) U.S. Treasury bills, long-term stock investment, bonds with maturities in ten years.

____ **6.** What type of firm generally has the highest proportion of inventory to total assets?

    (a) Retailers.

    (b) Wholesalers.

    (c) Manufacturers.

    (d) Service-oriented firms.

____ **7.** Why is the method of valuing inventory important?

    (a) Inventory valuation is based on the actual flow of goods.

    (b) Inventories always account for over 50 percent of total assets and therefore have a considerable impact on a company's financial position.

    (c) Companies desire to use the inventory valuation method which minimizes the cost of goods sold expense.

    (d) The inventory valuation method chosen determines the value of inventory on the balance sheet and the cost of goods sold expense on the income statement, two items having considerable impact on the financial position of a company.

____ **8.** What are three major cost-flow assumptions used by U.S. companies in valuing inventory?

    (a) LIFO, FIFO, average market.

    (b) LIFO, FIFO, actual cost.

    (c) LIFO, FIFO, average cost.

    (d) LIFO, FIFO, double-declining balance.

____ **9.** Assuming a period of inflation, which statement is true?

    (a) The FIFO method understates balance sheet inventory.

    (b) The FIFO method understates cost of goods sold on the income statement.

    (c) The LIFO method overstates balance sheet inventory.

    (d) The LIFO method understates cost of goods sold on the income statement.

____ **10.** Why would a company switch to the LIFO method of inventory valuation?

    (a) By switching to LIFO, reported earnings will be higher.

    (b) A new tax law requires companies using LIFO for reporting purposes also to use LIFO for figuring taxable income.

    (c) LIFO produces the largest cost of goods sold expense in a period of inflation and thereby lowers taxable income and taxes.

    (d) A survey by *Accounting Trends and Techniques* revealed that the switch t LIFO is a current accounting "fad."

____ **11.** Where can one most typically find the cost-flow assumption used for inventory valuation for a specific company?

    (a) In Robert Morris Associates, *Annual Statement Studies*.

    (b) In the statement of retained earnings.

    (c) On the face of the balance sheet with the total current asset amount.

    (d) In the notes to the financial statements.

____ **12.** What type of firm generally has the highest proportion of fixed assets to total assets.

    (a) Manufacturers.

(b) Retailers.

(c) Wholesalers.

(d) Retailers and wholesalers.

___ **13.** Companies A, B, and C:

	A	B	C
Inventory	$ 90,000	$120,000	$180,000
Property, Plant, and Equipment	$ 75,000	$ 30,000	$ 45,000
Total Assets	$300,000	$300,000	$300,000

Which company is most likely a retailer? a wholesaler? a manufacturer?

(a) Company A, retailer; Company B, wholesaler; Company C, manufacturer.

(b) Company A, wholesaler; Company B, manufacturer; Company C, retailer.

(c) Company A, manufacturer; Company B, wholesaler; Company C, retailer.

(d) Company A, manufacturer; Company B, retailer; Company C, wholesaler.

___ **14.** Which group of items would most likely be included in the other assets account on the balance sheet?

(a) Inventories, marketable securities, bonds.

(b) Land held for investment, start-up costs, long-term prepayments.

(c) One-year pre-paid insurance policy, stock investments, copyrights.

(d) Inventories, franchises, patents.

___ **15.** What do current liabilities and current assets have in common?

(a) Current assets are claims against current liabilities.

(b) If current assets increase, then there will be a corresponding increase in current liabilities.

(c) Current liabilities and current assets are converted into cash.

(d) Current liabilities and current assets are those items that will be satisfied and converted into cash, respectively, in one year or one operating cycle, whichever is longer.

___ **16.** What is the difference between notes payable—banks and current maturities of long-term debt?

(a) Notes payable—banks are short-term obligations, while current maturities of long-term are the portion of long-term debt that will be repaid during the upcoming year.

(b) There is no difference.

(c) Notes-payable—banks are usually included under current liabilities, and current maturities of long-term debt are included under long-term debt.

(d) Notes payable—banks are long-term liabilities, and current maturities of long-term debt are current liabilities.

___ **17.** Which of the following items could cause the recognition of accrued liabilities?

(a) Sales, interest expense, rent.

(b) Sales, taxes, interest income.

(c) Salaries, rent, insurance.

(d) Salaries, interest expense, interest income.

____ **18.** Which statement is false?

     (a) Deferred taxes are the product of temporary differences in the recognition of revenue and expense for taxable income relative to reported income.

     (b) Deferred taxes arise from the use of the same method of depreciation for tax and reporting purposes.

     (c) Deferred taxes arise when taxes actually paid are less than tax expense reported in the financial statements.

     (d) Temporary differences causing the recognition of deferred taxes may arise from the methods used to account for items such as depreciation, installment sales, leases, and pensions.

____ **19.** Which of the following would be classified as long-term debt?

     (a) Mortgages, current maturities of long-term debt, bonds.

     (b) Mortgages, long-term notes payable, bonds due in ten years.

     (c) Accounts payable, bonds, obligations under leases.

     (d) Accounts payable, long-term notes payable, long-term warranties.

____ **20.** What accounts are most likely to be found in the stockholders' equity section of the balance sheet?

     (a) Common stock, long-term debt, preferred stock.

     (b) Common stock, additional paid-in capital, liabilities.

     (c) Common stock, retained earnings, dividends payable.

     (d) Common stock, additional paid-in capital, retained earnings.

____ **21.** What does the additional paid-in capital account represent?

     (a) The difference between the par and the stated value of common stock.

     (b) The price changes that result for stock trading subsequent to its original issue.

     (c) The market price of all common stock issued.

     (d) The amount by which the original sales price of stock exceeds the par value.

____ **22.** What does the retained earnings account measure?

     (a) Cash held by the company since its inception.

     (b) Payments made to shareholders in the form of cash or stock dividends.

     (c) All undistributed earnings.

     (d) Financial resources currently available to satisfy financial obligations.

23. Listed below are balance sheet accounts for Elf's Gift Shop. Mark current accounts with "C" and noncurrent accounts with "NC."

____   **(a)** Long-term debt

____   **(b)** Inventories

____   **(c)** Accounts payable

____   **(d)** Prepaid expenses

____   **(e)** Equipment

____   **(f)** Accrued liabilities

____   **(g)** Accounts receivable

____   **(h)** Cash

____   **(i)** Bonds payable

____   **(j)** Patents

24. Dot's Delicious Donuts has the following accounts on its balance sheet:
   (1) Current assets
   (2) Property, plant, and equipment
   (3) Intangible assets
   (4) Other assets
   (5) Current liabilities
   (6) Deferred Federal Income Taxes
   (7) Long-term debt
   (8) Stockholders' equity
   How would each of the following items be classified?

____ **(a)** Land held for speculation
____ **(b)** Current maturities on mortgage
____ **(c)** Common stock
____ **(d)** Mortgage payable
____ **(e)** Balances outstanding on credit sales to customers
____ **(f)** Accumulated depreciation
____ **(g)** Buildings used in business
____ **(h)** Accrued payroll
____ **(i)** Preferred stock
____ **(j)** Debt outstanding from credit extended by suppliers
____ **(k)** Patents
____ **(l)** Land on which warehouse is located
____ **(m)** Allowance for doubtful accounts
____ **(n)** Liability due to difference in taxes paid and taxes reported
____ **(o)** Additional paid-in capital

25. Match the following terms to the correct definition.

____ **(a)** Consolidated financial statements
   (1) Used up within one year or operating cycle, whichever is longer.

____ **(b)** Current assets
   (2) Expenses incurred prior to cash outflow.

____ **(c)** Depreciation
   (3) Value unrelated to selling price of stock.

____ **(d)** Deferred taxes
   (4) Estimation of uncollectible accounts receivable.

____ **(e)** Allowance for doubtful accounts
   (5) Cost allocation of fixed assets other than land.

____ **(f)** Prepaid expenses
   (6) Expenses paid in advance.

____ **(g)** Current maturities
   (7) Combined statements of parent company and controlled subsidiary companies.

____ **(h)** Accrued expense
   (8) Price at which stock trades.

____ **(i)** Par value of stock
   (9) Difference in taxes reported and taxes paid.

____ **(j)** Market value of stock
   (10) Portion of debt to be repaid during the upcoming year.

STUDY QUESTIONS AND PROBLEMS

2.1 How can the allowance for doubtful accounts be used to assess earnings quality?

2.2 Why is the valuation of inventories important in financial reporting?

2.3 Why would a company switch to the LIFO method of inventory valuation in an inflationary period?

2.4 Discuss the difference between the straight-line method of depreciation and the accelerated method. Why do companies use different depreciation methods for tax reporting and financial reporting?

2.5 How is it possible for a company with positive retained earnings to be unable to pay a cash dividend?

2.6 The following data are available for three companies, A, B, and C:

	A	B	C
Inventories	$ 280,000	$ 280,000	$ 280,000
Net Fixed Assets	400,000	65,000	70,000
Total Assets	1,000,000	430,000	650,000

Which company is most likely a retailer? A wholesaler? A manufacturer?

2.7 The FLAC Corporation sells a single product. The following is information on inventory, purchase, and sales for the first quarter:

		NUMBER OF UNITS	UNIT COST	SALE PRICE
January 1	Inventory	10,000	$3.00	
January 10	Purchase	4,000	3.50	
January 1-31	Sales	8,000		$5.00
February 6	Purchase	5,000	4.00	
February 25	Purchase	5,000	4.00	
February 1-28	Sales	11,000		5.50
March 10	Purchase	6,000	4.50	
March 15	Purchase	8,000	5.00	
March 1-31	Sales	12,000		6.50

(a) Compute the inventory balance on March 31 and the cost of goods sold expense reported in the quarterly income statement using the following methods: FIFO, LIFO, and average cost.

(b) Discuss the effect of each method on the balance sheet and income statement during periods of inflation.

2.8 The IOU Corporation has a $150,000 note outstanding with 14% annual interest due in semiannual installments on January 31 and July 31. What amount will be shown as accrued interest on a December 31 balance sheet?

2.9 The King Corporation has total annual revenue of $800,000; expenses other than depreciation of $350,000; depreciation expense of $200,000 for tax purposes; and depreciation expense of $130,000 for reporting purposes. The tax rate is 34%. Calculate net income for reporting purposes and for tax purposes. What is the deferred tax liability?

2.10 Explain how treasury stock affects the stockholders' equity section of the balance sheet and the calculation of earnings per share.

2.11 Energaire Inc. reported the following in its consolidated balance sheets at December 31, 19X9:

	19X9	19X8
Accounts receivable, net of allowance accounts (19X9 $28,704; 19X8 $18,466)	$289,363	$276,204

Analyze Energaire's allowance for doubtful accounts for 19X9 and 19X8.

2.12 From the following accounts, prepare a balance sheet for Chester Co. at December 31, 19X9.

Accrued interest payable	$1,400
Property, plant, and equipment	34,000
Inventory	12,400
Additional paid-in capital	7,000
Deferred taxes payable (noncurrent)	1,600
Cash	1,500
Accumulated depreciation	10,500
Bonds payable	14,500
Accounts payable	4,300
Common stock	2,500
Prepaid expenses	700
Land held for sale	9,200
Retained earnings	?
Current portion of long-term debt	1,700
Accounts receivable	6,200
Notes payable	8,700

MAYTAG CORPORATION MINI-CASE

Maytag Corporation is one of the leading appliance manufacturers in the world. The Company is in two industry segments: home appliances and vending equipment. The vending equipment segment comprises only 5% of net sales, while the home appliances segment accounts for 95% of Maytag's net sales. The Company manufactures and distributes laundry equipment, ranges, refrigerators, freezers, dishwashers, food waste disposers and floor care products. The Company holds a number of trademarks including Admiral, Hoover, Jenn-Air, Magic Chef, Maytag, and Norge. In 1989, Maytag acquired Chicago Pacific Corporation which operated in the home appliances and the furniture segments. The furniture segment has been sold. As of December 31, 1992, Maytag had over 20,000 employees in its home appliances segment. Selected information from Maytag's 1992 and 1991 annual reports is given on pages 71–75.

REQUIRED

1. Which two current assets are the most significant? What percentage is each relative to total current assets? Calculate the percentages for 1992, 1991, and 1990. Why do you think the percentage of one of the current assets is trending upward while the other is trending downward?

2. Analyze the allowance for doubtful accounts relative to accounts receivable and net sales.

3. What percentage is the inventories account relative to total assets? Analyze the trend of the percentages from 1990 to 1992 relative to current assets as well as to total assets. Analyze the percentage trend in the specific components of the inventories accounts, i.e., finished products, work in process, and raw materials.

4. What inventory method does Maytag use? Estimate the current cost of inventory for December 31, 1992, 1991, and 1990.

5. Based on the inventory valuation method Maytag uses, would you expect Maytag to have tax savings or pay more in taxes because of their choice of inventory method? Explain your answer. (You do not need to do any calculations.)

6. Which other assets are significant to Maytag Corporation? What percentage is each relative to total assets? Are the relative proportions of these assets what you would expect for an appliance manufacturer? Explain.

7. Discuss the types of liabilities Maytag Corporation holds and note any significant changes in the liability structure.

8. When did Maytag adopt Financial Accounting Standard No. 109, "Accounting for Income Taxes?" Explain the effects on the financial statements caused by the adoption of this standard. Under which classifications do deferred income taxes appear in 1992? Explain why deferred income taxes appear in more than one classification. What are the principal sources of timing differences? Discuss why these items result in timing differences.

9. Approximately how much did Maytag Corporation's common stock originally sell for? What is the market value of one share of Maytag stock today? (Maytag trades on the New York Stock Exchange.)

10. Has Maytag experienced gains or losses due to foreign currency translation of its financial statements?

Statements of Consolidated Income—Maytag Corporation
Thousands of Dollars Except Per Share Data
Year ended December 31

	1992	1991	1990
Net sales	**$3,041,223**	$2,970,626	$3,056,833
Cost of sales	**2,339,406**	2,254,221	2,309,138
Gross Profit	**701,817**	716,405	747,695
Selling, general and administrative expenses	**528,250**	524,898	517,088
Reorganization expenses	**95,000**		
Operating Income	**78,567**	191,507	230,607
Interest expense	**(75,004)**	(75,159)	(81,966)
Other—net	**3,983**	7,069	10,764
Income before income taxes and cumulative effect of accounting changes	**7,546**	123,417	159,405
Income taxes	**15,900**	44,400	60,500
Income (loss) before cumulative effect of accounting changes	**(8,354)**	79,017	98,905
Cumulative effect of accounting changes for postretirement benefits other than pensions and income taxes	**(307,000)**		
Net Income (loss)	**$ (315,354)**	$ 79,017	$ 98,905
Income (loss) per average share of Common stock:			
Income (loss) before cumulative effect of accounting changes	**$ (.08)**	$ .75	$ .94
Cumulative effect on accounting changes	**$ (2.89)**		
Net income (loss) per Common share	**$ (2.97)**	$ .75	$ .94

Statements of Consolidated Financial Condition—Maytag Corporation
Thousands of Dollars
December 31

Assets	1992	1991	1990
Current Assets			
Cash and cash equivalents	$ 57,032	$ 48,752	$ 69,587
Accounts receivable, less allowance—			
(1992—$16,380; 1991—$14,119; 1990—$17,600)	476,850	457,773	487,726
Inventories	401,083	489,082	535,787
Deferred income taxes	52,261	24,858	22,937
Other current assets	28,309	56,168	52,484
Total current assets	1,015,535	1,076,633	1,168,521
Noncurrent Assets			
Deferred income taxes	71,442		
Pension investments	215,433	232,231	235,264
Intangibles, less allowance for amortization—			
(1992—$37,614; 1991—$28,295; 1990—$18,980)	328,980	338,275	347,090
Miscellaneous	35,989	52,436	45,209
Total noncurrent assets	651,844	622,942	627,563
Property, Plant and Equipment			
Land	47,370	51,147	50,613
Buildings and improvements	286,368	296,684	282,828
Machinery and equipment	962,006	895,025	828,464
Construction in progress	90,847	92,954	61,775
	1,386,591	1,335,810	1,223,680
Less allowance for depreciation	552,480	500,317	433,223
Total property, plant and equipment	834,111	835,493	790,457
Total Assets	$2,501,490	$2,535,068	$2,586,541

Liabilities and Shareowners' Equity	1992	1991	1990
Current Liabilties			
Notes payable	$ 19,886	$ 23,504	$ 56,601
Accounts payable	218,142	273,731	266,190
Compensation to employees	89,245	63,845	53,753
Accrued liabilities	180,894	165,384	154,369
Income taxes payable	11,323	17,574	13,736
Current maturities of long-term debt	43,419	23,570	11,070
Total current liabilities	562,909	567,608	555,719
Noncurrent Liabilities			
Deferred income taxes	89,011	75,210	71,548
Long-term debt	789,232	809,480	857,941
Postretirement benefits other than pensions	380,376		
Other noncurrent liabilities	80,737	72,185	86,602
Total noncurrent liabilities	1,339,356	956,875	1,016,091
Shareowner's Equity			
Common stock:			
Authorized—200,000,000 shares			
(par value $1.25)			
Issued—117,150,593 shares,			
including shares in treasury	146,438	146,438	146,438
Additional paid-in capital	478,463	479,833	487,034
Retained earnings	328,122	696,745	670,878
Cost of Common stock in treasury			
(1992—10,545,915 shares:1991—10,808,			
116 shares; 1990—11,424,154 shares)	(234,993)	(240,848)	(254,576)
Employee stock plans	(65,638)	(66,711)	(63,590)
Foreign currency translation	(53,167)	(4,872)	28,547
Total shareowners' equity	599,225	1,010,585	1,014,731
Total Liabilities and Shareowners' Equity	$2,501,490	$2,535,068	$2,586,541

Notes to Consolidated Financial Statements—Maytag Corporation

Summary of Significant Accounting Policies:
Principles of Consolidation: The consolidated financial statements include the accounts and transactions of the Company and its wholly owned subsidiaries. Subsidiaries located outside the United States are consolidated as of a date one month earlier than subsidiaries in the United States. Intercompany accounts and transactions are eliminated in consolidation.

Exchange rate fluctuations from translating the financial statements of subsidiaries located outside the United States into U.S. dollars and exchange gains and losses from designated foreign currency transactions are recorded in a separate component of shareowners' equity. All other foreign exchange gains and losses are included in current income.

Certain reclassifications have been made to prior years' financial statements to conform with the 1992 presentation.

Cash Equivalents: Highly liquid investments with a maturity of 90 days or less when purchased are considered by the Company to be cash equivalents.

Inventories: Inventories are stated at the

lower of cost or market. Cost is determined by the last-in, first-out (LIFO) method for approximately 76% and 72% of the Company's inventory at December 31, 1992 and 1991. The remaining inventories, which are primarily outside the United States, are stated using the first-in, first-out (FIFO) method.

Property, Plant and Equipment: Property, plant and equipment is stated on the basis of cost. Depreciation expense is calculated principally on the straight-line method for financial reporting purposes. The depreciation methods are designed to amortize the cost of the assets over their estimated useful lives.

Intangibles: Intangibles principally represent the cost of business acquisitions in excess of the fair value of identifiable net tangible assets and are amortized over 40 years on a straight-line basis.

Income Taxes: Certain expenses (principally related to accelerated tax depreciation, employee benefits and various other accruals) are recognized in different periods for financial reporting and income tax purposes.

Short and Long-Term Debt: The carrying amounts of the Company's borrowings under its short-term revolving credit agreements, including multicurrency loans, approximate their fair value. The fair values of the Company's long-term debt are estimated based on quoted market prices of comparable instruments.

Inventories In Thousands	1992	1991	1990
Finished products	$ **249,289**	$ 314,493	$ 335,417
Work in process, raw materials and supplies	**151,794**	174,589	200,370
	$ **401,083**	$ 489,082	$ 535,787

If the first-in, first-out (FIFO) method of inventory accounting, which approximates current cost, had been used for all inventories, they would have been $78.1 million, $72.3 million and $76.8 million higher than reported at December 31, 1992, 1991 and 1990.

Income Taxes

Effective January 1, 1992, the Company adopted Statement of Financial Accounting Standards No. 109, "Accounting for Income Taxes." which requires recognition of deferred tax liabilities and assets for the expected future tax consequences of events that have been included in the financial statements for tax returns. Under this method, deferred tax liabilities and assets are determined based on the difference between the financial statement and tax bases of assets and liabilities using enacted tax rates in effect for the year in which the differences are expected to reverse. Prior to 1992, the provision for income taxes was based on income and expenses included in the accompanying consolidated statements of income. As permitted under the new rules, prior years' financial statements have not been restated. The cumulative effect of adopting Statement 109 was to decrease net income by $85 million or $.80 per share as of January 1, 1992.

At December 31, 1992, the Company has available for tax purposes approximately $101 million of net operating loss of carryforwards outside the United States, of which $22 million expire in various years through 1998 and $79 million is available indefinitely. Of this amount, $32 million relates to pre-acquisition net operating losses which will be used to reduce intangibles when utilized.

Deferred income taxes reflect the net tax effects of temporary differences between the amount of assets and liabilities for financial reporting purposes and the amounts used for income tax purposes. Significant components of the Company's deferred tax assets and liabilities as of December 31, 1992 are as follows:

In thousands	**1992**
Deferred tax items:	
Tax over book depreciation	$(116,725)
Postretirement benefit obligation	143,197
Product warranty accruals	20,221
Pensions and other employee benefits	(58,704)
Reorganization accrual	23,586
Net operating loss carryforward	23,178
Other	15,812
	50,565
Less valuation allowance for deferred tax assets	(15,873)
Net deferred tax assets	$ 34,692
Recognized in statement of consolidated financial condition:	
Deferred tax assets—current	$ 52,261
Deferred tax assets—noncurrent	71,442
Deferred tax liabilities	(89,011)
Net deferred tax assets	$ 34,692

The valuation allowance for deferred tax assets increased $12 million in 1992.

Income (loss) before income taxes and cumulative effect of accounting changes consists of the following:

In thousands	**Year ended December 31**		
	1992	1991	1990
United States	$ 80,013	$ 112,988	$ 163,278
Non-United States	(72,467)	10,429	(3,873)
	$ 7,546	$ 123,417	$ 159,405

3

The Income Statement
and Statement of
Retained Earnings

Never ask of money spent
Where the spender thinks it went.
Nobody was ever meant
To remember or invent
What he did with every cent.

—Robert Frost, *The Hardship of Accounting**

The operating performance of a business has traditionally been measured by its success in generating earnings—the "bottom line." Investors, creditors, and analysts eagerly await a company's earnings report. One objective of this book is to broaden the reader's perspective of operating success to consider such yardsticks as "cash flow from operations" as well as net income. In this chapter, however, the focus is on the income statement and how a company arrives at its "bottom line."

The *income statement*, also called the *statement of earnings*, presents revenues, expenses, net income, and earnings per share for an accounting period, generally a year or a quarter. (The terms *income* and *earnings* are used interchangeably throughout.) Closely related to the income statement is the *statement of retained earnings*. This statement documents the changes in the balance sheet retained earnings account from one accounting period to the next.   Usually this reconciliation consists of the beginning retained earnings balance plus/minus any profit/loss for the period and less the deduction for any dividends. Annual reports include income statements and statements of retained earnings for three years.

Many firms, like R.E.C. Inc., combine the presentation of the income and retained earnings statements.   Both statements are considered here, using the R.E.C.   Inc. Consolidated Statements of Earnings and Retained Earnings (Exhibit 3.1) as the basis for a description of each statement and the accounts that typically appear in the statements. An alternative to the statement of retained earnings is the statement of shareholders' equity, which provides a reconciliation of the changes in all of the equity accounts.   This statement is also discussed and illustrated.

EXHIBIT 3.1 R.E.C., Inc.
Consolidated Statements of Earnings and Retained Earnings
for the Years Ended December 31, 19X9, 19X8, and 19X7
(In thousands except per share amounts)

	19X9	19X8	19X7
Statements of Consolidated Earnings			
Net Sales	$215,600	$153,000	$140,700
Cost of goods sold (note A)	129,364	91,879	81,606
Gross profit	86,236	61,121	59,094
Selling and administrative expenses (note A)	32,664	26,382	25,498
Advertising	14,258	10,792	9,541
Lease payments (note E)	13,058	7,111	7,267
Depreciation and amortization (note A)	3,998	2,984	2,501
Repairs and maintenance	3,015	2,046	3,031
Operating profit	19,243	11,806	11,256
Other income (expense)			
Interest income	422	838	738
Interest expense	(2,585)	(2,277)	(1,274)
Earnings before income taxes	17,080	10,367	10,720
Income taxes (notes A and D)	7,686	4,457	4,824
Net Earnings	$ 9,394	$ 5,910	$ 5,896
Earnings per common share (note G)	$ 1.96	$ 1.29	$ 1.33
Statements of Consolidated Retained Earnings			
Retained earnings at beginning of year	$ 32,363	$ 28,315	$ 24,260
Net earnings	9,394	5,910	5,896
Cash dividends (19X9—$.33 per share; 19X8 and 19X7—$.41 per share)	(1,582)	(1,862)	(1,841)
Retained earnings at end of year	$ 40,175	$ 32,363	$ 28,315

The accompanying notes are an integral part of these statements.

THE INCOME STATEMENT

Regardless of the perspective of the financial statement user—investor, creditor, employee, competitor, supplier, regulator—it is essential to understand and analyze the earnings statement. But it is also important that the analyst realize that a company's report of earnings and other information presented on the income statement are not complete and exact barometers of financial performance. The income statement is one of many pieces of a financial statement package. Like the other pieces, the income statement is partially the product of a wide range of accounting choices, estimates, and judgments that affect reported results, just as business policies, economic conditions, and many other variables affect results. How these issues, introduced in Chapter 1, affect reported earnings is considered throughout this chapter.

It has previously been explained that earnings are measured on an accrual rather than a cash basis, which means that income reported on the income statement is not the same as cash generated during the accounting period. Cash flow from operations and its importance to analysis is covered in Chapter 4. The purpose of this chapter is not to minimize the importance of the income statement, but to provide a clear context for its interpretation.

The income statement comes in two basic formats and with considerable variation in the detail presented. The earnings statement for R.E.C., Inc. is presented in a *multiple-step* format, which provides several intermediate profit measures—gross profit, operating profit, and earnings before income tax—prior to the amount of net earnings for the period. The *single-step* version of the income statement groups all items of revenue, then deducts all categories of expense to arrive at a figure for net income. Exhibit 3.2 illustrates the single-step approach if R.E.C., Inc. used that method to report earnings.

EXHIBIT 3.2 R.E.C., Inc.
Consolidated Statements of Earnings
for Years Ended December 31, 19X9, 19X8, 19X7
(in thousands except per share amounts)

	19X9	19X8	19X7
Income			
Net sales	$215,600	$153,000	$140,700
Interest income	422	838	738
	216,022	153,838	141,438
Costs and Expenses			
Cost of goods sold	129,364	91,879	81,606
Marketing, administrative and other expenses	66,993	49,315	47,838
Interest expense	2,585	2,277	1,274
Income taxes	7,686	4,457	4,824
Net Earnings	$ 9,394	5,910	5,896
Earnings per Common Share	$1.96	$1.29	$1.33

Certain special items, if they occur during an accounting period, must be disclosed separately on an income statement, regardless of format. These include discontinued operations, extraordinary transactions, and the cumulative effect of changes in accounting principles. *Discontinued operations* occur when a firm sells a major portion of its business. The results of continuing operations are shown separately from the operating results of the discontinued portion of the business. Any gain or loss on the disposal is also disclosed separately. *Extraordinary gains and losses* are items that meet two criteria: unusual in nature and not expected to recur in the foreseeable future, considering the firm's operating environment. The *cumulative effect of a change in accounting principles* is disclosed when a firm changes an accounting policy, for example from the FIFO method of accounting for inventory to LIFO.

Data are presented in corporate income statements for three years to facilitate comparison and to provide evidence regarding trends of revenues, expenses, and net earnings. The statements for R.E.C., Inc. are consolidated, which means that the information presented is a combination of the results for R.E.C., Inc. and its wholly owned subsidiaries. The accounting methods used for subsidiary investments are discussed later under the heading "Other Issues—Cost vs. Equity Method."

Net Sales

Total sales revenue for each year of the three-year period is shown net of returns and allowances. A *sales return* is a cancellation of a sale, and a *sales allowance* is a deduction from the original sales invoice price. Since sales are the major revenue source for most companies, the trend of this figure is a key element in performance measurement. Although most of the analysis of R.E.C., Inc.'s financial statements is conducted in Chapter 5, the reader can look for clues on the income statement. It would appear, for instance, that R.E.C., Inc. had a much better sales year in 19X9 than 19X8: sales increased 40.9% ($62.6 million) between 19X8 and 19X9, compared with an 8.7% ($12.3 million) growth between 19X7 and 19X8. The remainder of the income statement reveals management's ability to translate sales dollars into profits.

Cost of Goods Sold

The first expense deduction from sales is the cost to the seller of products sold to customers. This expense is called *cost of goods sold* or *cost of sales.* The amount of cost of goods sold for any accounting period, as explained in Chapter 2, will be affected by the cost-flow assumption used to value inventory. R.E.C., Inc. uses the LIFO method, which means that the last purchases made during the year have been charged to expense. The relationship between cost of goods sold and net sales—called the *cost of goods sold percentage*—is an important one for profit determination because cost of goods sold is the largest expense item for many firms.

	19X9	19X8	19X7
$\dfrac{\text{Cost of goods sold}}{\text{Net Sales}}$	$\dfrac{129,364}{215,600} = 60.0\%$	$\dfrac{91,879}{153,000} = 60.1\%$	$\dfrac{81,606}{140,700} = 58.0\%$

The cost of goods sold percentage for R.E.C., Inc. increased between 19X7 and 19X8. Since then, the firm has either controlled costs more effectively and/or has been able to pass along price increases to customers. The cost of goods sold percentage will vary significantly by industry, according to markup policies and other factors. For example, the cost of goods sold percentage for jewelry retailers averages 55%, compared with 77% for retailers of groceries and meats.[1]

Gross Profit

The difference between net sales and cost of goods sold is called *gross profit* or *gross margin*. Gross profit is the first step of profit measurement on the multiple-step income statement and is a key analytical tool in assessing a firm's operating performance. The gross profit figure indicates how much profit the firm is generating after deducting the cost of products sold. Gross profit, expressed as a percentage of net sales, is the gross profit margin.

	19X9	19X8	19X7
$\dfrac{\text{Gross profit}}{\text{Net sales}}$	$\dfrac{86,236}{215,600} = 40.0\%$	$\dfrac{61,121}{153,000} = 39.9\%$	$\dfrac{59,094}{140,700} = 42.0\%$

Operating Expense

R.E.C., Inc. discloses five categories of operating expense: selling and administrative, advertising, lease payments, depreciation and amortization, and repairs and maintenance. These are all areas over which management exercises discretion and which have considerable impact on the firm's current and future profitability. Thus it is important to track these accounts carefully in terms of trends, absolute amounts, relationship to sales, and relationship to industry competitors.

Selling and administrative expenses are expenses that relate to the sale of products or services and to the management of the business. They include salaries, rent, insurance, utilities, supplies, and sometimes depreciation and advertising expense. R.E.C., Inc. provides separate disclosures for advertising, lease payments, and for depreciation and amortization. Note A to the R.E.C., Inc. financial statements indicates that the firm includes the expenses related to the opening of new stores in selling and administrative expense.

Advertising costs are (or should be) a major expense in the budgets of companies for which marketing is an important element of success. This topic was discussed in Chapter 1. As a retail firm operating in a competitive industry, recreational products, R.E.C., Inc. spends 6 to 7 cents of every sales dollar for advertising, as indicated by the ratio of advertising to net sales:

	19X9	19X8	19X7
$\dfrac{\text{Advertising}}{\text{Net sales}}$	$\dfrac{14,258}{215,600} = 6.6\%$	$\dfrac{10,792}{153,000} = 7.1\%$	$\dfrac{9,541}{140,700} = 6.8\%$

Lease payments include the costs of rentals of leased facilities for retail outlets. Note E to the financial statements explains the agreements that apply to the rental arrange-

---

[1] Robert Morris Associates, *Annual Statement Studies*, Philadelphia, PA, 1992.

ments and presents a schedule of minimum annual rental commitments. The sharp rise in lease payments for R.E.C., Inc. between 19X8 and 19X9, from $7.1 million to $13.1 million—an increase of 84% —indicates an expansion of the firm's use of leased space.

The property leasing arrangement used by R.E.C., Inc. is an *operating lease*, which is a conventional rental agreement with no ownership rights transferring to the lessee at the termination of the rental contract. Another commonly used type of leasing arrangement is a *capital lease*. Capital leases are, in substance, a "purchase" rather than a "lease." If a lease contract meets any one of four criteria—transfers ownership to the lessee, contains a bargain purchase option, has a lease term of 75% or more of the leased property's economic life, or has minimum lease payments with a present value of 90% or more of the property's fair value–then the lease must be capitalized by the lessee according to the requirements of FASB Statement No. 13, "Accounting for Leases."

Both the balance sheet and the income statement are affected by a capital lease. An asset and a liability are recorded on the lessee's balance sheet equal to the present value of the lease payments to be made under the contract. The asset account reflects what is, in essence, the purchase of an asset; and the liability is the obligation incurred in financing the purchase. Each lease payment is apportioned partly to reduce the outstanding liability and partly to interest expense. The asset account is amortized with amortization expense recognized on the income statement, just as a purchased asset would be depreciated.

Depreciation and Amortization

The cost of assets other than land that will benefit a business enterprise for more than a year is allocated over the asset's service life rather than expensed in the year of purchase. Land is an exception to the rule because land is considered to have an unlimited useful life. The cost allocation procedure is determined by the nature of the long-lived asset. *Depreciation* is used to allocate the cost of tangible fixed assets such as buildings, machinery, equipment, furniture and fixtures, and motor vehicles. *Amortization* is the term applied to the cost expiration of intangible assets such as patents, copyrights, trademarks, licenses, franchises, and goodwill. The cost of acquiring and developing natural resources—oil and gas, other minerals, and standing timber—is allocated through *depletion*. The amount of expense recognized in any accounting period will depend on the level of investment in the relevant asset; estimates with regard to the asset's service life and residual value; and for depreciation, the method used.

R.E.C., Inc. recognizes annual depreciation expense for the firm's buildings and equipment and amortization expense for the leasehold improvements on rental property. Note A to the R.E.C., Inc. financial statements explains the company's procedures relating to depreciation and amortization: "Depreciation and Amortization: Property, plant, and equipment is stated at cost. Depreciation expense is calculated principally by the straight-line method based upon estimated useful lives for buildings. Estimated useful lives of leasehold improvements represent the remaining term of the lease in effect at the time the improvements are made." Remember that for tax purposes, most firms use the Modified Accelerated Cost Recovery System for depreciation.

With any expense on the income statement the analyst should evaluate the amount and trend of the expenditure as well as its relationship to the volume of firm activity that is relevant to the expense. For a firm like R.E.C., Inc. one would expect a fairly constant relationship between the investment in buildings, leasehold improvements, and equipment on the balance sheet and the annual expense recorded for depreciation and amortization on the income statement.

	19X9	19X8
Depreciation and amortization	$\dfrac{3,998}{39,796} = 10.0\%$	$\dfrac{2,984}{25,696} = 11.6\%$
Buildings, leasehold improvements, equipment		

The percentage of depreciation and amortization expense has decreased somewhat, possibly because new assets were placed in service during 19X9 for only part of the year, resulting in less than a full year's depreciation and amortization. To help put these accounts in a broader context, Chapter 5 includes an analysis of long-term trends by using data from earlier years as well as the current year's financial statements.

Repairs and maintenance are the annual costs of repairing and maintaining the firm's property, plant, and equipment. Expenditures in this area should correspond to the level of investment in capital equipment and to the age and condition of the company's fixed assets. Similar to research and development and advertising and marketing expenses, inadequate allowance for repair and maintenance can impair the ongoing success of an organization. This category, like depreciation, should be evaluated in relation to the firm's investments in fixed assets.

	19X9	19X8
Repairs and maintenance	$\dfrac{3,015}{39,796} = 7.6\%$	$\dfrac{2,046}{25,696} = 8.0\%$
Buildings, leasehold improvements, equipment		

Operating Profit

Operating profit (also called EBIT or *earnings before interest and taxes*) is the second step of profit determination on the R.E.C., Inc. earnings statement and measures the overall performance of the company's operations: sales revenue less the expenses associated with generating sales. The figure for operating profit provides a basis for assessing the success of a company apart from its financing and investing activities and separate from tax considerations. The *operating profit margin* is calculated as the relationship between operating profit and net sales:

	19X9	19X8	19X7
Operating profit	$\dfrac{19,243}{215,600} = 8.9\%$	$\dfrac{11,806}{153,000} = 7.7\%$	$\dfrac{11,256}{140,700} = 8.0\%$
Net sales			

The ratio indicates that R.E.C., Inc. strengthened its return on operations in 19X9 after a dip in 19X8.

Other Income (Expense)

This category includes revenues and costs other than from operations, such as dividend and interest income, interest expense, gains (losses) from investments, and gains (losses) from the sale of fixed assets. R.E.C., Inc. recognizes as other income the interest earned on its investments in marketable securities and as other expense the interest paid on its debt. The relative amounts depend on the level of investments and the amount of debt outstanding, as well as the prevailing level of interest rates.

Under the requirements of FASB Statement No. 115, discussed in Chapter 2, firms (primarily financial institutions and insurance companies) which carry debt and equity securities classified as "trading securities" report these investments on the balance sheet at market value with any unrealized gains and losses included in earnings. The Financial Accounting Standards Board has proposed an accounting rule that would require companies to deduct the value of executive stock options from earnings, beginning in 1997.

In the assessment of earnings quality (discussed in Chapter 1 and Appendix A) it is important that the analyst consider the materiality and the variability of the nonoperating items of income, for example, gains and losses on the sale of major capital assets, investment income from temporary investments in cash equivalents, and investment income recognized under the equity method (covered later in this chapter).

Earnings Before Income Taxes

Earnings before income taxes is the profit recognized before the deduction of income tax expense. Income taxes are discussed in notes to the financial statements describing the difference between the reported figure for income taxes and the actual amount of income taxes paid (see the discussion of deferred income taxes in Chapter 2). For R.E.C., Inc., refer to Note A, which explains why the differences occur, and Note D, which quantifies the reconciliation between taxes paid and tax expense reported on the income statement. R.E.C., Inc.'s average reported tax rate is calculated by dividing income taxes on the income statement by earnings before taxes.

	19X9	19X8	19X7
$\dfrac{\text{Income taxes}}{\text{Earnings before income taxes}}$	$\dfrac{7,686}{17,080} = 45.0\%$	$\dfrac{4,457}{10,367} = 43.0\%$	$\dfrac{4,824}{10,720} = 45.0\%$

Net Earnings

Net earnings or "the bottom line" represents the firm's profit after consideration of all revenue and expense reported during the accounting period. The *net profit margin* shows the percentage of profit earned on every sales dollar.

	19X9	19X8	19X7
$\dfrac{\text{Net earnings}}{\text{Net sales}}$	$\dfrac{9,394}{215,600} = 4.4\%$	$\dfrac{5,910}{153,000} = 3.9\%$	$\dfrac{5,896}{140,700} = 4.2\%$

Earnings Per Common Share

Earnings per common share is the net earnings for the period divided by the average number of common stock shares outstanding. This figure shows the return to the common stock shareholder for every share owned. R.E.C., Inc. earned $1.96 per share in 19X9, compared with $1.29 per share in 19X8 and $1.33 per share in 19X7.

Companies with complex capital structures—which means existence of convertible securities (such as bonds convertible into common stock), stock options, and warrants—must calculate two amounts for earnings per share: *primary* and *fully diluted*. If convertible securities were converted into common stock and/or the options and warrants—were exercised, there would be more shares outstanding for every dollar earned, and the potential for dilution is accounted for by the dual presentation. Dual presentation is required if the potential dilution would reduce earnings per share by 3% or more. In Note G to the financial statements R.E.C., Inc. reports that the potential for dilution is less than 3% of earnings per share and, thus, the firm reports only one earnings per share amount. The primary earnings per share figure is based on the assumption that some[2] of the potentially dilutive securities have been converted into common stock, while fully diluted earnings per share includes all potentially dilutive securities in the number of shares outstanding.

THE STATEMENT OF RETAINED EARNINGS

The retained earnings statement is ordinarily the shortest and least complicated of the four financial statements. This statement details the transactions—primarily net income (loss) and dividends—that affect the balance sheet retained earnings account during an accounting period. The starting point is the retained earnings balance at the beginning of the accounting period. To that balance net earnings are added or net losses are deducted. Dividends, both cash and stock, are subtracted to arrive at the ending balance. (R.E.C., Inc.'s dividend payment policy is discussed in Chapter 5.)

The statements of consolidated retained earnings for R.E.C., Inc., like the income statements, are presented for three years. (See Exhibit 3.3.) The net earnings for each year have been added to the beginning balance of retained earnings. The only deduction for R.E.C., Inc. has been the annual payment of cash dividends. In 19X9 R.E.C., Inc. paid cash dividends of $.33 per share on average shares outstanding (Note G) of 4,792,857 for a total of $1,581,643. The amount of the dividend payment was reduced from $.41 per share in 19X8 and 19X7. Although R.E.C., Inc. paid no stock dividends, the financial statement user should be aware of the accounting treatment of these dividends.

EXHIBIT 3.3

Statements of Consolidated Retained Earnings

Retained earnings at beginning of year	$32,363	$28,315	$24,260
Net earnings	9,394	5,910	5,896
Cash dividends (19X9—$.33 per share; 19X8 and 19X7—$.41 per share)	(1,582)	(1,862)	(1,841)
Retained earnings at end of year	$40,175	$32,363	$28,315

The accompanying notes are an integral part of these statements.

[2] Included are those securities considered to be dilutive common stock equivalents. Accounting Principles Board Opinion No. 15 defines common stock equivalents as securities that contain a provision that enables the owner to convert them into common stock.

Stock dividends are the issuance to existing shareholders of additional shares of stock in proportion to those shares currently owned. When a stock dividend is declared, the retained earnings account is decreased by the market value of the shares issued in the case of a *small stock dividend* (less than 20 to 25% of the number of shares outstanding) or by the par value of the stock in the case of a large *stock dividend* (more than 20 to 25% of the number of shares outstanding). For example, if a company with 100,000 ($1 par) common shares outstanding issues a 10% stock dividend at a time when the market value of the stock is $3, the retained earnings account would be reduced by $30,000:

$$(100,000 \times .10) \times \$3 = \$30,000.$$

If a 50% stock dividend were paid, the deduction would be $50,000:

$$(100,000 \times .5) \times \$1 = \$50,000.$$

From the stockholders' viewpoint, receipt of stock dividends, unlike a cash dividend, represents nothing of tangible value. When a cash dividend is paid the shareholder receives cash, and the company's assets and retained earnings are reduced. Payment of a stock dividend does not affect assets or liabilities but results only in an adjustment within the equity section of the balance sheet: the retained earnings' balance is reduced, and the stock account (or stock and paid-in capital) is increased by the same amount. The shareholder has more shares, but the *proportion of ownership* in the company is exactly the same; and the net asset value (assets minus liabilities) of the company is exactly the same. The market value of the stock should drop in proportion to the additional shares issued.

Stock splits also result in the issuance of additional shares to the shareholder and are generally executed by a company in order to lower the market price of the firm's shares. For example, assume that a company with 2,000,000 outstanding shares of $4 par value stock, selling at $100 per share, declares a 4 for 1 stock split. A shareholder with 100 shares would end up with 400 shares after the split. There is no accounting entry required for the issuing company, but a memorandum item would note the change in the par value of the stock from $4 to $1, and the change in the total number of shares outstanding from 2,000,000 to 8,000,000. Theoretically, the price would fall to $25, and the value of shareholders' holdings would remain unchanged. Companies frequently execute stock splits in order to make common shares more affordable for the average investor.

Transactions other than the recognition of net profit/loss and the payment of dividends can cause changes in the retained earnings balance. These include prior period adjustments and certain changes in accounting principles. Prior period adjustments result primarily from the correction of errors made in previous accounting periods; the beginning retained earnings balance is adjusted for the year in which the error is discovered. Some changes in accounting principles, such as a change from LIFO to any other inventory valuation method, also cause an adjustment to retained earnings for the cumulative effect of the change. Retained earnings can also be affected by transactions in a firm's own shares.

STATEMENT OF SHAREHOLDERS' EQUITY

Some companies adopt a broader approach and prepare a statement that summarizes changes in the entire shareholders' equity section of the balance sheet, including not only retained earnings but also all of the other equity accounts. Exhibit 3.4 shows the

EXHIBIT 3.4 Consolidated Statements of Stockholders' Equity

Columbine Corporation and Subsidiaries Three years ended June 30, 19X9

In thousands.

	Common Stock Shares	Common Stock Dollars	Treasury Stock Shares	Treasury Stock Dollars	Additional Paid-in Capital	Retained Earnings	Foreign Currency Translation Effects	Total
Balance at June 30, 19X6	95,645	$95,645	(5,905)	$(166,435)	$102,305	$1,344,394	$4,130	$1,380,039
Purchase of treasury stock	—	—	(2,286)	(90,541)	—	—	—	(90,541)
Foreign currency translation adjustments, net of deferred taxes of $2,048,000							3,975	3,975
Sale of treasury stock to employee stock purchase program			1,095	31,993	12,694	—	—	44,687
Cash dividends declared						(51,402)		(51,402)
Net income						316,354		316,354
Balance at June 30, 19X7	95,645	95,645	(7,096)	(224,983)	114,999	1,609,346	8,105	1,603,112
Purchase of treasury stock	—	—	(4,690)	(198,823)				(198,823)
Foreign currency translation adjustments, net of deferred taxes of $1,416,000							(2,749)	(2,749)
Sale of treasury stock to employee stock purchase program			1,158	36,460	12,989			49,449
Acquisition of SLIDE Systems			1,283	57,145	2,752			59,897
Exercise of stock options			38	1,525	52			1,577
Cash dividends declared						(53,129)		(53,129)
Net income						323,504		323,504
Balance at June 30, 19X8	95,645	95,645	(9,307)	(328,676)	130,792	1,879,721	5,356	1,782,838
Purchase of treasury stock	—	—	(8,907)	(369,982)				(369,982)
Foreign currency translation adjustments, net of deferred taxes of $1,586,000							3,079	3,079
Sale of treasury stock to employee stock purchase program			1,335	50,439	1,580			52,019
Exercise of stock options			82	3,050	(25)			3,025
SLIDE earn out			284	10,430	403			10,833
Cash dividends declared						(48,663)		(48,663)
Net income						290,347		290,347
Balance at June 30, 19X9	95,645	$95,645	(16,513)	$(634,739)	$132,750	$2,121,405	$8,435	$1,723,496

The accompanying notes are an integral part of these financial statements.

Consolidated Statements of Stockholders' Equity for Columbine Corporation and Subsidiaries from the 19X9 Annual Report. This statement provides a reconciliation in dollars and shares of all of the accounts from the stockholders' equity section of Columbine's balance sheet: common stock, treasury stock, additional paid-in capital, retained earnings and foreign currency translation effects. These accounts were discussed in Chapter 2.

The stockholders' equity statement enables the analyst to trace any changes in equity accounts. Consider, for example, the treasury stock account. Exhibit 3.4 shows that Columbine acquired 2,286 thousand shares in fiscal 19X7, 4,690 thousand in 19X8, and 8,907 thousand in 19X9, resulting in a decrease of equity (for the cost to acquire the shares) of $90,541 thousand in 19X7, $198,823 thousand dollars in 19X8 and $369,982 in 19X9. Columbine sold treasury stock in each of the three periods to the employee stock purchase program—1,095 thousand shares 1,158 thousand shares, and 1,335 thousand shares—with resulting increases in equity of $31,993 thousand, $36,460 thousand, and $50,439 thousand. Other treasury stock transactions included the sale of shares through stock options, 38 thousand ($1,525 thousand) in 19X8 and 82 thousand ($3,050 thousand) in 19X9; and the use of treasury shares for an acquisition of SLIDE Systems in 19X8, involving 1,283 thousand shares ($57,145 thousand). In fiscal 19X9, 284 thousand shares ($10,430 thousand) were issued to SLIDE Systems stockholders as part of the acquisition agreement.

Purchases of treasury shares reduce equity, and sales of treasury shares increase equity; treasury stock is shown as a contra equity account in the balance sheet. The beginning and ending account balances of the account are shown for each year. The analyst could trace, in the same way, the transactions for all of the equity accounts.

OTHER ISSUES—COST vs. EQUITY METHOD

An additional issue that users sometimes encounter in attempting to evaluate financial statement data is the method—cost or equity—employed to account for investments in the voting stock of other companies. This method is not an issue for R.E.C., Inc. because the parent owns 100% of the voting stock in its subsidiaries; R.E.C., Inc. and its subsidiaries are, in substance, one consolidated entity. When one firm owns more than 50% of the voting stock of another company, the parent company can obviously control the business operations, financial policies, and dividend declarations of the subsidiary, and consolidated financial statements are prepared with the disclosures relating to consolidation policies provided in the financial statement notes. The accounting rules underlying the preparation of consolidated financial statements, while similar to the equity method, are extremely complicated and beyond the scope of this book.[3] Questions regarding use of cost or equity comes into play for stock investments of less than 50%, when consolidated financial statements are not prepared.

---

[3] Accounting for consolidated financial statements is fully discussed and explained in advanced accounting textbooks.

Accounting rules permit two different methods to account for stock investments of less than 50%. The *equity method* allows the investor proportionate recognition of the investee's net income, irrespective of the payment or nonpayment of cash dividends; under the *cost method*, the investor recognizes investment income only to the extent of any cash dividends received. At issue in the choice of accounting methods is whether the investor exercises control over the investee.

Accounting Principles Board Opinion No. 18 specifies that the equity method of accounting should be used when the investor can exercise *significant influence* over the investee's operating and financing policies. No problem exists where there is ownership of 50% or more because, clearly, one company can control the other. But at what level below 50% ownership can one firm *substantially influence* the affairs of another firm? Although there can be exceptions, 20% ownership of voting stock is generally considered to be evidence of substantial influence. There are, however, cases in which less than 20% ownership reflects control and cases in which more than 20% does not. Such factors as the extent of representation on investee's board of directors, major intercompany transactions, technological dependence, and other relationships would be considered in the determination.

What difference does it make whether a company uses the cost or equity method? An illustration should help provide the answer.

Assume that Company A acquires exactly 20% of the voting common stock of Company B for $400,000. Company B reports $100,000 earnings for the year and pays $25,000 in cash dividends. For Company A, the income recognition in the earnings statement and the noncurrent investment account on the balance sheet would be entirely different depending on the accounting method used for the investment.

	Cost	**Equity**
Income Statement: Investment Income	$ 5,000	$ 20,000
Balance Sheet: Investment Account	$400,000	$415,000

The cost method allows recognition of investment income only to the extent of any cash dividends actually received ($25,000 × .20), and the investment account is carried at cost.[4] The equity method permits the investor to count as income the percentage interest in investee's earnings.

Company B's earnings	$100,000
Company A's percent ownership	× .20
Company A's investment income	$ 20,000

Under the equity method, the investment account is increased by the amount of investment income recognized and is reduced by the amount of cash dividends received.

---

[4] Or market, depending on the provisions of FASB Statement No. 115. This statement does not apply to investments accounted for under the equity method.

Investment at cost	$400,000
Investment income	+ 20,000
Cash dividends received	– 5,000
Investment account	$415,000

Use of the equity method distorts earnings somewhat in the sense that income is recognized even though no cash may ever be received. The theoretical justification for the equity method is that it is presumed that the investor (Company A), through its control of voting shares, could cause Company B to pay dividends. In reality, this may not be true, and Company A is permitted to recognize more income than is received in cash.

One of the adjustments to net income (illustrated in Chapter 4) to calculate cash flow from operations is to deduct the amount by which income recognized under the equity method of accounting exceeds cash received from dividends. For Company A this amount would be $15,000 (investment income $20,000 less cash dividends $5,000). It is also equal to the increase in the balance sheet investment account (ending balance $415,000 less original cost $400,000).

EARNINGS QUALITY, INFLATION, CASH FLOW, SEGMENTAL ACCOUNTING

Other topics which are directly related to the income statement are covered in other sections of the book. The assessment of the quality of reported earnings is an essential element of income statement analysis. The qualitative interpretation of earnings is discussed in Chapter 1 and Appendix A.

The impact of inflation on reported earnings is covered in Chapter 1.

The earnings figure reported on the income statement is rarely the same as the cash generated during an accounting period. Because it is cash that a firm needs to service debt, to pay suppliers, to invest in new capital assets, to pay cash dividends, cash flow from operations is a key ingredient in analyzing operating performance. The calculation of cash flow from operations, how it differs from reported earnings, and the interpretation of cash flow as a performance measure are discussed in Chapter 4.

Appendix B deals with the supplementary information reported by companies that operate in several different business segments. Segmental data include revenue, operating profit or loss, identifiable assets, depreciation and amortization, and capital expenditures by industry components. These disclosures facilitate the analysis of operating performance and the contribution by each segment of a diversified company.

SELF-TEST SOLUTIONS ARE PROVIDED IN APPENDIX D

____ **1.** What does the income statement measure for a firm?

  (a) The changes in assets and liabilities that occurred during a period.

  (b) The financing and investment activities for a period.

    (c) The results of operations for a period.

    (d) The financial position of a firm for a period.

____ **2.** Which two financial statements are frequently combined for presentation purposes?

    (a) The statement of financial position and the balance sheet.

    (b) The income and retained earnings statements.

    (c) The statement of cash flows and the retained earnings statement.

    (d) The balance sheet and the income statement.

____ **3.** Which of the items below need *not* be disclosed separately in the income statement?

    (a) Salary expense.

    (b) Selling a major business segment.

    (c) Extraordinary transactions.

    (d) Cumulative effect of changes in accounting principles.

____ **4.** Why are data presented in income statements for three years?

    (a) The IRS requires a three-year presentation for tax purposes.

    (b) A three-year presentation discourages manipulation of earnings by management.

    (c) Income statements for three years facilitate comparison and provide evidence regarding trends of revenues, expenses, and net earnings.

    (d) An income statement for only one year would be meaningless.

____ **5.** What is the largest expense item for most firms?

    (a) Gross profit.

    (b) Depreciation.

    (c) Operating expense.

    (d) Cost of goods sold.

____ **6.** What is the basic difference between an operating lease and a capital lease?

    (a) A capital lease is, in substance, a purchase, whereas an operating lease is a rental agreement.

    (b) An operating lease transfers ownership to the lessee.

    (c) Capital leases must meet four criteria.

    (d) Capital leases must have a lease term of 90% or more of the leased property's economic life.

____ **7.** Which of the following statements is incorrect with regard to capital leases?

    (a) The balance sheet and the income statement are affected by a capital lease.

    (b) Each lease payment is apportioned partly to interest expense and partly to reduce a liability.

    (c) The liability account is amortized just as a purchased asset would be depreciated.

    (d) An asset and a liability are recorded on the lessee's balance sheet equal to the present value of the lease payments to be made under the contract.

____ **8.** Which of the following assets will not be depreciated over its service life?

    (a) Buildings.

    (b) Furniture.

    (c) Equipment.

    (d) Land.

____ **9.** How are costs of assets that benefit a firm for more than one year allocated?

    (a) Depreciation.

    (b) Depletion and amortization.

    (c) Costs are divided by service lives of assets and allocated to repairs and maintenance.

    (d) Both (a) and (b).

____ **10.** Why should the expenditures for repairs and maintenance correspond to the level of investment in capital equipment and to the age and condition of that equipment?

    (a) Repairs and maintenance expense is calculated in the same manner as depreciation expense.

    (b) Inadequate repairs of equipment can impair the operating success of a business enterprise.

    (c) It is a generally accepted accounting principle that repairs and maintenance expense is generally between 5% and 10% of fixed assets.

    (d) Repairs and maintenance are depreciated over the remaining life of the assets involved.

____ **11.** Why is the figure for operating profit important?

    (a) This is the figure used for calculating federal income tax expense.

    (b) The figure for operating profit provides a basis for assessing the success of a company apart from its financing and investment activities and separate from its tax status.

    (c) The operating profit figure includes all operating revenues and expenses as well as interest and taxes related to operations.

    (d) The figure for operating profit provides a basis for assessing the wealth of a firm.

____ **12.** What are three profit measures calculated from the income statement?

    (a) Gross profit margin, operating profit margin, net profit margin.

    (b) Gross profit margin, cost of goods sold percentage, EBIT.

    (c) Operating profit margin, net profit margin, repairs and maintenance to fixed assets.

    (d) None of the above.

____ **13.** When is a dual presentation of primary and fully diluted earnings per share required?

    (a) If the potential dilution would reduce earnings per share by 3% or more.

    (b) If convertible securities were in fact converted.

    (c) If a company has a complex capital structure.

    (d) If a company has stock options and warrants outstanding.

____ **14.** What is the impact of a stock dividend on the financial statements?

   (a) Cash is reduced on the balance sheet, and common stock is increased.

   (b) The proportion of ownership in the company will increase.

   (c) The retained earnings balance is reduced, and the stock account is increased by the same amount.

   (d) The retained earnings account is decreased by the par value of the shares issued in the case of a small stock dividend or by the market value in the case of a large dividend.

____ **15.** Which of the following cause a change in the retained earnings account balance?

   (a) Prior period adjustment.

   (b) Payment of dividends.

   (c) Net profit or loss.

   (d) All of the above.

____ **16.** What is a statement of shareholders' equity?

   (a) It is the same as a retained earnings statement.

   (b) It is a statement that reconciles only the treasury stock account.

   (c) It is a statement that summarizes changes in the entire shareholders' equity section of the balance sheet.

   (d) It is a statement reconciling the difference between stock issued at par value and stock issued at market value.

____ **17.** What additional shareholder equity accounts can be found on a statement of shareholders' equity as compared to a statement of retained earnings?

   (a) Investments in other companies.

   (b) Treasury stock, unrealized gains (losses) on marketable equity securities, and cumulative translation adjustment.

   (c) Market value of treasury stock.

   (d) Both (a) and (c).

____ **18.** Why can the equity method of accounting for investments in the voting stock of other companies cause distortions in net earnings?

   (a) Income is recognized when no cash may ever be received.

   (b) Significant influence may exist even if the ownership of voting stock is less than 20%.

   (c) Income should be recognized in accordance with the accrual method of accounting.

   (d) Income is recognized only to the extent of cash dividends received.

19. Match the following terms with the correct definitions:

   ____ **(a)** Depreciation   ____ **(d)** Gross profit

   ____ **(b)** Depletion   ____ **(e)** Operating profit

   ____ **(c)** Amortization   ____ **(f)** Net profit

___(g) Equity method   ___ (k) Primary earnings per share

___(h) Cost method   ___ (l) Fully diluted earnings per share

___ (i) Single-step format   ___ (m) Operating lease

___ (j) Multiple-step form   ___ (n) Capital lease

Definitions:

(1) Proportionate recognition of investee's net income for investments in voting stock of other companies.

(2) Presentation of income statement that provides several intermediate profit measures.

(3) Conventional rental agreement with no ownership rights transferring to the lessee at the termination of the contract.

(4) Allocation of costs of tangible fixed assets.

(5) Difference between sales revenue and expenses associated with generating sales.

(6) Recognition of income from investments in voting stock of other companies to the extent of cash dividend received.

(7) Rental agreement which is, in substance, a purchase.

(8) Difference between net sales and cost of goods sold.

(9) Allocation of costs of acquiring and developing natural resources.

(10) Earnings per share figure based on the assumption that some of the potentially dilutive securities have been converted to common stock.

(11) Presentation of income statement that groups all revenue items, then deducts all expenses, to arrive at net income.

(12) Earnings per share figure based on the assumption that all potentially dilutive securities have been converted to common stock.

(13) Allocation of costs of intangible assets.

(14) Difference between all revenues and expenses.

20. The following categories appear on the income statement of Joshua Jeans Company:

(a) Net sales

(b) Cost of sales

(c) Operating expenses

(d) Other revenue / expense

(e) Income tax expense

Classify the following items according to income statement category:

___   (1) Depreciation expense

___   (2) Interest revenue

___   (3) Sales revenue

___   (4) Advertising expense

___   (5) Interest expense

___   (6) Sales returns and allowance

____ **(7)** Federal income taxes

____ **(8)** Repairs and maintenance

____ **(9)** Selling and administrative expenses

____ **(10)** Cost of products sold

____ **(11)** Dividend income

____ **(12)** Lease payments

STUDY QUESTIONS AND PROBLEMS

3.1 What is the difference between a multiple-step and a single-step format of the earnings statement?

3.2 Under what circumstances must a lease be capitalized?

3.3 Discuss the differences between depreciation, amortization, and depletion.

3.4 What is the importance of evaluating the repairs and maintenance expense account on an income statement?

3.5 What is the difference between a retained earnings statement and a statement of shareholders' equity?

3.6 Why is the bottom line figure, net income, not necessarily a good indicator of a firm's financial success?

3.7 An excerpt from the Sun Company's annual report is presented below. Calculating any profit measures deemed necessary, discuss the implications of the profitability of the company.

Sun Company
Income Statements
For the Years Ended December 31, 19X3, 19X2, and 19X1:
(In thousands)

	19X3	19X2	19X1
Net Sales	$ 236,000	$ 195,000	$ 120,000
Cost of goods sold	186,000	150,000	85,000
Gross profit	$ 50,000	$ 45,000	$ 35,000
Operating expenses	22,000	18,000	11,000
Operating profit	$ 28,000	$ 27,000	$ 24,000
Income taxes	12,000	11,500	10,500
Net Income	$ 16,000	$ 15,500	$ 13,500

3.8 Star, Inc. has 400,000 $1 par common shares outstanding currently valued at $20. If the company issues a 15% stock dividend, what will be the effect on the equity section of the balance sheet? What about a 40% stock dividend?

3.9 Using the information presented for Dandy Corporation on p. 96 explain the following:

(a) How Dandy Corporation reduced the number of common stock shares outstanding from 103,856,000 at June 30, 19X6 to 88,647,000 at June 30, 19X9.

(b) The reasons for the change in retained earnings from $691,105,000 to $1,103,357,000 between June 30, 19X6, and June 30, 19X9.

3.10 Big Company purchased 25% of the voting common stock of Little Company on January 1 and paid $500,000 for the investment. Little Company reported $250,000 of earnings for the year and paid $50,000 cash dividends. Calculate investment income and the balance sheet investment account for Big Company under the cost method and under the equity method.

3.11 Prepare a multi-step income statement for Coyote, Inc. from the following single-step statement.

Net Sales	$ 1,833,000
Interest Income	13,000
	1,846,000
Costs and expenses:	
Cost of goods sold	1,072,000
Selling expense	279,000
General and Administrative expense	175,000
Depreciation	14,000
Interest expense	16,000
Income tax expense	116,000
Net Income	$ 174,0000

Consolidated Statements of Stockholders' Equity
Dandy Corporation and Subsidiaries
Three Years Ended June 30, 19X9
In thousands

| | Shares | | | Amount | | | | | |
	Issued	Treasury Stock	Outstanding	Common Stock	Additional Paid-in Capital	Retained Earnings	Foreign Currency Translation Effects	Treasury Stock	Total
Balance at June 30, 19X6	105,645	(1,789)	103,856	$105,645	$39,627	$691,105	$(12,317)	$(11,383)	$812,677
Foreign currency translation adjustments for the period	—	—	—	—	—	—	(3,980)	—	(3,980)
Sale of treasury stock to employee stock purchase program	—	813	813	—	28,484	—	—	5,170	33,654
Net income	—	—	—	—	—	278,521	—	—	278,521
Balance at June 30, 19X7	105,645	(976)	104,669	105,645	68,111	969,626	(16,297)	(6,213)	1,120,872
Purchase and retirement of stock through tender offer	(10,000)	—	(10,000)	(10,000)	(7,800)	(337,200)	—	—	(355,000)
Purchase of treasury stock	—	(2,785)	(2,785)	—	—	—	—	(92,535)	(92,535)
Foreign currency translation adjustments for the period	—	—	—	—	—	—	(5,375)	—	(5,375)
Sale of treasury stock to employee stock purchase program	—	1,042	1,042	—	15,102	—	—	23,761	38,863
Net income	—	—	—	—	—	281,871	—	—	281,871
Balance at June 30, 19X8	95,645	(2,719)	92,926	95,645	75,413	914,297	(21,672)	(74,987)	988,696
Purchase of treasury stock	—	(5,651)	(5,651)	—	—	—	—	(144,448)	(144,448)
Foreign currency translation adjustments for the period	—	—	—	—	—	—	(7,743)	—	(7,743)
Sale of treasury stock to employee stock purchase program	—	1,372	1,372	—	1,417	—	—	36,472	37,889
Net income	—	—	—	—	—	189,060	—	—	189,060
Balance at June 30, 19X9	95,645	(6,998)	88,647	$95,645	$76,830	$1,103,357	$(29,415)	$(182,963)	$1,063,454

IBM CORPORATION—MINI-CASE

IBM Corporation has been a world leader in providing advanced information services, products and technologies. The Consolidated Statements of Earnings and Stockholders' Equity for IBM for the years ended December 31, 1992, 1991, and 1990, and selected notes to the financial statements are given on pages 98–100. When preparing their earnings statements, IBM segregates revenues and costs of goods sold into five industry segments: Sales, Software, Maintenance, Services, and Rentals and Financing.

REQUIRED:

1. Analyze the profitability of IBM by calculating and discussing profit measures for all three years. Your analysis should also include an explanation of the year-to-year changes in gross profit by pinpointing the specific causes of those changes, a discussion of amounts spent on research and development, and an explanation of the income tax rate.

2. Using the Statements of Stockholders' Equity, answer the following questions:

   a. The Retained Earnings account for IBM has declined from 1990 to 1992. Calculate percentages to show which items are primarily responsible for this decline.

   b. How was IBM able to pay cash dividends in 1992 when the company experienced a loss of $5 billion?

   c. What is the reason for the change in the treasury stock account from 1990 to 1992?

   d. Explain the effects of the foreign currency translation adjustments on the equity of IBM for the years 1990 to 1992.

CONSOLIDATED STATEMENT OF EARNINGS
International Business Machines Corporation and Subsidiary Companies
(Dollars in millions
except per share amounts)

For the year ended December 31:	1992	1991*†	1990*
Revenue:			
Sales	$33,755	$37,093	$43,959
Software	11,103	10,498	9,865
Maintenance	7,635	7,414	7,198
Services	7,352	5,582	4,124
Rentals and financing	4,678	4,179	3,785
	64,523	64,766	68,931
Cost:			
Sales	19,698	18,571	19,401
Software	3,924	3,865	3,118
Maintenance	3,430	3,379	3,302
Services	6,051	4,531	3,315
Rentals and financing	1,966	1,727	1,579
	35,069	32,073	30,715
Gross Profit	29,454	32,693	38,216
Operating Expenses:			
Selling, general and administrative	19,526	21,375	20,709
Research, development and engineering	6,522	6,644	6,554
Restructuring charges	11,645	3,735	—
	37,693	31,754	27,263
Operating Income	(8,239)	939	10,953
Other Income, principally interest	573	602	495
Interest Expense	1,360	1,423	1,324
Earning before Income Taxes	(9,026)	118	10,124
Provision for Income Taxes	(2,161)	716	4,157
Net Earnings before Changes in Accounting Principles	(6,865)	(598)	5,967
Effect of Changes in Accounting Principles‡	1,900	(2,263)	—
Net Earnings	$(4,965)	$(2,861)	$5,967
Per Share Amounts:			
Before Changes in Accounting Principles	$(12.03)	$(1.05)	$10.42
Effects of Changes in Accounting Principles‡	3.33	(3.96)	—
Net Earnings	$(8.70)	$(5.01)	$10.42

Average Number of Shares Outstanding:
1992—570,896,489; 1991—572,003,382; 1990—572,647,906

*Restated for the American Institute of Certified Public Accountants Statement of Position, "Software Revenue Recognition."
†Reclassified to conform with 1992 presentation.
‡1992, cumulative effect of Statement of Financial Accounting Standards (SFAS) 109, "Accounting for Income Taxes"; and 1991, transition effect of SFAS 106, "Employers' Accounting for Postretirement Benefits Other Than Pensions."

CONSOLIDATED STATEMENT OF STOCKHOLDERS' EQUITY
International Business Machines Corporation and Subsidiary Companies

(Dollars in millions)	Capital Stock	Retained Earnings	Translation Adjustments	Treasury Stock	Total
1990*					
Stockholders' Equity, January 1, 1990........	$6,341	$30,208	$1,710	$(7)	$38,252
Net earnings..		5,967			5,967
Cash dividends declared..		(2,774)			(2,774)
Capital stock issued under employee plans					
(686,159 shares).......................................	47				47
Purchases (7,346,528 shares) and sales					
(7,194,647 shares) of treasury stock under					
employee plans—net†............................		(117)		(18)	(135)
Capital stock purchased and retired					
(3,842,924 shares).................................	(43)	(372)			(415)
Tax reductions—employee plans........................	12				12
Translation adjustments..			1,599		1,599
Stockholders' Equity, December 31, 1990...	6,357	32,912	3,309	(25)	42,553
1991*					
Net earnings..		(2,861)			(2,861)
Cash dividends declared..		(2,771)			(2,771)
Capital stock issued under employee plans					
(1,857,904 shares).......................................	172				172
Purchases (7,306,058 shares) and sales					
(7,201,997 shares) of treasury stock under					
employee plans—net†............................		(125)		(6)	(131)
Capital stock purchased and retired					
(2,127,400 shares).................................	(24)	(172)			(196)
Tax reductions—employee plans........................	26				26
Translation adjustments..			(113)		(113)
Stockholders' Equity, December 31, 1991...	6,531	26,983	3,196	(31)	36,679
1992					
Net earnings..		(4,965)			(4,965)
Cash dividends declared..		(2,765)			(2,765)
Capital stock issued under employee plans					
(442,581 shares).......................................	26				26
Purchases (8,097,681 shares) and sales					
(8,073,124 shares) of treasury stock under					
employee plans—net............................		(129)		6	(123)
Tax reductions—employee plans........................	6				6
Translation adjustments..			(1,234)		(1,234)
Stockholders' Equity, December 31, 1992	$6,563	$19,124	$1,962	$(25)	$27,624

*Restated for the American Institute of Certified Public Accountants Statement of Position, "Software
   Revenue Recognition."
†Number of shares purchased and sold restated to conform with 1992 presentation.

NOTES TO CONSOLIDATED FINANCIAL STATEMENTS
International Business Machines Corporation and Subsidiary Companies

Taxes (Dollars in millions)	1992	1991	1990
Earnings before income taxes:			
U.S. operations	$(7,678)	$(3,379)	$ 2,337
Non-U.S. operations	(1,348)	3,497	7,787
	$(9,026)	$ 118	$10,124
The provision for income taxes by geographic operations is as follows:			
U.S. operations	$(2,179)	$ (857)	$ 905
Non-U.S. operations	18	1,573	3,252
Total provision for income taxes	$(2,161)	$ 716	$ 4,157

4

Statement of Cash Flows

Joan and Joe: A Tale of Woe

Joe added up profits and went to see Joan
Assured of obtaining a much-needed loan.

When Joe arrived, he announced with good cheer
"My firm has had an outstanding year.

"And now I need a loan from your bank."
Eyeing the statements, Joan's heart sank.

"Your profits are fine," Joan said to Joe.
"But where, oh where, is your company's cash flow?
I'm sorry to say: the answer is 'no'."

—L. Fraser

The statement of cash flows, required by Statement of Financial Accounting Standards No. 95, provides information about cash inflows and outflows during an accounting period. On the statement, cash flows are segregated by *operating activities*, *investing activities*, and *financing activities*.[1] The statement of cash flows, which replaced the statement of changes in financial position (or sources and uses of funds statement) in 1988, represents a major advancement for users of financial statement data because of its relevance for analytical purposes. The mandated focus on cash in this statement results in a more useful document than its predecessor.

In this chapter I will explain how the statement of cash flows is prepared and how to interpret the information presented in the statement, including a discussion of the significance of cash flow from operations as an analytical tool in assessing financial performance.

---

[1] Financing and investing activities not involving cash receipts and payments—such as the exchange of debt for stock or the exchange of property—are reported in a separate schedule on the statement of cash flows.

EXHIBIT 4.1 R.E.C., Inc.
Consolidated Statements of Cash Flows
for the Years Ended December 31, 19X9, 19X8, and 19X7
(In thousands)

	19X9	19X8	19X7
Cash Flow from Operating Activities—Direct Method			
Cash received from customers	$214,990	$149,661	$140,252
Interest received	422	838	738
Cash paid to suppliers for inventory	(132,933)	(99,936)	(83,035)
Cash paid to employees (S&A expenses)	(32,664)	(26,382)	(25,498)
Cash paid for other operating expenses	(29,728)	(21,350)	(20,848)
Interest paid	(2,585)	(2,277)	(1,274)
Taxes paid	(7,478)	(4,321)	(4,706)
Net cash provided (used) by operating activities	$10,024	($3,767)	$5,629
Cash Flow from Investing Activities			
Additions to property, plant, and equipment	(14,100)	(4,773)	(3,982)
Other investing activities	295	0	0
Net cash provided (used) by investing activities	($13,805)	($4,773)	($3,982)
Cash Flow from Financing Activities			
Sales of common stock	256	183	124
Increase (decrease) in short-term borrowings (includes current maturities of long-term debt)	(30)	1,854	1,326
Additions to long-term borrowings	5,600	7,882	629
Reductions of long-term borrowings	(1,516)	(1,593)	(127)
Dividends paid	(1,582)	(1,862)	(1,841)
Net cash provided (used) by financing activities	$2,728	$6,464	$111
Increase (decrease) in cash and marketable securities	($1,053)	($2,076)	$1,758
Supplementary Schedule			
Cash Flow from Operating Activities—Indirect Method			
Net income	$9,394	$5,910	$5,896
Noncash revenue and expense included in net income:			
Depreciation	3,998	2,984	2,501
Deferred income taxes	208	136	118
Cash provided (used) by current assets and liabilities:			
Accounts receivable	(610)	(3,339)	(448)
Inventories	(10,272)	(7,006)	(2,331)
Prepaid expenses	247	295	(82)
Accounts payable	6,703	(1,051)	902
Accrued liabilities	356	(1,696)	(927)
Net cash provided (used) by operations	$10,024	($3,767)	$5,629

The accompanying notes are an integral part of these statements.

This chapter also provides a far more extensive treatment of the preparation of the statement of cash flows than the chapters on the balance sheet and income statement for several reasons: its relative newness as a requirement by the Financial Accounting Standards Board; its seeming complexity to users and preparers; and its importance as an analytical tool. Research suggests that the cash flow statement is more widely read, more readily understood, and substantially more useful than the previously required statement of changes in financial position.[2] A positive net income figure on the income statement is ultimately insignificant unless a company can translate its earnings into cash, and the only source in financial statement data for learning about the generation of cash from operations is the statement of cash flows. Understanding this statement can be enhanced by understanding how it is developed from the balance sheet and income statement.

The Consolidated Statements of Cash Flows for R.E.C., Inc. (Exhibit 4.1), will serve as the background for an explanation of how the statement is prepared and a discussion of its usefulness for financial analysis.

PREPARING A STATEMENT OF CASH FLOWS

Preparing the statement of cash flows begins with a return to the balance sheet (Chapter 2). The statement of cash flows requires a reordering of the information presented on a balance sheet. The balance sheet shows account balances at the end of an accounting period, while the statement of cash flows shows changes in those same account balances between accounting periods. The statement is called a statement of flows because it shows *changes over time rather than the absolute dollar amount of the accounts at a point in time*. Because a balance sheet balances, the changes in all of the balance sheet accounts balance; and the changes which reflect cash inflows less the changes which result from cash outflows will equal the changes in the cash account.

The statement of cash flows is prepared in exactly that way: by calculating the changes in all of the balance sheet accounts, including *cash*; then listing the changes in all of the accounts except cash as *inflows* or *outflows*; and categorizing the flows by *operating*, *financing*, or *investing* activities. The *inflows less the outflows balance to and explain the change in cash*.

In order to classify the account changes on the balance sheet, it is first necessary to review the definitions of the four parts of a statement of cash flows:

> cash;
> operating activities;
> investing activities; and
> financing activities.

Cash

Cash includes cash and highly liquid short-term marketable securities, also called cash equivalents. Marketable securities are included as cash because they represent, as explained in Chapter 2, short-term highly liquid investments that can be readily converted

---

[2] Epstein, M. and Pava, M. "How Useful Are Corporate Annual Reports?" *Business Credit*, April 1993.

into cash. They include U.S. Treasury bills, certificates, notes, and bonds; negotiable certificates of deposit at financial institutions; and commercial paper.

Operating activities

Operating activities include delivering or producing goods for sale and providing services; and the cash effects of transactions and other events that enter into the determination of income.

> **Inflows**
> Sales of goods
> Revenue from services
> Returns on interest earning assets (interest)
> Returns on equity securities (dividends)
>
> **Outflows**
> Payments for purchases of inventories
> Payments for operating expenses (salaries, rent, insurance, etc.)
> Payments for purchases from suppliers other than inventory
> Payments to lenders (interest)
> Payments for taxes

Investing Activities

Investing activities include acquiring and selling, or otherwise disposing of (a) securities that are not cash equivalents and (b) productive assets that are expected to benefit the firm for long periods of time; and lending money and collecting on loans.

> **Inflows**
> Sales of long-lived assets such as property, plant, and equipment
> Sales of debt or equity securities of other entities
> Returns from loans (principal) to others
>
> **Outflows**
> Acquisitions of long-lived assets
> Purchases of debt or equity securities of other entities
> Loans (principal) to others

Financing Activities

Financing activities include borrowing from creditors and repaying the principal; and obtaining resources from owners and providing them with a return on the investment.

> **Inflows**
> Proceeds from borrowing
> Proceeds from issuing the firm's own equity securities
>
> **Outflows**
> Repayment of debt principal
> Repurchase of a firm's own shares
> Payment of dividends

With these definitions in mind, consider Exhibit 4.2 a worksheet for preparing the statement of cash flows which shows comparative 19X9 and 19X8 balance sheet accounts for R.E.C., Inc. Included in this exhibit is a column with the account balance changes and the category (or categories) which applies to each account. Explanations of how each account change is used in a statement of cash flow will be provided later in the chapter.

EXHIBIT 4.2 R.E.C., Inc.
                     Worksheet for Preparing Statement of Cash Flows
                     (In thousands)

		19X9	19X8	Change (19X8-19X9)	Category
Assets					
(1)	Cash	$ 4,061	$ 2,382	$ 1,679	Cash
(2)	Marketable securities	5,272	8,004	(2,732)	Cash
(3)	Accounts receivable (net)	8,960	8,350	610	Operating
(4)	Inventories	47,041	36,769	10,272	Operating
(5)	Prepaid expenses	512	759	(247)	Operating
(6)	Property, plant, and equipment	40,607	26,507	14,100	Investing
(7)	Accumulated depreciation and amoriti-zation	(11,528)	(7,530)	(3,998)	Operating
(8)	Other assets	373	668	(295)	Investing
Liabilities and Stockholders' Equity					
Liabilities					
(9)	Accounts payable	14,294	7,591	6,703	Operating
(10)	Notes payable—banks	5,614	6,012	(398)	Financing
(11)	Current maturities of long-term debt	1,884	1,516	368	Financing
(12)	Accrued liabilities	5,669	5,313	356	Operating
(13)	Deferred income taxes	843	635	208	Operating
(14)	Long-term borrowings*	21,059	16,975	4,084	Financing
Stockholders' Equity					
(15)	Common stock	4,803	4,594	209	Financing
(16)	Additional paid-in capital	957	910	47	Financing
(17)	Retained earnings**	40,175	32,363	7,812	**
*(14)	Additions to long-term borrowings			$ 5,600	
(14)	Reductions of long-term borrowings			(1,516)	
(14)	Net Change in long-term debt			$ 4,084	
**(18)	Net income (operating)			$ 9,394	Operating
(19)	Dividends paid (financing)			(1,582)	Financing
(17)	Change in retained earnings			$ 7,812	

(1)(2) Cash and marketable securities are cash. The changes in these two accounts —a net decrease of $1,053 thousand (decrease in marketable securities of $2,732 thousand less increase in cash of $1,679 thousand) will be explained by the changes in all of the other accounts. This means that for the year ending 19X9, the cash outflows have exceeded the cash inflows by $1,053 thousand.

(3)(4)(5) Accounts receivable, inventories, and prepaid expenses are all operating accounts relating to sales of goods, purchases of inventories, and payments for operating expenses.

(6) The net increase in property, plant, and equipment is an investing activity reflecting purchases of long-lived assets.

(7) The change in accumulated depreciation and amortization is classified as operating because it will be used as an adjustment to operating expenses or net income to determine cash flow from operating activities.

(8) Other assets are land held for resale, representing an investing activity.

(9) Accounts payable is an operating account because it arises from purchases of inventory.

(10) (11) Notes payable and current maturities of long-term debt result from borrowing (debt principal), a financing activity.

(12) Accrued liabilities are operating because they result from the accrual of operating expenses such as wages, rent, salaries, and insurance.

(13) The change in deferred income taxes is categorized as operating because it is part of the adjustment of tax expense to calculate cash flow from operating activities.

(14) The change in long-term debt, principal on borrowings, is a financing activity.

(15)(16) Common stock and paid-in capital are also financing activities because the changes result from sales of the firm's own equity shares.

(17) The change in retained earnings (Chapter 3), is the product of two activities: (18) net income for the period, which is operating; and (19) the payment of cash dividends, which is a financing activity.

The next step is to transfer the account changes to the appropriate area of a statement of cash flows.[3] In doing so, a determination must also be made of what constitutes an inflow and what constitutes an outflow when analyzing the change in an account balance. The following table should help:

Inflow	**Outflow**
− Asset account	+ Asset account
+ Liability account	− Liability account
+ Equity account	− Equity account

The table indicates that a decrease in an asset balance and an increase in liability and equity accounts are inflows.[4] Examples from Exhibit 4.2 are the decrease in other assets

---

[3] Several alternative formats can be used for presenting the statement of flows, provided that the statement is reconciled to the change in cash and shows cash inflows and outflows from operating, financing, and investing activities.

[4] In accounting terminology, an *inflow* results from the decrease in a debit balance account or an increase in a credit balance account; an *outflow* results from the increase in a debit balance account or the decrease in a credit balance.

(cash inflow from the sale of property not used in the business); the increase in long-term debt (cash inflow from borrowing); and the increase in common stock and additional paid-in capital (cash inflow from sales of equity securities). Outflows are represented by the increase in inventories (cash outflow to purchase inventory); and the decrease in notes payable (cash outflow to repay borrowings).

Note that accumulated depreciation appears in the asset section but actually is a contra-asset or credit balance account because it reduces the amount of total assets. Accumulated depreciation is shown in parentheses on the balance sheet and has the same effect as a liability account.

Another complication occurs from the impact of two *transactions in one account*. For example, the net increase in retained earnings resulted from the combination of net income for the period, which increases the account, and the payment of dividends, which reduces the account. Multiple transactions can also affect other accounts, such as property, plant, and equipment if a firm both acquires and sells capital assets during the period; and debt accounts, if a firm both borrows and repays principal.

CALCULATING CASH FLOW FROM OPERATING ACTIVITIES

The R.E.C., Inc. Consolidated Statements of Cash Flows begins with cash flow from operating activities. This represents the cash generated *internally*. In contrast, investing and financing activities provide cash from *external* sources. Two methods are used for calculating and presenting cash flow from operating activities: the direct method and the indirect method.[5] Both methods are illustrated for R.E.C., Inc. and explained in the chapter. The *direct method* shows cash collections from customers; interest and dividends collected; other operating cash receipts; cash paid to suppliers and employees; interest paid; taxes paid; and other operating cash payments. The *indirect method* starts with net income and adjusts for deferrals; accruals; noncash items, such as depreciation and amortization; and nonoperating items, such as gains and losses on asset sales. (A supplement is provided at the end of the chapter to illustrate how to adjust net income from an accrual to a cash basis, a process similar to the indirect method.) The direct and indirect methods yield identical figures for net cash flow from operating activities because the underlying accounting concepts are the same.

Direct Method

Exhibit 4.3 illustrates the calculation of net cash flow from operating activities by the direct method. This method translates each item on the accrual-based income statement to a cash revenue or expense item. The calculation of cash flow from operating activities in Exhibit 4.3 represents an approximation of the *actual* receipts and payments of cash required by the direct method.

[5] FASB Statement No. 95 recommends presentations of the direct method in the primary statement with the indirect method provided as supplementary information. Firms are permitted to use either method.

EXHIBIT 4.3 R.E.C., Inc.
            Net Cash Flow from Operating Activities
            Direct Method

Sales	− Increase in accounts receivable + Decrease in accounts receivable + Increase in deferred revenue − Decrease in deferred revenue	= Cash collections from customers
Cost of Goods Sold	+ Increase in inventory − Decrease in inventory − Increase in accounts payable + Decrease in accounts payable	= Cash paid to suppliers
Salary Expense	− Increase in accrued salaries payable + Decrease in accrued salaries payable	= Cash paid to employees

Other
Operating
Expenses
	− Depreciation, amortization, depletion
	  expense for period
	+ Increase in prepaid expenses
	− Decrease in prepaid expenses
	− Increase in accrued operating ex-
	  penses
	+ Decrease in accrued operating ex-
	  penses
		= Cash paid for other operating
		  expenses

Interest Revenue	− Increase in interest receivable + Decrease in interest receivable	= Cash revenue from interest
Interest Expense	− Increase in accrued interest payable + Decrease in accrued interest payable	= Cash paid for interest

Investment
Income
	− Increase in investment account from
	  equity income*
	+ Decrease in investment account from
	  equity income**
		= Cash revenue from dividends

Tax Expense	− Increase in deferred tax liability + Decrease in deferred tax liability − Decrease in deferred tax asset + Increase in deferred tax asset − Increase in accrued taxes payable + Decrease in accrued taxes payable − Decrease in prepaid tax + Increase in prepaid tax	= Cash paid for taxes

Net cash flow from operating activities

*Amount by which equity income recognized exceeds cash dividends received.
**Amount by which cash dividends received exceed equity income recognized.

The steps shown in Exhibit 4.3 will be used to explain the calculation of net cash flow from operating activities on the R.E.C, Inc. Statement of Cash Flows for 19X9.

R.E.C., Inc. Direct Method

Sales	$215,600	
Increase in accounts receivable	(610)	
Cash collections on sales		214,990
Cost of goods sold	129,364	
Increase in inventory	10,272	
Increase in accounts payable	(6,703)	
Cash payments for supplies		132,933
Selling and administrative expenses		32,664
Other operating expenses	34,329	
Depreciation and amortization	(3,998)	
Decrease in prepaid expense	(247)	
Increase in accrued liabilities	(356)	
Cash paid for other operating expense		29,728
Interest revenue		422
Interest expense		2,585
Tax expense	7,686	
Increase in deferred tax liability	(208)	
Cash paid for taxes		(7,478)
Net cash flow from operating activities		$10,024

The increase in *accounts receivable* is subtracted from sales revenue because more sales revenue was recognized in the income statement than was received in cash.

The increase in *inventories* is added to cost of goods sold because more cash was paid to purchase inventories than was included in cost of goods sold expense, that is, cash was used to purchase inventory that has not yet been sold. The increase in *accounts payable* is subtracted from cost of goods sold because R.E.C., Inc. was able to defer some payments to suppliers for purchases of inventory; more cost of goods sold expense was recognized than was actually paid in cash.

Depreciation and amortization expense is subtracted from other operating expenses. Remember that depreciation represents a cost allocation, not an outflow of cash. The acquisition of the capital asset was recognized as an investing cash outflow (unless it was exchanged for debt or stock) in the statement of cash flows for the period in which the asset was acquired. So depreciation itself does not require any outflow of cash in the year it is recognized. To deduct depreciation expense in the current year's statement of cash flows would be double counting. Amortization is similar to depreciation—an expense that enters into the determination of net income but which does not require an outflow of cash. Depletion would be handled in the same manner as depreciation and amortization.

The depreciation and amortization expense for R.E.C., Inc. in 19X9 is equal to the change in the balance sheet accumulated depreciation and amortization account. If the firm had dispositions of capital assets during the accounting period, however, the balance sheet change would not equal the expense recognition for the period because some of the account change would have resulted from the elimination of accumulated depreciation for the asset which was removed. The appropriate figure to subtract would be depreciation and amortization expense from the earnings statement.

The decrease in *prepaid expense* is subtracted from other operating expenses because the firm is recognizing as expense in 19X9 items for which cash was paid in the previous year, that is, the firm is utilizing on a net basis some of the prior years' prepayments.

The increase in *accrued liabilities* is subtracted from other operating expenses because R.E.C., Inc. has recognized more in expense on the income statement than has been paid in cash.

Finally, the increase in the *deferred tax liability* account is subtracted from tax expense to obtain cash payments for taxes. The deferred tax liability, explained in Chapter 2, was created as a reconciliation between the amount of tax expense reported on the income statement and the cash actually paid or payable to the IRS. If a deferred tax liability increases from one year to the next, tax expense deducted on the earnings statement to arrive at net income has exceeded cash actually paid for taxes. Thus, an increase in the deferred tax liability account is subtracted from tax expense to arrive at cash from operations. A decrease in deferred tax liabilities would be added. A change in deferred tax assets would be handled in the opposite way from the deferred tax liability.

Exhibit 4.3 includes other possible adjustments, not present for R.E.C., Inc., which would be made to calculate net cash flow from operating activities by the direct method.

Indirect Method

Exhibit 4.4 illustrates the steps necessary to convert net income to cash flow from operating activities.

The steps shown in Exhibit 4.4 will be used to explain the calculation of cash flow from operating activities for R.E.C., Inc. using the indirect method. Exhibit 4.4 includes some adjustments not present for R.E.C., Inc.

Depreciation and amortization are added back to net income because they reflect the recognition of a noncash expense (see preceding discussion).

The *deferred tax liability* account, as discussed in Chapter 2 and the preceding section, reconciles the difference between tax expense recognized in the calculation of net income and the tax expense actually paid. The increase in the liability account for R.E.C., Inc. is added back to net income because more tax expense was recognized in the calculation of net income than was actually paid for taxes.

The increase in *accounts receivable* is deducted because more sales revenue has been included in net income than has been collected in cash from customers.

The increase in *inventory* is subtracted because R.E.C., Inc. has purchased more inventory than has been included in cost of goods sold. Cost of goods sold used in calculating net income includes only the inventory actually sold.

EXHIBIT 4.4 R.E.C., Inc.
Net Cash Flow from Operating Activities
Indirect Method

Net income*
Noncash/Nonoperating revenue and expense included in income:
+   Depreciation, amortization, depletion expense for period

+   Increase in deferred tax liability
−   Decrease in deferred tax liability
+   Decrease in deferred tax asset
−   Increase in deferred tax asset

−   Increase in investment account from equity income**
+   Decrease in investment account from equity income***

+   Increase in deferred revenue
−   Decrease in deferred revenue

−   Gain on sale of assets
+   Loss on sale of assets

Cash provided (used) by current assets and liabilities
+   Decrease in accounts receivable
−   Increase in accounts receivable

+   Decrease in inventory
−   Increase in inventory

+   Decrease in prepaid expenses
−   Increase in prepaid expenses

+   Decrease in interest receivable
−   Increase in interest receivable

+   Increase in accounts payable
−   Decrease in accounts payable

+   Increase in accrued liabilities
−   Decrease in accrued liabilities

Net cash flow from operating activities

*Before extraordinary items, accounting changes, discontinued operations
**Amount by which equity income exceeds cash dividends received.
***Amount by which cash dividends received exceed equity income recognized.

R.E.C., Inc. Indirect Method

Net Income	$9,394
Noncash nonoperating items	
+ Depreciation and amortization expense	3,998
+ Increase in deferred tax liability	208
Cash provided (used) by current assets, liabilities	
- Increase in accounts receivables	(610)
- Increase in inventory	(10,272)
+ Decrease in prepaid expenses	247
+ Increase in accounts payable	6,703
+ Increase in accrued liabilities	356
Net cash flow from operating activities	$10,024

The decrease in *prepaid expenses* is added back because the firm has recognized an expense in the current period for which cash was paid in an earlier period, on a net basis.

The increase in *accounts payable* is added because less has been paid to suppliers for purchases of inventory than was included in cost of goods sold.

The increase in *accrued liabilities* is an addition to net income because it reflects the recognition of expense, on a net basis, prior to the payment of cash.

There are other potential adjustments, not required for R.E.C. Inc., that enter into the net income adjustment for noncash expense and revenues. One such item is the recognition of investment income from unconsolidated subsidiaries by the equity method of accounting, (Chapter 3). When a company uses the equity method, earnings can be recognized in the income statement in excess of cash actually received from dividends; or the reverse can occur, for example in the case of a loss recorded by an investee. For a firm using the equity method, there would be a deduction from net income for the amount by which investment income recognized exceeded cash received. Other potential adjustment items include changes relating to deferred income, deferred expense, the amortization of bond discounts and premiums, extraordinary items, and gains or losses on sales of long-lived assets.

Although *gains and losses from asset sales* are included in the calculation of net income, they are not considered an operating activity. A gain should be deducted from net income, and a loss should be added to net income to determine cash flow from operating activities. The entire proceeds from sales of long-lived assets are included as investing inflows.

Cash Flow from Investing Activities

Additions to *property, plant,* and *equipment* represent a net addition to R.E.C. Inc.'s buildings, leasehold improvements, and equipment, a cash outflow of $14,100 thousand. Other investing activities for R.E.C., Inc. result from a decrease in the *other assets* account on the balance sheet, which represent holdings of investment properties. The sale of these assets has provided a cash inflow of $295 thousand.

Cash Flow from Financing Activities

As a result of the exercise of stock options, R.E.C., Inc. issued new shares of stock during 19X9. The total cash generated from stock sales amounted to $256 thousand. Note that two accounts on the balance sheet *common stock* and *additional paid-in capital*—combine to explain this change:

Common stock	$209 Inflow
Additional paid-in capital	47 Inflow
	256 Total inflow

The two accounts *notes payable to banks* and *current maturities of long-term debt* (carried as a current liability since the principal is payable within a year) jointly explain R.E.C. Inc.'s net reduction in short-term borrowings in 19X9 of $30 thousand:

Notes payable—banks	($398) Outflow
Current maturities of long-term debt	368 Inflow
	($ 30) Net outflow

In preparing the statement of cash flows, long-term borrowings should be segregated into two components: additions to long-term borrowings and reductions of long-term borrowings. This information is provided in Note C Long-Term Debt to the R.E.C., Inc. financial statements in which detail on the various long-term notes is provided. The two figures—additions to long-term debt and reductions of long-term debt—on the R.E.C., Inc. statement of cash flows reconcile the change in the *long-term debt* account on the R.E.C., Inc. balance sheet:

Additions to long-term borrowings	$5,600 Inflow
Reductions of long-term borrowings	(1,516) Outflow
Increase in long-term debt	$4,084

The payment of cash dividends by R.E.C., Inc. in 19X9 of $1,582 thousand is the final item in the financing activities section. The change in *retained earnings* results from the combination of net income recognition and the payment of cash dividends; this information is provided in the R.E.C., Inc. Statement of Retained Earnings:

Net income	$9,394 Inflow
Dividends paid	(1,582) Outflow
Change in retained earnings	$7,812

It should be noted that the *payment* of cash dividends is the financing outflow; the *declaration* of a cash dividend would not affect cash.

Change in Cash

To summarize the cash inflows and outflows for 19X9 for R.E.C., Inc., the net cash provided by operating activities, plus the net cash provided by financing activities, less the

EXHIBIT 4.5 R.E.C., Inc.
Consolidated Statements of Cash Flows
for the Years Ended December 31, 19X9, 19X8, and 19X7
(In thousands)

	19X9	19X8	19X7
Cash Flow from Operating Activities—Direct Method			
Cash received from customers	$214,990	$149,661	$140,252
Interest received	422	838	738
Cash paid to suppliers for inventory	(132,933)	(99,936)	(83,035)
Cash paid to employees (S&A Expenses)	(32,664)	(26,382)	(25,498)
Cash paid for other operating expenses	(29,728)	(21,350)	(20,848)
Interest paid	(2,585)	(2,277)	(1,274)
Taxes paid	(7,478)	(4,321)	(4,706)
Net cash provided (used) by operating activities	$ 10,024	($ 3,767)	$ 5,629
Cash Flows from Investing Activities			
Additions to property, plant, and equipment	(14,100)	(4,773)	(3,982)
Other investing activities	295	0	0
Net cash provided (used) by investing activities	($ 13,805)	($ 4,773)	($ 3,982)
Cash Flow from Financing Activities			
Sales of common stock	256	183	124
Increase (decrease) in short-term borrowings (includes current maturities of long-term debt)	(30)	1,854	1,326
Additions to long-term borrowings	5,600	7,882	629
Reductions of long-term borrowings	(1,516)	(1,593)	(127)
Dividends paid	(1,582)	(1,862)	(1,841)
Net cash provided (used) by financing activities	$ 2,728	$ 6,464	$ 111
Increase (decrease) in cash & marketable securities	($ 1,053)	($ 2,076)	$ 1,758
Supplementary Schedule			
Cash Flow from Operating Activities—Indirect Method			
Net income	$ 9,394	$ 5,910	$ 5,896
Noncash revenue and expense included in net income			
Depreciation and amortization	3,998	2,984	2,501
Deferred income taxes	208	136	118
Cash provided (used) by current assets and liabilities			
Accounts receivable	(610)	(3,339)	(448)
Inventories	(10,272)	(7,006)	(2,331)
Prepaid expenses	247	295	(82)
Accounts payable	6,703	(1,051)	902
Accrued liabilities	356	(1,696)	(927)
Net cash provided (used) by operations	$ 10,024	($ 3,767)	$ 5,629

net cash used by investing activities produced a net decrease in *cash* and *marketable securities* for the period:

Net cash provided by operating activities	$10,024
Net cash provided by financing activities	2,728
Net cash used by investing activities	(13,805)
Decrease in cash and marketable securities	($1,053)

The three-year statements of cash flows for R.E.C., Inc. are provided in Exhibit 4.5. The statement for 19X8 and 19X7 would be prepared using the same process that was illustrated for 19X9.

ANALYZING THE STATEMENT OF CASH FLOWS

The statement of cash flows is an important analytical tool for creditors, investors, and other users of financial statement data in order to help determine the following about a business firm:

> its ability to generate cash flows in the future;
>
> its capacity to meet obligations for cash;
>
> its future external financing needs;
>
> its success in productively managing investing activities; and
>
> its effectiveness in implementing financing and investing strategies.

To begin the analysis of a statement of cash flows, it is essential to understand the importance of cash flow from operations, the first category on the statement.

Cash Flow from Operations

It is possible for a firm to be highly profitable and not be able to pay dividends or invest in new equipment. It is possible for a firm to be highly profitable and not be able to service debt. It is also possible for a firm to be highly profitable and go bankrupt. W.T. Grant is one of the classic examples.[6] How? The problem is cash. Consider the following questions:

1. You are a banker evaluating a loan request from a prospective customer. What is your primary concern when making a decision regarding approval or denial of the loan request?
2. You are a wholesaler of goods and have been asked to sell your products on credit to a potential buyer. What is the major determining factor regarding approval or denial of the credit sale?

---

[6] Largay, J.A. and Stickney, C.P. "Cash Flows, Ratio Analysis, and the W.T. Grant Bankruptcy," *Financial Analysts Journal,* July-August 1980.

3. You are an investor in a firm and rely on the receipt of regular cash dividends as part of your return on investment. What must the firm generate in order to pay dividends?

In each case, the answer is *cash*. The banker must decide whether or not the prospective borrower will have the cash to meet interest and principal payments on the debt. The wholesaler will sell goods on credit only to those customers who can satisfy their accounts. A company can pay cash dividends only by producing cash.

The ongoing operation of any business depends upon its success in generating cash from operations. It is cash that a firm needs to satisfy creditors and investors. Temporary shortfalls of cash can be satisfied by borrowing or other means, such as selling long-lived assets, but ultimately a company must generate cash.

Cash flow from operations has become increasingly important as an analytical tool to determine the financial health of a business. Periods of high interest rates and inflation contributed to the enhanced attention paid to cash flow by investors and creditors. When interest rates are high, the cost of borrowing to cover short-term cash shortages can be out of reach for many firms. Periods of inflation distort the meaningfulness of net income, through the understatement of depreciation and cost of goods sold expenses, making other measures of operating performance and financial success important. Even when interest rates and inflation are low, there are other factors which limit the usefulness of net income as a barometer of financial health. Consider the case of the Nocash Corporation.

The Nocash Corporation

The Nocash Corporation had sales of $100,000 in its second year of operations, up from $50,000 in the first year. Expenses, including taxes, amounted to $70,000 in year 2, compared with $40,000 in year 1. The comparative income statements for the two years indicate substantial growth, with year 2 earnings greatly improved over those reported in year 1.

Nocash Corporation
Income Statement for Year 1 and Year 2

	Year 1	Year 2
Sales	$50,000	$100,000
Expenses	40,000	70,000
Net Income	$10,000	$ 30,000

So far, so good—a tripling of profit for Nocash. There are some additional facts, however, which are relevant to Nocash's operations but which do not appear on the firm's income statement:

1. In order to improve sales in year 2, Nocash eased its credit policies and attracted customers of a substantially lower quality than these in year 1.
2. Nocash purchased a new line of inventory near the end of year 1. It became apparent during year 2 that the inventory could not be sold, except at substantial reductions below cost.

3. Rumors regarding Nocash's problems with accounts receivable and inventory management prompted some suppliers to refuse goods on credit to Nocash.

The effect of these additional factors can be found on Nocash's balance sheet.

Nocash Corporation
Balance Sheet at December 31,

	Year 2	Year 2	$ Change
Cash	$2,000	$2,000	0
Accounts Receivable	10,000	30,000	+20,000 (1)
Inventories	10,000	25,000	+15,000 (2)
Total assets	22,000	57,000	+35,000
Accounts payable	7,000	2,000	− 5,000 (3)
Notes payable—to banks	0	10,000	+10,000
Equity	15,000	45,000	+30,000
Total liabilities and equity	$22,000	$57,000	+35,000

(1) Accounts receivable increased at a faster pace than sales as a result of deterioration in customer quality.

(2) Ending inventory increased and included items that would ultimately be sold at a loss.

(3) Nocash's inability to purchase goods on credit caused a reduction in accounts payable.

If Nocash's net income is recalculated on a cash basis, the following adjustments would be made, using the account balance changes between year 1 and year 2:

Net income	$30,000
(1) Accounts receivable	(20,000)
(2) Inventories	(15,000)
(3) Accounts payable	(5,000)
Cash income	($10,000)

(1) The increase in accounts receivable is subtracted because more sales revenue was recognized in computing net income than was collected in cash.

Sales recognized in net income		$100,000
Sales collected		
Beginning accounts receivable	$10,000	
Plus: sales, year 2	100,000	
Less: ending accounts receivable	(30,000)	80,000
Difference between net income and cash flow		$ 20,000

(2) The increase in inventory is deducted, reflecting the cash outflow for inventory purchases in excess of the expense recognized through cost of goods sold.

Purchases for inventory*	$75,000
Less: cost of goods sold	(60,000)
Difference between net income and cash flow	$15,000

(3) The decrease in accounts payable is deducted because the cash payments to suppliers in year 2 were greater than the amount of expense recorded. (In essence, cash was paid for some year 1 accounts as well as for year 2 accounts.)

Payments to suppliers**	$80,000
Less: Purchases for inventory*	(75,000)
Difference between net income and cash flow	$ 5,000
*Ending inventory	$25,000
Plus: Cost of goods sold	60,000
Less: Beginning inventory	(10,000)
*Purchases	$75,000
**Beginning accounts payable	$ 7,000
Plus: Purchases	75,000
Less: Ending accounts payable	(2,000)
**Payments	$80,000

How did Nocash cover its $10,000 cash shortfall? Note the appearance of a $10,000 note payable to banks on the year 2 balance sheet. The borrowing enabled Nocash to continue to operate, but unless the company can begin to generate cash from operations, its problems will compound. Bankers sometimes refer to this problem as a company's "selling itself out of business." The higher the cost of borrowing, the more costly and difficult it will be for Nocash to continue to operate.

Help From a Statement of Cash Flows

The statement of cash flows provides the figure, "net cash flow from operating activities." A condensed Statement of Cash Flows for R.E.C., Inc. (using the indirect method because it provides detail on changes in relevant balance sheet accounts) is shown in Exhibit 4.6. The analyst should be concerned with the following in reviewing this information:

The success or failure of the firm in generating cash from operations.

The underlying causes of the positive or negative operating cash flow.

The magnitude of positive or negative operating cash flow.

Fluctuations in cash flow from operations over time.

For R.E.C., Inc. the first point of significance is the negative cash flow from operations in 19X8 ($3,767 thousand). It should be noted that the negative *cash flow* occurred in a year in which the company reported *positive net income* of $5,910 thousand. The cash flow crunch apparently was caused primarily by a substantial growth in accounts receivable and inventories. Those increases were partly the result of the firm's expansion policies; and it would also be important to evaluate the quality of receivables and inventory that is, are they collectable and salable? R.E.C., Inc. was able to recover in 19X9, returning to

EXHIBIT 4.6 R.E.C., Inc.
Condensed Consolidated Statements of Cash Flows
for the Years Ended December 31, 19X9, 19X8, and 19X7
(In thousands)

	19X9	19X8	19X7
Cash Flow from Operating Activities			
Net income	$9,394	$5,910	$5,896
Noncash expenses and revenues included in income			
Depreciation and amortization	3,998	2,984	2,501
Deferred income taxes	208	136	118
Cash Provided by (used for) Current Assets and Liabilities			
Accounts receivable	(610)	(3,339)	(448)
Inventories	(10,272)	(7,006)	(2,331)
Prepaid expenses	247	295	(82)
Accounts payable	6,703	(1,051)	902
Accrued liabilities	356	(1,696)	(927)
Net cash provided (used) by operating activities	$10,024	($3,767)	$5,629

strongly positive cash generation of $10,024 thousand, in spite of the continuation of inventory growth to support the expansion.

The company obtained good supplier credit in 19X9 and controlled the growth in accounts receivable. It will be necessary to monitor R.E.C., Inc.'s cash flow from operations closely and, in particular, the management of inventories. Inventory growth is desirable when supporting an expansion of sales but undesirable when like Nocash Corporation, the inventory is not selling or is selling only at discounted prices.

The calculation of cash flow from operations illustrated for R.E.C., Inc. can be made for any company from its balance sheet and income statement, using the procedures outlined in the examples. Cash flow from operations is especially important for those firms that are heavily invested in inventories and that use trade accounts receivables and payables as a major part of ordinary business operations. Such problems as sales growth that is too rapid, slow-moving or obsolete inventory, price discounting within the industry, a rise in accounts receivable of inferior quality, and the tightening of credit by suppliers can all impair the firm's ability to generate cash from operations and lead to serious financial problems, including bankruptcy.

Summary Analysis of the Statement of Cash Flows

EXHIBIT 4.7 R.E.C., Inc.
Summary Analysis Statement of Cash Flows

	19X9	19X8	19X7
Inflows (thousands)			
Operations	$10,024	$ 0	$5,629
Sales of other assets	295	0	0
Sales of common stock	256	183	124
Additions of short-term debt	0	1,854	1,326
Additions to long-term debt	5,600	7,882	629
Total	$16,175	$ 9,919	$7,708
Outflows (thousands)			
Operations	$ 0	$ 3,767	$ 0
Purchase of property, plant, and equipment	14,100	4,773	3,982
Reductions of short-term debt	30	0	0
Reductions of long-term debt	1,516	1,593	127
Dividends paid	1,582	1,862	1,841
Total	$17,228	$11,995	$5,950
Change in cash and marketable securities	($1,053)	($2,076)	$1,758
Inflows (percent of total)			
Operations	62.0%	0.0%	73.0%
Sales of other assets	1.8	0.0	0.0
Sales of common stock	1.6	1.8	1.6
Additions to short-term debt	0.0	18.7	17.2
Additions to long-term debt	34.6	79.5	8.2
Total	100.0%	100.0%	100.0%
Outflows (percent of total)			
Operations	0.0%	31.4%	0.0%
Purchase of property, plant, and equipment	81.8	40.0	66.9
Reductions in short-term debt	0.2	0.0	0.0
Reductions in long-term debt	8.8	13.2	2.1
Dividends paid	9.2	15.4	31.0
Total	100.0%	100.0%	100.0%

Exhibit 4.7 presents a summary table to facilitate the analysis of a statement of cash flows, including cash flow from operating activities. The top part of the exhibit shows the inflows and outflows over the three-year period from 19X7 to 19X9 for R.E.C., Inc. in dollars. The lower portion of Exhibit 4.7 shows the cash inflows as a percentage of total inflows and the outflows as a percentage of total outflows.

First consider the dollar amounts. It is apparent that the magnitude of R.E.C., Inc.'s activity has increased sharply over the three-year period, with total cash inflows increasing from $7.7 million to $16.2 million and cash outflows from $6.0 million to $17.2 million. The major increase in cash outflows is capital asset expansion, while the increases in inflows have been the result of operations and long-term borrowing. The firm also has used liquid cash assets to support growth: note that cash and marketable securities decreased in 19X8 and 19X9.

In percentage terms, it is noteworthy that operations supplied 62% of needed cash in 19X9 and 73% in 19X7. As a result of negative cash from operations in 19X8, the firm had to borrow heavily, with debt (short-term and long-term) accounting for 98% of 19X8 inflows. The stronger operating cash production in 19X9 supported the substantial capital expansion (82% of cash outflow for investments in property, plant, and equipment) with only 35% external debt financing. Also noteworthy is the trend of R.E.C., Inc.'s dividend payments reduction—in dollar amounts in 19X9, and in percentage terms in both 19X8 and 19X9. This decision will be discussed in the next chapter.

The purpose of the summary table is to provide an approach to analyzing a statement of cash flows. This type of analysis can be used for any firm which provides comparative cash flow data. The information in the summary table underlines the importance of internal cash generation—from operations—and the implications for investing and financing activities when this does and does not occur.

The next step is to integrate the analysis of cash flows into an overall analysis of R.E.C., Inc.'s financial condition and performance.

Supplement To Chapter 4

Adjusting Net Income from Accrual to Cash: An Illustration

According to the accrual basis of accounting (discussed in Chapter 1), which underlies the preparation of published financial statements, net income is determined by a process of allocating revenue and expense to appropriate accounting periods: revenue is recognized when earned, and expense is recorded when incurred, regardless of when cash is actually received or paid. If a credit sale is made to a customer in December and the cash is collected in January, the revenue is recognized in the accounting period that ends in December. If a purchase is made in December and paid for in January, the expense is recorded for the accounting period ending in December. Further, expenses such as "depreciation" are "noncash" deductions in the sense that depreciation (discussed in Chapter 3) is an expense on the income statement but is actually an allocation of the cost of capital assets and involves no outflow of cash in the current period. Converting an income statement from an accrual to a cash basis involves "backing up" through the income statement to adjust for noncash, accrued, and deferred revenue and expense items that were recorded under accrual accounting. The process, which requires the same adjustments used to calculate cash flow from operating activities by the indirect method, is as follows:

Step One: Begin with net income from the income statement.

Step Two: Adjust for any "noncash" items, such as expenses recorded for depreciation, amortization and depletion.

Step Three: Adjust for any accrual/deferral accounts, such as accounts receivable and deferred revenue, that resulted in a difference between revenue recognized and cash received.

Step Four: Adjust for any accrual/deferral accounts—such as accounts payable, prepaid expenses, accrued expenses payable, and deferred taxes—that resulted in a difference between expense recorded and cash paid.

Step Five: The adjusted amount is net income (loss) on a cash basis.

Remember that changes in asset accounts will be treated the opposite of changes in liability accounts. For a complete list of adjustments see Exhibit 4.4.

Example: Assume that WJR Corporation, a supplier of golf equipment to R.E.C. Inc., reported the following balance sheet at December 31, 19X9, and income statement for the year ended December 31, 19X9.

WJR Corporation
Balance Sheet at 12/31/X9
(Thousands of Dollars)

	19X9	19X8
Cash	$2,500	$2,000
Accounts Receivable	7,000	4,800
Inventory	4,500	5,700
Prepaid Expenses	1,200	1,000
Property, Plant, Equipment	21,000	17,000
Less: Accumulated Depreciation	(9,500)	(7,000)
Property, Plant, Equipment (Net)	11,500	10,000
TOTAL ASSETS	$26,700	$23,500
Accounts Payable	3,000	2,600
Accrued Interest Payable	400	900
Long-term Debt	9,600	8,100
Deferred Taxes	1,400	1,200
Common Stock	5,000	5,000
Additional Paid-In Capital	3,000	3,000
Retained Earnings	4,300	2,700
TOTAL LIABILITIES AND STOCKHOLDERS' EQUITY	$ 26,700	$ 23,500

Income Statement For Year Ended 12/31/X9
(Thousands of Dollars)

Sales		$ 23,000
Cost of Goods Sold		16,100
Gross Profit Margin		6,900
Operating Expenses		
Depreciation	2,500	
Other	600	3,100
Operating Profit		3,800
Interest Expense		1,000
Earnings Before Tax		2,800
Income Taxes		1,200
Net Income		$1,600

To convert net income from an accrual to a cash basis, the following adjustments are made (all amounts in thousands of dollars):

Step One: Net income (accrual basis)	1,600
Step Two: Adjust for noncash items	
Add: depreciation expense	2,500
(Depreciation is an allocation of a capital outlay—an expense that did not involve a current outlay of cash.)	
Step Three: Adjustments to revenue	
Deduct: increase in accounts receivable	(2,200)
(More revenue was recognized than was collected in cash)	
Step Four: Adjustments to expense	
Add: decrease in inventory	1,200
(Some expense was recognized in cost of goods sold for inventory purchased in prior periods)	
Deduct: increase in prepaid expenses	(200)
(More cash was paid out than was recorded as expense)	
Add: increase in accounts payable	400
(More expense was recorded for cost of goods sold than was paid for in cash)	
Deduct: decrease in accrued interest payable	(500)
(Less interest expense was recorded than was paid in cash)	
Add: increase in deferred taxes payable	200
(More income tax expense was reported than was paid in cash)	
Step Five: Net income (cash basis)	3,000

SELF-TEST SOLUTIONS ARE PROVIDED IN APPENDIX D

____ **1.** The Statement of Cash Flows segregates cash inflows and outflows by:
- **(a)** Operating and financing activities.
- **(b)** Financing and investing activities.
- **(c)** Operating and investing activities.
- **(d)** Operating, financing, and investing activities.

____ **2.** How would short-term investments in marketable securities be classified?
- **(a)** Cash.
- **(b)** Operating activities.
- **(c)** Financing activities.
- **(d)** Investing activities.

____ **3.** How would revenue from sales of goods and services be classified?
- **(a)** Operating outflow.
- **(b)** Operating inflow.
- **(c)** Investing inflow.
- **(d)** Financing inflow.

____ **4.** How would payments for taxes be classified?
- **(a)** Operating outflow.
- **(b)** Operating inflow.
- **(c)** Investing outflow.
- **(d)** Financing outflow.

____ **5.** How would the sale of a building be classified?
- **(a)** Operating outflow.
- **(b)** Operating inflow.
- **(c)** Investing inflow.
- **(d)** Financing inflow.

____ **6.** How would the repayment of debt principal be classified?
- **(a)** Operating outflow.
- **(b)** Operating inflow.
- **(c)** Investing outflow.
- **(d)** Financing outflow.

____ **7.** What type of accounts are accounts receivable and inventory?
- **(a)** Cash accounts.
- **(b)** Operating accounts.
- **(c)** Financing accounts.
- **(d)** Investing accounts.

____ **8.** What type of accounts are notes payable and current maturities of long-term debt?
- **(a)** Cash accounts.
- **(b)** Operating accounts.
- **(c)** Financing accounts.
- **(d)** Investing accounts.

___ **9.** The change in retained earnings is affected by which of the following?
   (a) Net income and common stock.
   (b) Net income and paid-in capital.
   (c) Net income and payment of dividends.
   (d) Payment of dividends and common stock.

___ **10.** Which method of calculating cash flow from operations requires the adjustment of net income for deferrals, accruals, noncash, and nonoperating expenses?
   (a) The direct method.
   (b) The indirect method.
   (c) The inflow method.
   (d) The outflow method.

___ **11.** An outflow of cash would result from which of the following?
   (a) The increase in an asset account.
   (b) The decrease in an asset account.
   (c) The decrease in an equity account.
   (d) The decrease in a liability account.

___ **12.** An outflow of cash would result from which of the following?
   (a) The decrease in an asset account.
   (b) The increase in a liability account.
   (c) The decrease in a liability account.
   (d) The increase in an equity account.

___ **13.** What are internal sources of cash?
   (a) Cash inflows from operating activities.
   (b) Cash inflows from investing activities.
   (c) Cash inflows from financing activities.
   (d) All of the above.

___ **14.** What are external sources of cash?
   (a) Cash inflows from operating activities.
   (b) Cash inflows from investing activities.
   (c) Cash inflows from financing activities.
   (d) Both (b) and (c).

___ **15.** Which of the following items is included in the adjustment of net income to obtain cash flow from operating activities?
   (a) Depreciation expense for the period.
   (b) The change in deferred taxes.
   (c) The amount by which equity income recognized exceeds cash received.
   (d) All of the above.

___ **16.** Which statement is true for gains and losses from capital asset sales?
   (a) They do not affect cash and are excluded from the statement of cash flows.
   (b) They are included in cash flows from operating activities.
   (c) They are included in cash flows from investing activities.
   (d) They are included in cash flows from financing activities.

___ **17.** Which of the following current assets is included in the adjustment of net income to obtain cash flow from operating activities?

   (a) Accounts receivable.
   (b) Inventory.
   (c) Prepaid expenses.
   (d) All of the above.

___ **18.** Which of the following current liability accounts is included in the adjustment of expenses to obtain cash flow from operating activities?

   (a) Accounts payable.
   (b) Notes payable and current maturities of long-term debt.
   (c) Accrued liabilities.
   (d) Both (a) and (c).

___ **19.** How is it possible for a firm to be profitable and still go bankrupt?

   (a) Earnings have increased more rapidly than sales.
   (b) The firm has positive net income but has failed to generate cash from operations.
   (c) Net income has been adjusted for inflation.
   (d) Sales have not improved even though credit policies have been eased.

___ **20.** Why has cash flow from operations become increasingly important as an analytical tool?

   (a) Inflation has distorted the meaningfulness of net income.
   (b) High interest rates can put the cost of borrowing to cover short-term cash needs out of reach for many firms.
   (c) Firms may have uncollected accounts receivable and unsalable inventory on the books.
   (d) All of the above.

___ **21.** Which of the following statements is false?

   (a) A negative cash flow can occur in a year in which net income is positive.
   (b) An increase in accounts receivable represents accounts not yet collected in cash.
   (c) An increase in accounts payable represents accounts not yet collected in cash.
   (d) To obtain cash flow from operations, the reported net income must be adjusted.

___ **22.** Which of the following could lead to cash flow problems?

   (a) Obsolete inventory, accounts receivable of inferior quality, easing of credit by suppliers.
   (b) Slow-moving inventory, accounts receivable of inferior quality, tightening of credit by suppliers.
   (c) Obsolete inventory, increasing notes payable, easing of credit by suppliers.
   (d) Obsolete inventory, improved quality of accounts receivable, easing of credit by suppliers.

Questions 23-30 are based on the *direct method* of presenting cash flow from operating activities. Indicate whether the following items will be added (A) or subtracted (S) to/from the relevant revenue or expense item in the calculation of cash flow from operating activities.

____ 23. Decrease in accounts receivable to calculate cash collections from sales.

____ 24. Decrease in inventories to calculate cash paid to suppliers.

____ 25. Increase in accounts payable to calculate cash paid to suppliers.

____ 26. Decrease in accrued salaries payable to calculate cash paid to employees.

____ 27. Depreciation expense for the period to calculate cash paid for operating expenses.

____ 28. Increase in prepaid expenses to calculate cash paid for operating expense.

____ 29. Decrease in accrued interest payable to calculate cash paid for interest expense.

____ 30. Increase in deferred tax liability to calculate cash paid for tax expense.

The following information is available for Jaqui's Jewelry and Gift Store:

Net Income	$ 5,000
Depreciation expense	2,500
Increase in deferred tax liabilities	500
Decrease in cash	3,000
Increase in marketable securities	1,000
Decrease in accounts receivable	2,000
Increase in inventories	9,000
Decrease in accounts payable	5,000
Increase in accrued liabilities	1,000
Increase in property and equipment	14,000
Increase in short-term notes payable	19,000
Decrease in long-term bonds payable	4,000

Use the *indirect method* to answer questions 31-34.

____ 31. What is net cash flow from operating activities?
  (a) ($3,000)
  (b) ($1,000)
  (c) $5,000
  (d) $13,000

____ 32. What is net cash flow from investing activities?
  (a) $14,000
  (b) ($14,000)
  (c) $21,000
  (d) ($16,000)

____ 33. What is net cash flow from financing activities?
  (a) $15,000

      (b) ($15,000)
      (c) $17,000
      (d) ($14,000)

____ **34.** What is the change in cash?
      (a) ($3,000)
      (b) $3,000
      (c) $2,000
      (d) ($2,000)

STUDY QUESTIONS AND PROBLEMS

4.1 Identify the following as financing activities (F) or investing activities (I):

    (a) Purchase of equipment   _____

    (b) Purchase of treasury stock   _____

    (c) Reduction of long-term debt   _____

    (d) Sale of building   _____

    (e) Resale of treasury stock   _____

    (f) Increase in short-term debt   _____

    (g) Issuance of common stock   _____

    (h) Purchase of land   _____

    (i) Purchase of common stock of another firm   _____

    (j) Payment of cash dividends   _____

    (k) Gain on sale of land   _____

    (l) Repayment of debt principal   _____

4.2 Indicate which of the following current assets and current liabilities are operating accounts (O) and thus included in the adjustment of net income to cash flow from operating activities and which are cash (C), investing (I), or financing (F) accounts.

    (a) Accounts payable   _____

    (b) Accounts receivable   _____

    (c) Notes payable (to bank)   _____

    (d) Marketable securities   _____

    (e) Accrued expenses   _____

    (f) Inventory   _____

    (g) Notes receivable—officers   _____

    (h) Current portion of long-term debt   _____

    (i) Dividends payable   _____

    (j) Income taxes payable   _____

    (k) Interest payable   _____

    (l) Certificates of deposit   _____

4.3 Comparative balance sheets for 19X8 and 19X7 and an income statement for 19X8 are presented for Leon Company.   Prepare a statement of cash flows for 19X8.

Leon Corporation
Comparative Balance Sheets
December 31, 19X7 and 19X8

	19X8	19X7
Current Assets		
Cash	$ 1,378	$ 512
Marketable securities	276	200
Accounts receivable	9,921	9,016
Inventories	12,217	12,651
Prepaid expenses	247	161
Total current assets	$24,039	$22,540
Noncurrent Assets		
Plant and equipment	$12,461	11,209
Less accumulated depreciation	(7,638)	(7,140)
Net plant and equipment	4,823	4,069
Patents	420	0
Investments (land held for resale)	1,520	1,720
Total Assets	$30,802	$28,329
Current Liabilities		
Accounts payable	$ 3,418	$ 4,211
Notes payable	2,788	857
Accrued expenses	4,110	3,872
Current portion of long-term debt	493	493
Total current liabilities	$10,809	$ 9,433
Noncurrent Liabilities		
Deferred taxes	$ 1,447	$ 1,475
Bonds payable	9,200	9,693
Total noncurrent liabilities	$10,647	$11,168
Owner's Equity		
Common stock (par $1.00)	$ 100	$ 100
Additional paid-in capital	2,000	2,000
Retained earnings	7,246	5,628
Total equity	$ 9,346	$ 7,728
Total Liabilities and Equity	$30,802	$28,329

Leon Corporation
Statement of Income
for Year Ended December 31, 19X8

Net sales		$51,224
Cost of goods sold		38,162
Gross profit		13,062
Operating expense		
Administrative	$ 7,953	
Depreciation	498	8,451
Net operating income		4,611
Interest expense		1,237
Earnings before taxes		3,374
Income tax expense		1,606
Net income		$ 1,768

4.4 Condensed financial statements for Luna Enterprises are provided below.

   (a) Prepare a statement of cash flows using the indirect method.

   (b) Compute cash flow from operating activities by the direct method.

Luna Enterprises
Comparative Balance Sheets
December 31, 19X9 and 19X8

	19X9	19X8
Cash	$ 1,200	$ 950
Accounts receivable	1,750	1,200
Inventory	1,150	1,450
Plant and equipment	4,500	3,900
Accumulated depreciation	(1,200)	(1,100)
Long-term investments	900	1,150
Total Assets	8,300	7,550
Accounts payable	1,100	800
Accrued wages payable	250	350
Bonds payable	1,100	1,400
Capital stock	1,000	1,000
Paid-in Capital	400	400
Retained earnings	4,450	3,600
Total Liability and Equity	$ 8,300	$ 7,550

Income Statement
For Year Ended December 31, 19X9

Sales	$ 9,500
Cost of Goods Sold	6,650
Gross Profit	2,850
Other Expenses	
Selling	1,200
Depreciation	100
Interest	150
Income Tax	350
Net Income	1,050
Cash Dividends	200

4.5 The following income statement and balance sheet information are available for two firms: Firm A operates in a retail trade industry and Firm B in a service oriented industry.   Firm A paid $5,000 in dividends, Firm B paid $35,000 in dividends during 19X9.

(a) Prepare a statement of cash flows for each firm.

(b) Analyze the difference in the two firms.

Income Statement
for Year Ended December 31, 19X9

	Firm A	Firm B
Sales	$1,000,000	$1,000,000
Cost of Goods Sold	700,000	700,000
Gross Profit	300,000	300,000
Other Expenses		
Selling and administrative	120,000	115,000
Depreciation	10,000	30,000
Interest Expense	20,000	5,000
Earnings before taxes	150,000	150,000
Income Tax Expense	75,000	75,000
Net Income	$ 75,000	$ 75,000

Changes in Balance Sheet Accounts
December 31, 19X8 to December 31, 19X9

	Firm A	Firm B
Cash	$+ 5,000	$+ 5,000
Marketable Securities	− 5,000	+ 5,000
Accounts Receivable	+ 40,000	+ 5,000
Inventory	+ 40,000	− 10,000
Property, plant, and equipment	+ 20,000	+ 70,000
Less accumulated depreciation	(+ 10,000)	(+ 30,000)
Total Assets	$+ 90,000	$+ 45,000
Accounts payable	$− 20,000	$− 5,000
Notes payable (current)	+ 17,000	+ 2,000
Long-term debt	+ 20,000	− 10,000
Deferred taxes (noncurrent)	+ 3,000	+ 18,000
Stockholders' equity	+ 70,000	+ 40,000
Total Liability and Equity	$+ 90,000	$+ 45,000

4.6 The following comparative balance sheets, income statement, and additional information are available for Little Bit, Inc.

Required: Prepare a statement of cash flows for 19X9 and analyze the statement.

December 31, 19X9 and 19X8

	19X9	19X8
Cash	$ 12,000	$ 7,000
Accounts receivable (net)	190,000	125,000
Inventory	280,000	210,000
Prepaid rent	25,000	18,000
Total current assets	$ 507,000	$360,000
Plant and equipment	500,000	450,000
Less accumulated depreciation	(105,000)	(95,000)
Plant and equipment (net)	$ 395,000	$355,000
Land held for investment	165,000	150,000
Total Assets	$1,067,000	$865,000
Accounts payable	$ 175,000	$150,000
Notes payable—banks	179,000	61,000
Accrued salaries payable	43,000	52,000
Total current liabilities	$ 397,000	$263,000
Long-term debt	210,000	190,000
Deferred taxes	105,000	95,000
Total liabilities	712,000	548,000
Common stock ($1 par)	110,000	100,000
Additional paid-in capital	70,000	60,000
Retained earnings	175,000	157,000
Total Liabilities and Equity	$1,067,000	$865,000

Income Statement for 19X9

Sales		$950,000
Cost of Goods Sold		650,000
Gross Profit		$300,000
Selling and administrative	$ 100,000	
Depreciation	60,000	
Other operating	45,000	205,000
Operating Profit		$ 95,000
Other income		
Gain on Sale of building		5,000
Other expense		
Interest		40,000
Earnings before tax		$ 60,000
Tax expense		20,000
Net Income		$ 40,000

Additional Information

1. A building with original cost of $100,000 and accumulated depreciation of $50,000 was sold for $55,000.

2. Land for investment was purchased at a cost of $15,000.

3. Long-term debt of $20,000 was repaid.

4. 10,000 shares of common stock were sold for $2 per share.

4.7 Using the balance sheet and income statement given prepare a Statement of Cash Flows for FSA Corporation.   Using both the direct and indirect method to calculate cash flow from operating activities.

FSA Corporation
Balance Sheet at December 31, 19X2 and 19X3

	19X2	19X3
Assets		
Cash	$ 80,000	$ 100,000
Accounts receivable	240,000	200,000
Inventories	500,000	420,000
Prepaid expenses	30,000	50,000
Total current assets	$ 850,000	$ 770,000
Property, plant and equipment	500,000	350,000
Less accumulated depreciation	(140,000)	(100,000)
Property, Plant, and Equipment (net)	360,000	250,000
Total Assets	$1,210,000	$1,020,000
Liabilities and Equity		
Accounts Payable	$ 175,000	$ 150,000
Notes Payable	150,000	120,000
Accrued wages payable	50,000	75,000
Interest payable	35,000	25,000
Income taxes payable	10,000	15,000
Total Current Liabilities	$ 420,000	$ 385,000
Long-term debt	325,000	250,000
Deferred taxes	90,000	70,000
Total liabilities	$ 835,000	$ 705,000
Common stock	100,000	100,000
Paid-in capital	50,000	50,000
Retained earnings	225,000	165,000
Total Liabilities and Equity	$1,210,000	$1,020,000

Income Statement for Year Ended 19X2

Sales		$1,000,000
Cost of Goods Sold		650,000
Gross Profit		$ 350,000
Operating expenses		
Selling and administrative	$ 60,000	
Depreciation	40,000	
Other	50,000	150,000
Operating Profit		$ 200,000
Interest expense		55,000
Earnings before tax		$ 145,000
Income tax expense		35,000
Net Income		$ 110,000

4.8 The following financial statements are provided for Deerco, Inc. a manufacturer of farm equipment and machinery. The sluggish economic conditions in the farming industry have affected Deerco, but the firm still maintained a profit in 19X9.

Deerco's accountant has prepared a statement showing sources and uses of funds (working capital) for the period 19X7 through 19X9.

(a) Convert the Deerco sources and uses of funds statement to a statement of cash flows. (Use the indirect method to calculate cash flow from operating activities.)

(b) Analyze the Deerco statement of cash flows for the years 19X7 to 19X9.

Deerco, Inc.
Sources and Uses of Funds
(In thousands)

	19X9	19X8	19X7
Sources			
Net Income	$ 52,000	$150,000	$128,000
Add (deduct)			
Depreciation	128,000	165,000	147,000
Undistributed earnings of			
unconsolidated subsidiaries	(83,000)	(88,000)	(39,000)
Deferred income taxes	1,000	64,000	71,000
Working capital from operations	$98,000	$291,000	$307,000
Additions to long-term debt	65,000	16,000	150,000
Issuance of common stock	3,000	195,000	50,000
Total Sources of Funds	$166,000	$502,000	$507,000
Uses			
Property and equipment	109,000	345,000	420,000
Investments in unconsolidated			
subsidiaries	19,000	51,000	95,000
Dividends	98,000	133,000	116,000
Retirement of long-term debt	37,000	42,000	68,000
Total Uses of funds	$263,000	$571,000	$699,000
Increase (decrease in working capital)	(97,000)	(69,000)	(192,000)
Components of working capital			
Current assets increase (decrease)			
Cash and equivalents	(15,000)	(2,000)	16,000
Trade receivables	303,000	269,000	491,000
Inventories	(92,000)	(61,000)	(8,000)
Prepaid expenses	6,000	(4,000)	7,000
Current liabilities increase (decrease)			
Accounts payable	(171,000)	104,000	116,000
Notes payable	474,000	98,000	543,000
Accrued liabilities	13,000	73,000	37,000
Dividends payable	(17,000)	(4,000)	2,000

Additional Information
(In thousands)

	19X9	19X8	19X7
1. Investment Income (equity method)	$92,000*	$95,000*	$50,000*
2. Cash dividends received from unconsolidated subsidiary investments	9,000	7,000	11,000

*Investment income on income statement

4.9 The following cash flows were reported by Techno Inc. in 19X8 and 19X7: (In thousands)

(In thousands)

	19X8	19X7
Cash provided by operations		
Net income	$316,354	$242,329
Noncash charges (credits) to income		
Depreciation and Amoritization	68,156	62,591
Deferred Taxes	15,394	22,814
	399,904	327,734
Cash Provided (Used) by Operating assets and liabilities:		
Receivables	(288,174)	(49,704)
Inventories	(159,419)	(145,554)
Other current assets	(1,470)	3,832
Accounts payable, accrued liabilities	73,684	41,079
Total Cash Provided by Operations	24,525	177,387
Investment Activities		
Additions to plant and equipment	(94,176)	(93,136)
Other investment activities	14,408	(34,771)
Net Investment Activities	(79,768)	(127,907)
Financing Activities		
Purchases of treasury stock	(45,854)	(39,267)
Dividends paid	(49,290)	(22,523)
Net changes in short-term borrowings	125,248	45,067
Additions to long-term borrowings	135,249	4,610
Repayments of long-term borrowings		(250,564)
Net Financing Activities	165,353	(262,677)
Increase (Decrease) in Cash	110,110	(213,197)
Beginning Cash Balance	78,114	291,311
Ending Cash Balance	188,224	78,114

(a) What method does Techno use to calculate cash flows from operating activities?

(b) Explain the difference between net income and cash flow from operating activities for Techno in 19X8.

(c) Analyze Techno, Inc.'s cash flows for 19X8 and 19X7.

4.10 Analyze the 1989 Consolidated Statement of Cash Flows for Reebok International Ltd.

Reebok International Ltd.
Consolidated Statements of Cash Flows
(In Thousands)

	Year ended December 31		
	1989	1988	1987
Cash flows from operating activities			
Net Income	**$174,998**	$137,002	$165,200
Adjustment to reconcile net income to net cash provided by operating activities:			
Depreciation and amortization	**13,512**	8,850	5,777
Amortization of intangibles	**14,427**	14,216	12,453
Amortization of unearned compensation	**596**	287	1,882
Deferred income taxes	**(3,988)**	(5,157)	(12,587)
Gain on sale of Frye	**(3,642)**	—	—
Foreign currency transaction gain	**(3,332)**	—	—
Changes in operating assets and liabilities, exclusive of those arising from business acquisitions:			
Decrease (increase) in assets:			
Accounts receivable	**(6,477)**	(66,684)	(43,106)
Inventory	**35,603**	(53,960)	(81,406)
Prepaid expenses	**(1,252)**	1,522	(7,221)
Other	**(3,775)**	(6,631)	(4,715)
Increase (decrease) in liabilities:			
Accounts payable and accrued expenses	**33,463**	1,335	20,380
Income taxes payable	**14,817**	(1,491)	4,463
Total adjustments	**89,952**	(107,713)	(104,080)
Net Cash provided by operating activities	**264,950**	29,289	61,120
Cash Flows from investing activities:			
Payments to acquire property and equipment	**(18,400)**	(31,923)	(28,638)
Payments for business acquisitions, net of cash acquired	**(32,850)**	(14,768)	(198,905)
Cash received from sale of Frye	**1,109**		
Net cash used by investing activities	**(50,141)**	(46,691)	(227,543)

Year ended December 31

	1989	1988	1987
Cash flows from financing activities:			
Net borrowings (repayments) under line of credit	**(73,680)**	10,623	6,498
Net borrowings (repayments) of interest-bearing accounts payable	**(31,878)**	(25,377)	38,540
Proceeds from issuance of common stock to public			125,628
Proceeds from issuance of common stock to employees	**8,381**	2,878	2,084
Other Payments			(279)
Dividends paid	**(33,965)**	(25,396)	(22,158)
Shares retired		(58)	(117)
Repayments of long-term debt	**(11,762)**	(120)	(248)
Proceeds from long-term debt		96,465	7,765
Net Cash (used) provided by financing activities	**(142,904)**	59,015	157,713
Effect of exchange rate changes on cash	**170**	(2,431)	2,800
Net increase (decrease) in cash and cash equivalents	**72,075**	39,182	(5,910)
Cash and cash equivalents at beginning of year	**99,349**	60,167	66,077
Cash and cash equivalents at end of year	**$171,424**	$99,349	$60,167

ROYAL APPLIANCE MFG. CO. AND SUBSIDIARIES MINI-CASE

As the Vice-President of Lending for Gilbert National Bank, you are in charge of giving final approval on all loan applications. Gilbert National Bank is currently trying to acquire new corporate clients and Royal Appliance Mfg. Co. and Subsidiaries has approached the bank to request a substantial line of credit. Kathy Kuebbing, one of your loan officers, has been working with the company and has recommended approval. She submitted the following summary of her analysis:

Royal Appliance Manufacturing Company
(Submitted by Kathy Kuebbing)

Royal Appliance owns numerous trademarks in the vacuum cleaner industry, including the famous product line introduced in 1984, the Dirt Devil Hand Vac. Since 1984, the Company has made significant progress in gaining market share. At the end of 1992 Royal had a 20% market share in the upright vacuum cleaner market, just 8% behind the industry leader. The tremendous gain in market share should continue since Royal has doubled advertising and promotion expenditures in each of the three past years. The company has also increased spending in engineering and product development. Net sales have increased 229% from 1990 to 1992. Despite the large increase in advertising and engineering expenditures, Royal has still managed to increase net earnings 72% from 1990 to 1992. The Company also has a strong working capital position. Current assets, comprised mainly of accounts receivable and inventories, are 2.5 times greater than current liabilities. Other noncurrent debt includes a revolving credit agreement and capital lease obligations. This company, which just began selling stock to the public in 1991, is a high growth company which I highly recommend for funding.

You note that Kathy's analysis did not consider the statement of cash flows, which you decide to review before making a final decision.

REQUIRED:

1. Analyze the statement of cash flows for Royal Appliance Mfg. Company for the past three years, 1990 through 1992.
2. Using the statement submitted by Kathy and your cash flow analysis, evaluate the credit worthiness of Royal Appliance Mfg. Co. and Subsidiaries.
3. Explain what information you gain from the statement of cash flows that cannot be found directly from the balance sheet or income statement.
4. What information, other than the financial statements, would be helpful in making this credit decision?

Royal Appliance Mfg. Co. and Subsidiaries
CONDENSED CONSOLIDATED STATEMENTS OF CASH FLOWS
For the years ended December 31

(Dollars in thousands)	1990	1991	1992
Cash flows from operating activities:			
Net income	$11,714	$32,800	$20,151
Adjustments to reconcile net income to net cash provided by (used in) operating activities			
Depreciation and amortization	1,404	2,868	6,246
Compensatory effect of stock options	—	—	39
(Increase) decrease in assets:			
Trade accounts receivable, net	(17,933)	(7,213)	(2,557)
Inventories	(9,847)	(30,317)	(35,281)
Refundable and deferred income taxes	—	(2,935	(1,154)
Prepaid expenses and other	(313)	(80)	(1,891)
Other	515	(780)	(767)
Increase (decrease) in liabilities:			
Trade accounts payable	4,524	14,306	(8,166)
Accrued advertising and promotion	3,972	2,149	2,908
Accrued salaries, benefits, and payroll taxes	181	1,986	(725)
Accrued warranty and customer returns	—	2,041	5,011
Accrued income taxes	—	—	5,894
Accrued interest and other	390	591	236
Other	—	—	(183)
Total adjustments	(17,107)	(17,384)	(30,390)
Net cash (used in) provided by operations	(5,393)	15,416	(10,239)
Cash flows from investing activities:			
Purchases of tooling, property, plant, and equipment net	(4,663)	(9,512)	(31,876)
Increase in tooling deposits	—	(4,622)	(618)
Net cash (used in) investing activities	(4,663)	(14,134)	(32,494)
Cash flows from financing activities:			
Proceeds from bank debt	31,992	108,010	210,928
Payments on bank debt	(17,500)	(122,273)	(154,564)
Purchase of treasury shares	—	—	(12,973)
Payments on capital lease obligations	(46)	(61)	(206)
S corporation dividends	(4,975)	(28,429)	—
Proceeds of share offering	—	42,327	—
Proceeds from (payment on) note payable	2,000	(2,000)	—
Other	24	(150)	—
Net cash provided by (used in) financing activities	11,495	(2,666)	43,185
Effect of exchange rate changes on cash	(137)	62	(452)
Net increase (decrease) in cash	1,302	(1,322)	—
Cash at beginning of year	20	1,322	—
Cash at the end of year	$ 1,322	$ —	$ —
Supplemental disclosure of cash flow information:			
Cash payments for:			
Interest, net of capitalized interest	$ 2,629	$ 2,846	$ 3,057
Income taxes	$ —	$15,686	$ 8,136
Supplemental schedule of noncash investing and financing activities:			
Capital assests acquired under capital leases	$ —	$ 7,270	$ —
Reinstatement of deferred tax benefit	$ —	$ 923	$ —

5

The Analysis of Financial Statements

Only a rank degenerate would drive 1,500 miles across Texas without eating a chicken fried steak
—Larry McMurtry, *In a Narrow Grave: Essays on Texas*

The preceding chapters have covered in detail the form and content of the four basic financial statements found in the annual reports of U.S. firms: the balance sheet, the income statement, the statement of retained earnings or statement of shareholders' equity, and the statement of cash flows. This chapter develops tools and techniques for the interpretation and analysis of financial statements.

Objectives of the Analysis

Before beginning the analysis of any firm's financial statements, it is necessary to specify the objectives of the analysis. The objectives will vary depending on the perspective of the financial statement user and the specific questions that are addressed by the analysis of the financial statement data.

A *creditor* is ultimately concerned with the ability of an existing or prospective borrower to make interest and principal payments on borrowed funds. The questions raised in a credit analysis should include:

What is the *borrowing cause*? What do the financial statements reveal about the reason a firm has requested a loan or the purchase of goods on credit?

What is the firm's *capital structure*? How much debt is currently outstanding? How well has debt been serviced in the past?

What will be the *source of debt repayment*? How well does the company manage working capital? Is the firm generating cash from operations?

The credit analyst will use the historical record of the company, as presented in the financial statements, to answer such questions and to predict the firm's potential to satisfy future demands for cash, including debt service.

The *investor* attempts to estimate a company's future earnings stream in order to attach a value to the securities being considered for purchase or liquidation. The investment analyst poses such questions as:

What is the company *performance record*, and what are its *future expectations*? What is its record of growth and stability of earnings? Of cash flow from operations?

How much *risk* is inherent in the firm's existing capital structure? What are the *expected returns*, given the firm's current condition and future outlook?

How successfully does the firm compete in its industry, and how well positioned is the company to hold or improve its *competitive position*?

The investment analyst also uses historical financial statement data to forecast the future. For the investor, the ultimate objective is to determine whether the objective is sound.

Financial statement analysis from the standpoint of *management* relates to all of the questions raised by creditors and investors because these groups must be satisfied in order for the firm to obtain capital as needed. Management must also consider its employees, the general public, regulators, and the financial press. Management looks to financial statement data to determine:

How *well* has the firm performed and *why*? What *operating areas* have contributed to success and which have not?

What are the *strengths and weaknesses* of the company's financial position?

What *changes* should be implemented to improve future performance?

Financial statements provide insight into the company's current status and lead to the development of policies and strategies for the future. It should be pointed out, however, that management also has responsibility for preparing the financial statements. The analyst should be alert to the potential for management to influence the outcome of financial statements in order to appeal to creditors, investors, and others. It is important that any analysis of financial statements include a careful reading of the notes to the financial statements. It may also be helpful to supplement the analysis with other material in the annual report and with other information outside the annual report.

SOURCES OF INFORMATION

The financial statement user has access to a wide range of data in the analysis of financial statements. The *objective* of the analysis dictates to a considerable degree not only the approach taken in the analysis, but also the particular resources that should be consulted. The beginning point, however, should always be the financial statements themselves and the notes to the financial statements. In addition, the analyst will want to consider the following resources.

Auditor's Report

The report of the independent auditor contains the expression of opinion as to the fairness of the financial statement presentation. Most auditor's reports are *unqualified*, which means that, in the opinion of the auditor, the financial statements present fairly the financial position, the results of operations, and the cash flows for the periods covered by the financial statements. A *qualified* report is a signal that the auditors believe the financial statements are fairly presented except for certain items or circumstances which the auditor discloses in the report, such as a scope limitation or uncertainties about future events that cannot be resolved or estimated. If an *adverse opinion* is rendered, the financial statements have not been presented fairly in accordance with generally accepted accounting principles. A *disclaimer of opinion* is given when the auditor cannot evaluate the fairness of the statements. (Also see discussion of auditor's report in Chapter 1.)

Management's Discussion and Analysis

Management's Discussion and Analysis of the Financial Condition and Results of Operations (Chapter 1) is a section of the annual report that is required and monitored by the Securities and Exchange Commission. In this section, management presents a detailed coverage of the firm's liquidity, capital resources, and operations. The material can be especially helpful to the financial analyst because it includes facts and estimates not found elsewhere in the annual report. For example, this report is expected to cover forward-looking information such as projections of capital expenditures and how such investments will be financed. There is information about the mix of price relative to volume increases for products sold. Management must disclose any favorable or unfavorable trends and any significant events or uncertainties that relate to the firm's historical or prospective financial condition and operations.

Supplementary Schedules

Certain supplementary schedules are required for inclusion in an annual report and are frequently helpful to the analysis. For example, companies that operate in several unrelated lines of business provide a breakdown by operating segment of key financial figures. (The analysis of segmental data is covered in Appendix B.)

Form 10-K and Form 10-Q   Form 10-K is a document filed annually with the Securities and Exchange Commission by companies that sell securities to the public. It contains much of the same information as the annual report issued to shareholders. It also shows additional detail that may be of interest to the financial analyst, such as schedules listing information about management, a description of material litigation and governmental actions, and elaborations of some financial statement disclosures. A less extensive document, Form 10-Q, provides quarterly financial information. Both reports are available to the public on request from the Securities and Exchange Commission.

Other Sources

There is a considerable body of material outside of the corporate annual report that can contribute to an analysis of financial statements. Most academic libraries and many public libraries have computerized search systems and computerized data bases that can greatly facilitate financial analysis.[1] Although not a replacement for the techniques that will be discussed, these research materials supplement and enhance the analytical process and save time. There are also available software packages that perform some of the ratio calculations and other analyses described here.

Other general resources for the analysis of financial statements may be found in the general reference section of public and university libraries. The following sources provide comparative statistical ratios to help determine a company's relative position within its industry:

1. Dun and Bradstreet Information Services, *Industry Norms and Key Business Ratios*. Murray Hill, NJ

2. Robert Morris Associates, *Annual Statement Studies*. Philadelphia, PA.

3. Standard & Poor's Corporation, *Ratings Handbook* and *Industry Surveys*. New York, NY

4. Gale Research Inc., M*anufacturing U.S.A. Industry Analyses*. Detroit, MI.

Also helpful to the analyst are the following which contain useful investment and financial information about particular companies, industries, and mutual funds:

1. Moody's Investor Service, *Moody's Manuals* and *Moody's Handbook*. New York, NY

2. Standard & Poor's Corporation, C*orporation Records, The Outlook, Stock Reports*, and *Stock Guide*. New York, NY

3. Value Line, Inc., Th*e Value Line Investment Survey*. New York, NY

4. Zack's Investment Research Inc., *Earnings Forecaster*. Chicago, IL.

5. Gale Research Inc., *Market Share Reporter*. Detroit, MI.

6. Dow Jones-Irwin, *The Financial Analyst's Handbook*. Homewood, IL.

7. For mutual funds: Morningstar, *Morningstar Mutual Funds*. Chicago, IL.

[1] One resource that is commonly available in both public and academic libraries is the Infotrak—General Business Index.This CD-Rom database provides indexing to approximately 800 business, trade and management journals. It has company profiles, investment analyst reports, and a wide range of business news. To learn about the availability and use of this system or other search systems and databases, consult the reference librarian or the business reference librarian.

Articles from current periodicals such as *Business Week*, *Forbes*, *Fortune*, and *The Wall Street Journal* can add insight into the management and operations of individual firms as well as provide perspective on general economic and industry trends.

Tools and Techniques

Various tools and techniques are used by the financial statement analyst to convert financial statement data into formats that facilitate the evaluation of a firm's financial condition and performance, both over time and in comparison with industry competitors. Among these are *common size financial statements,* which express each balance sheet account as a percentage of total assets and each income statement account as a percentage of net sales; *financial ratios,* which standardize financial data using mathematical relationships expressed as percentages or times; *trend analysis,* which evaluates financial data over several accounting periods; *structural analysis,* which looks at the internal structure of a business enterprise; *industry comparisons,* which compare one firm with averages compiled for the industry in which it operates; and most important of all, *common sense* and *judgment.*

These tools and techniques will be illustrated by a financial statement analysis of R.E.C., Inc. This first part covers number crunching, the preparation of common size financial statements and the calculation of key financial ratios. The second part involves the integration of these numbers with other information—such as the statement of cash flows from Chapter 4 and background on the economy and the environment in which the firm operates—in order to perform an analysis of R.E.C., Inc. over a 5-year period and to assess the firm's strengths, weaknesses, and future.

Common Size Financial Statements

Common size financial statements are a form of ratio analysis which allow comparison of firms with different levels of sales or total assets by introducing a common denominator. A *common size balance sheet* expresses each item on the balance sheet as a percentage of total assets; and a *common size income statement* expresses each income statement category as a percentage of net sales. Common size statements facilitate the internal or structural analysis of a firm. The common size balance sheet reveals the composition of assets within major categories; for example, cash and cash equivalents relative to other current assets; the distribution of assets in which funds are invested (current, long-lived, intangible); the capital structure of the firm (debt relative to equity); and the debt structure (long-term relative to short-term). The common size income statement shows the relative magnitude of various expenses relative to sales, the profit percentages (gross profit, operating profit, and net profit margins) and the relative importance of "other" revenues and expenses. Common size statements are also useful to evaluate trends and make industry comparisons. The common size balance sheets and income statements for R.E.C., Inc. are presented in Exhibits 5.1 and 5.2.

EXHIBIT 5.1 R.E.C., Inc.
Common Size Balance Sheets
(Percent)

	19X9	19X8	19X7	19X6	19X5
Assets					
Current Assets					
Cash	4.3	3.1	3.9	5.1	4.9
Marketable securities	5.5	10.6	14.9	15.3	15.1
Accounts receivable, less allowance for					
doubtful accounts	9.4	11.0	7.6	6.6	6.8
Inventories	49.4	48.4	45.0	40.1	39.7
Prepaid expenses	.5	1.0	1.6	2.4	2.6
Total current assets	69.1	74.1	73.0	69.5	69.1
Property, Plant, and Equipment					
Land	.8	1.1	1.2	1.4	1.4
Buildings and leasehold improvements	19.2	15.7	14.4	14.1	14.5
Equipment	22.6	18.1	17.3	15.9	16.5
Less accumulated depreciation and amortization	(12.1)	(9.9)	(6.9)	(3.1)	(3.0)
Net property, plant, and equipment	30.5	25.0	26.0	28.3	29.4
Other Assets	.4	.9	1.0	2.2	1.5
Total Assets	100.0	100.0	100.0	100.0	100.0
Liabilities and Stockholders' Equity					
Current Liabilities					
Accounts payable	15.0	10.0	13.1	11.4	11.8
Notes payable—banks	5.9	7.9	6.2	4.4	4.3
Current maturities of long-term debt	2.0	2.0	2.4	2.4	2.6
Accrued liabilities	5.9	7.0	10.6	7.7	5.7
Total current liabilities	28.8	26.9	32.3	25.9	24.4
Deferred Federal Income Taxes	.9	.8	.7	.5	.4
Long-Term Debt	22.1	22.4	16.2	14.4	14.9
Total liabilities	51.8	50.1	49.2	40.8	39.7
Stockholders' Equity					
Common stock	5.0	6.1	6.7	7.3	7.5
Additional paid-in capital	1.0	1.2	1.3	1.6	1.8
Retained earnings	42.2	42.6	42.8	50.3	51.0
Total stockholders' equity	48.2	49.9	50.8	59.2	60.3
Total Liabilities and Stockholders' Equity	100.0	100.0	100.0	100.0	100.0

EXHIBIT 5.2 R.E.C., Inc.
             Common Size Income Statements
             (Percent)

	19X9	19X8	19X7	19X6	19X5
Net sales	100.0	100.0	100.0	100.0	100.0
Cost of Goods Sold	60.0	60.1	58.0	58.2	58.2
Gross Profit	40.0	39.9	42.0	41.8	41.8
Operating Expenses					
Selling and administrative expenses	15.1	17.2	18.1	15.6	15.4
Advertising	6.6	7.1	6.8	6.4	6.3
Lease payments	6.1	4.6	5.1	4.7	4.6
Depreciation and amortization	1.9	2.0	1.8	1.4	1.2
Repairs and maintenance	1.4	1.3	2.2	2.7	2.7
Operating Profit	8.9	7.7	8.0	11.0	11.6
Other Income (Expense)					
Interest income	.2	.5	.5	.3	.3
Interest expense	(1.2)	(1.5)	(.9)	(.9)	(1.0)
Earnings before income taxes	7.9	6.7	7.6	10.4	10.9
Income Taxes	3.6	2.9	3.4	5.4	5.7
Net Earnings	4.3	3.8	4.2	5.0	5.2

The common size balance sheet in Exhibit 5.1, shows that inventories have become more dominant over the 5-year period in the firm's total asset structure and in 19X9 comprised almost half (49.4%) of total assets. Holdings of cash and marketable securities decreased from a 20% combined level in 19X5 and 19X6 to about 10% in 19X9. The company elected to make this shift in order to accommodate the inventory requirements of new store openings. The firm opened 43 new stores in the past two years, and the effect of this market strategy is also reflected in the overall asset structure. Buildings, leasehold improvements, equipment, and accumulated depreciation and amortization increased as a percentage of total assets. On the liability side, the proportion of debt required to finance investments in assets rose, primarily through long-term borrowing.

The common size income statement (Exhibit 5.2) reveals the trends of expenses and profit margins. Cost of goods sold increased slightly, resulting in a small decline in the gross profit percentage. To improve this margin, the firm will either have to raise its own retail prices, change the product mix, or figure ways to reduce costs on goods purchased for resale. Operating expenses, lease payments, depreciation, and amortization increased relative to sales, again reflecting costs associated with new store openings. Selling and administrative expenses also rose in 19X7 and 19X8, but the company controlled these costs more effectively in 19X9 relative to overall sales. Operating and net profit percentages are discussed more extensively in connection with the 5-year trends of financial ratios later in the chapter. The common size income statements show that both profit percentages deteriorated through 19X8 and rebounded in the most recent year as R.E.C., Inc. enjoyed the benefits of an economic recovery and profits from expansion.

Key Financial Ratios

The R.E.C., Inc. financial statements will be used to compute a set of key financial ratios for the years 19X9 and 19X8. Later, these ratios will be evaluated in the context of R.E.C., Inc.'s 5-year historical record and in comparison with industry competitors. The four categories of ratios to be covered are (1) *liquidity ratios,* which measure a firm's ability to meet cash needs as they arise; (2) *activity ratios,* which measure the liquidity of specific assets and the efficiency of managing assets; (3) *leverage ratios,* which measure the extent of a firm's financing with debt relative to equity and its ability to cover interest and other fixed charges; and (4) *profitability ratios,* which measure the overall performance of a firm and its efficiency in managing assets, liabilities, and equity.

Before delving into the R.E.C., Inc. financial ratios, a word of caution is necessary about the use of financial ratios generally. Although extremely valuable as analytical tools, financial ratios also have limitations. They can serve as screening devices, indicate areas of potential strength or weakness, and reveal matters that need further investigation. But financial ratios do not provide answers and they do not predict. Financial ratios should be used both with caution and common sense. They should be used in combination with other elements of financial analysis. There is no one definitive set of key financial ratios; there is no uniform definition for all ratios; and there is no standard which should be met for each ratio. Finally, there are no "rules of thumb" that apply to the interpretation of financial ratios. Each situation should be evaluated in the context of the particular firm, industry, and economic environment.

Figures from the R.E.C., Inc. Consolidated Balance Sheets and Statements of Retained Earnings, Exhibit 5.3, are used to illustrate the calculation of financial ratios for 19X9 and 19X8, and these financial ratios will subsequently be incorporated into a 5-year analysis of the firm.

Liquidity Ratios: Short-Term Solvency

Current Ratio

	19X9	19X8
$\dfrac{\text{Current assets}}{\text{Current liabilities}}$	$\dfrac{65,846}{27,461} = 2.40$ times	$\dfrac{56,264}{20,432} = 2.75$ times

The current ratio is a commonly used measure of short-run solvency, the ability of a firm to meet its debt requirements as they come due. Current liabilities are used as the denominator of the ratio because they are considered to represent the most urgent debts, requiring retirement within one year or one operating cycle. The available cash resources to satisfy these obligations must come primarily from cash or the conversion to cash of other current assets. Some analysts eliminate prepaid expenses from the numerator because they are not a potential source of cash but, rather, represent future obligations that have already been satisfied. The current ratio for R.E.C., Inc. indicates that at year-end 19X9 current assets covered current liabilities 2.4 times, down from 19X8. To interpret the significance of this ratio it is necessary to evaluate the trend of liquidity over a longer period and to compare R.E.C., Inc.'s coverage with industry competitors. It is also essential to assess the composition of the components that comprise the ratio.

EXHIBIT 5.3 R.E.C., Inc.
Consolidated Balance Sheets at December 31, 19X9 and 19X8
(In thousands)

	19X9	19X8
Assets		
Current Assets		
Cash	$ 4,061	$ 2,382
Marketable securities (note A)	5,272	8,004
Accounts receivable, less allowance for doubtful accounts of		
$448 in 19X9 and $417 in 19X8	8,960	8,350
Inventories (note A)	47,041	36,769
Prepaid expenses	512	759
Total current assets	65,846	56,264
Property, Plant, and Equipment (notes A, C, and E)		
Land	811	811
Buildings and leasehold improvements	18,273	11,928
Equipment	21,523	13,768
Less accumulated depreciation and amortization	11,528	7,530
Net property, plant, and equipment	29,079	18,977
Other Assets (note A)	373	668
Total Assets	$95,298	$75,909
Liabilities and Stockholders' Equity		
Current Liabilities		
Accounts payable	$14,294	$ 7,591
Notes payable—banks (note B)	5,614	6,012
Current maturities of long-term debt (note C)	1,884	1,516
Accrued liabilities	5,669	5,313
Total current liabilities	27,461	20,432
Deferred Federal Income Taxes (notes A and D)	843	635
Long-Term Debt (note C)	21,059	16,975
Total liabilities	49,363	38,042
Stockholders' Equity		
Common stock, par value $1, authorized, 10,000,000 shares;		
issued, 4,803,000 shares in 19X9 and 4,594,000 shares in		
19X8 (note F)	4,803	4,594
Additional paid-in capital	957	910
Retained earnings	40,175	32,363
Total stockholders' equity	45,935	37,867
Total Liabilities and Stockholders' Equity	$95,298	$75,909

The accompanying notes are an integral part of these statements.

EXHIBIT 5.3 R.E.C., Inc.
(Continued) Consolidated Statements of Earnings and Retained Earnings
For the Years ended December 31, 19X9, 19X8, and 19X7
(In thousands except per share amounts)

	19X9	19X8	19X7
Statements of Consolidated Earnings			
Net sales	$215,600	$153,000	$140,700
Cost of goods sold (note A)	129,364	91,879	81,606
Gross profit	86,236	61,121	59,094
Selling and administrative expenses (note A)	32,664	26,382	25,498
Advertising	14,258	10,792	9,541
Lease payments (note E)	13,058	7,111	7,267
Depreciation and amortization (note A)	3,998	2,984	2,501
Repairs and maintenance	3,015	2,046	3,031
Operating profit	19,243	11,806	11,256
Other income (expense)			
Interest income	422	838	738
Interest expense	(2,585)	(2,277)	(1,274)
Earnings before income taxes	17,080	10,367	10,720
Income taxes (notes A and D)	7,686	4,457	4,824
Net Earnings	$ 9,394	$ 5,910	$ 5,896
Earnings per common share (note G)	$ 1.96	$ 1.29	$ 1.33
Statements of Consolidated Retained Earnings			
Retained earnings at beginning of year	$ 32,363	$28,315	$ 24,260
Net earnings	9,394	5,910	5,896
Cash dividends (19X9—$.33 per share; 19X8 and 19X7—$.41 per share)	(1,582)	(1,862)	(1,841)
Retained earnings at end of year	$ 40,175	$ 32,363	$ 28,315

The accompanying notes are an integral part of these statements.

As a barometer of short-term liquidity, the current ratio is limited by the nature of its components. Remember that the balance sheet is prepared as of a particular date, and the actual amount of liquid assets may vary considerably from the date on which the balance sheet is prepared. Further, accounts receivable and inventory may not be truly liquid. A firm could have a relatively high current ratio but not be able to meet demands for cash because the accounts receivable are of inferior quality or the inventory is salable only at discounted prices. It is necessary to use other measures of liquidity, including cash flow from operations and other financial ratios which rate the liquidity of specific assets, to supplement the current ratio.

Quick or Acid-Test Ratio

	19X9	19X8
$\dfrac{\text{Current Assets - Inventory}}{\text{Current Liabilities}}$	$\dfrac{65{,}846 - 47{,}041}{27{,}461} = .68 \text{ times}$	$\dfrac{56{,}264 - 36{,}769}{20{,}432} = .95 \text{ times}$

The quick or acid-test ratio is a more rigorous test of short-run solvency than the current ratio because the numerator eliminates inventory, considered the least liquid current asset and the most likely source of losses. Like the current ratio and other ratios, there are alternative ways to calculate the quick ratio. Some analysts eliminate prepaid expenses and supplies if carried as a separate item from the numerator. The quick ratio for R.E.C., Inc. indicates some deterioration between 19X8 and 19X9; this ratio must also be examined in relation to the firm's own trends and to other firms in the same industry.

Cash-Flow Liquidity Ratio

	19X9	19X8
Cash + Marketing Securities + CFO*	$\dfrac{4{,}061 + 5{,}272 + 10{,}024}{27{,}461} = .70 \text{ times}$	$\dfrac{2{,}382 + 8{,}004 + (3{,}767)}{20{,}432} = .32 \text{ times}$
Current Liabilities		

*Cash Flow from Operating Activities

Another approach to measuring short-term solvency is the cash-flow liquidity ratio,[2] which considers cash flow from operating activities (from the statement of cash flows). The cash flow liquidity ratio uses in the numerator, as an approximation of cash resources: cash and marketable securities, which are truly liquid current assets; and cash flow from operating activities, which represents the amount of cash generated from the firm's operations, such as the ability to sell inventory and collect the cash.

Note that both the current ratio and the quick ratio decreased between 19X8 and 19X9, which could be interpreted as a deterioration of liquidity. But the cash-flow ratio increased, indicating an improvement in short-run solvency. Which is the correct assessment? With any ratio, the analyst must explore the underlying components. One major reason for the decreases in the current and quick ratios was the 88% growth in accounts payable in 19X9, which could actually be a plus if it means that R.E.C., Inc. strengthened its ability to obtain supplier credit. Also, the firm turned around from negative to positive its generation of cash from operations in 19X9, explaining the improvement in the cash flow liquidity ratio and indicating stronger short-term solvency.

[2] For additional reading about this ratio and its applications, see Fraser, L. "Cash Flow from Operations and Liquidity Analysis, A New Financial Ratio for Commercial Lending Decisions," *Cash Flow*, Robert Morris Associates, Philadelphia, PA, 1989. For other cash flow ratios, see Carslaw, C. and Mills, J. "Developing Ratios for Effective Cash Flow Statement Analysis," *Journal of Accountancy*, November 1991.

Activity Ratios: Asset Liquidity, Asset Management Efficiency

Average Collection Period

	19X9	19X8
$\dfrac{\text{Accounts receivable}}{\text{Average daily sales}}$	$\dfrac{8,960}{215,600/360} = 15 \text{ days}$	$\dfrac{8,350}{153,000/360} = 20 \text{ days}$

The average collection period of accounts receivable is the average number of days required to convert receivables into cash. The ratio is calculated as the relationship between net accounts receivable (net of the allowance for doubtful accounts) and average daily sales (sales/360 days). Some analysts use the average balance of accounts receivable in the numerator and 365 days to determine average daily sales. When available, the figure for credit sales can be substituted for net sales since credit sales produce the receivables. The ratio for R.E.C., Inc. indicates that during 19X9 the firm collected its accounts in 15 days on average, an improvement over the 20-day collection period in 19X8.

The average collection period helps gauge the liquidity of accounts receivable, the ability of the firm to collect from customers. It may also provide information about a company's credit policies. For example, if the average collection period increases over time or is higher than the industry average, then the firm's credit policies could be too lenient and accounts receivables not sufficiently liquid. The loosening of credit is necessary at times to boost sales, but at an increasing cost to the firm. If credit policies are too restrictive, as reflected in an average collection period that is shortening and less than industry competitors, the firm may be losing qualified customers.

The average collection period should be compared with the firm's stated credit policies. If the policy calls for collection within 30 days and the average collection period is 60 days, the implication is that the company is not stringent in collection efforts. There could be other explanations, however, such as temporary problems caused by a depressed economy. The analyst should attempt to determine the cause of a ratio that is too long or too short.

Another factor for consideration is the strength of the firm within its industry. There are circumstances that would enable a company in a relatively strong financial position within its industry to extend credit for longer periods than weaker competitors.

Accounts Receivable Turnover

	19X9	19X8
$\dfrac{\text{Net sales}}{\text{Accounts receivable}}$	$\dfrac{215,600}{8,960} = 24.06 \text{ times}$	$\dfrac{153,000}{8,350} = 18.32 \text{ times}$

The accounts receivable turnover indicates how many times, on average, accounts receivable are collected during the year. R.E.C., Inc. converted accounts receivable into cash 24 times in 19X9, up from 18 in 19X8. The turnover of receivables, like the average collection period, has improved; the two ratios are measuring the same thing—the quality of receivables and the efficiency of the firm's collection and credit policies. The turnover expresses this information in number of times, while the average collection period measures the process in days. Generally, a high turnover is good because it is evidence of efficiency in converting receivables into cash; but a turnover that is too high may indicate credit and collection policies that are overly restrictive.

Inventory Turnover

	19X9	19X8
$\dfrac{\text{Cost of goods sold}}{\text{Inventory}}$	$\dfrac{129{,}364}{47{,}041} = 2.75$ times	$\dfrac{91{,}879}{36{,}769} = 2.50$ times

Inventory turnover measures the efficiency of the firm in managing and selling inventory. It is a gauge of the liquidity of a firm's inventory. The ratio is sometimes calculated with net sales in the numerator and/or with average inventory as the denominator. The inventory turnover for R.E.C., Inc. was 2.75 times in 19X9, an improvement over 19X8.

Generally, a high turnover is a sign of efficient inventory management and profit for the firm; the faster inventory sells, the fewer funds tied up in inventory. But a high turnover can also mean understocking and lost orders, a decrease in prices, a shortage of materials, or more sales than planned. A relatively low turnover could be the result of a company's carrying too much inventory or stocking inventory that is obsolete, slow-moving, or inferior. Low turnover could also stem from stockpiling for legitimate reasons, such as increased demand or an expected strike. The analyst should explore the underlying causes of a turnover figure that is out of line either way.

The type of industry is important in assessing inventory turnover. We would expect florists and produce retailers to have a relatively high inventory turnover because they deal in perishable products, while retailers of jewelry or farm equipment would have lower turnover but higher profit margins. When making comparisons among firms, it is essential to check the cost flow assumption, discussed in Chapter 2, used to value inventory and cost of goods sold.

Fixed Asset Turnover

	19X9	19X8
$\dfrac{\text{Net sales}}{\text{Net property, plant, equipment}}$	$\dfrac{215{,}600}{29{,}079} = 7.41$ times	$\dfrac{153{,}000}{18{,}977} = 8.06$ times

Total Asset Turnover

	19X9	19X8
$\dfrac{\text{Net sales}}{\text{Total assets}}$	$\dfrac{215{,}600}{95{,}298} = 2.26$ times	$\dfrac{153{,}000}{75{,}909} = 2.02$ times

The fixed asset turnover and total asset turnover ratios are two approaches to assessing management's effectiveness in generating sales from investments in assets. The fixed asset turnover considers only the firm's investment in property, plant, and equipment, and is extremely important for a capital-intensive firm, such as a manufacturer with heavy investments in long-lived assets. The total asset turnover measures the efficiency of managing all of a firm's assets. Generally, the higher these ratios, the smaller the investment required to generate sales and thus the more profitable the firm. When the asset turnover-ratios are low relative to the industry or the firm's historical record, either the investment in assets is too heavy and/or sales are sluggish. There may, however, be plausible explanations; for example, the firm may have undertaken an extensive plant modernization or placed assets in service at year-end, which will generate positive results in the long-term.

For R.E.C., Inc. the fixed asset turnover has slipped slightly, while the total asset turnover has improved. The firm's investment in fixed assets has grown at a faster rate (53%) than sales (41%), and this occurrence should be examined within the framework of the overall analysis of R.E.C., Inc. The increase in total asset turnover is the result of improvements in inventory and accounts receivable turnover.

Leverage Ratios: Debt Financing and Coverage

Debt Ratio

	19X9	19X8
$\dfrac{\text{Total liabilities}}{\text{Total assets}}$	$\dfrac{49{,}363}{95{,}298} = 51.8\%$	$\dfrac{38{,}042}{75{,}909} = 50.1\%$

Long-term Debt to Total Capitalization

	19X9	19X8
$\dfrac{\text{Long-term debt}}{\text{Long-term debt + Stockholders' equity}}$	$\dfrac{21{,}059}{21{,}059 + 45{,}935} = 31.4\%$	$\dfrac{16{,}975}{16{,}975 + 37{,}867} = 31.0\%$

Debt to Equity

	19X9	19X8
$\dfrac{\text{Total liabilities}}{\text{Stockholders' equity}}$	$\dfrac{49{,}363}{45{,}935} = 107.5\%$	$\dfrac{38{,}042}{37{,}867} = 100.5\%$

Each of the three debt ratios measures the extent of the firm's financing with debt. The amount and proportion of debt in a company's capital structure are extremely important to the financial analyst because of the tradeoff between risk and return. Use of debt involves risk because debt carries a fixed commitment in the form of interest charges and principal repayment. Failure to satisfy the fixed charges associated with debt will ultimately result in bankruptcy. A lesser risk is that a firm with too much debt has difficulty obtaining additional debt financing when needed or finds that credit is available only at extremely high rates of interest. While debt implies risk, it also introduces the potential for increased benefits to the firm's owners. When debt is used successfully—if operating earnings are more than sufficient to cover the fixed charges associated with debt—the returns to shareholders are magnified through financial leverage, a concept that is explained and illustrated later in the chapter.

The debt ratio considers the proportion of all assets that are financed with debt. The ratio of long-term debt to total capitalization reveals the extent to which long-term debt is used for the firm's permanent financing (both long-term debt and equity). The debt to equity ratio measures the riskiness of the firm's capital structure in terms of the relationship between the funds supplied by creditors (debt) and investors (equity). The higher the proportion of debt, the greater is the degree of risk because creditors must be satisfied before owners in the event of bankruptcy. The equity base provides, in effect, a cushion of protection for the suppliers of debt. Each of the three ratios has increased somewhat for R.E.C., Inc. between 19X9 and 19X8, implying a slightly riskier capital structure.

The analyst should be aware that the debt ratios do not present the whole picture with regard to risk. There are fixed commitments, such as lease payments, that are similar to debt but are not included in debt. The fixed charge coverage ratio, illustrated below, considers such obligations. Off balance sheet financing arrangements, discussed in Chapter 1, also have the characteristics of debt and must be disclosed in notes to the financial statements according to the provisions of FASB Statement No. 105. These arrangements should be included in an evaluation of a firm's overall capital structure.

Times Interest Earned

	19X9	19X8
$\dfrac{\text{Operating profit}}{\text{Interest expense}}$	$\dfrac{19{,}243}{2{,}585} = 7.4 \text{ times}$	$\dfrac{11{,}806}{2{,}277} = 5.2 \text{ times}$

For a firm to benefit from debt financing, the fixed interest payments that accompany debt must be more than satisfied from operating earnings.[3] The more times a company can cover its annual interest expense from operating earnings, the better off will be the firm's investors. While R.E.C., Inc. increased its use of debt in 19X9, the company also improved its ability to cover interest payments from operating profits.

Fixed Charge Coverage

	19X9	19X8
$\dfrac{\text{Operating profit} + \text{Lease payments}}{\text{Interest expense} + \text{Lease payments}}$	$\dfrac{19{,}243 + 13{,}058}{2{,}585 + 13{,}058} = 2.1 \text{ times}$	$\dfrac{11{,}806 + 7{,}111}{2{,}277 + 7{,}111} = 2.0 \text{ times}$

The fixed charge coverage ratio is a broader measure of coverage capability than the times interest earned ratio because it includes the fixed payments associated with leasing. Lease payments are added back in the numerator because they were deducted as an operating expense to calculate operating profit. Lease payments are similar to interest expense in that they both represent obligations that must be met annually. The fixed charge cover-

---

[3] The operating return, operating profit divided by assets, must exceed the cost of debt, interest expense divided by liabilities.

age ratio is important for firms that operate extensively with leasing arrangements—either operating leases, used by R.E.C., Inc., or capital leases, a form of property financing described in Chapter 3. R.E.C., Inc. experienced a significant increase in the amount of annual lease payments in 19X9 but was still able to improve its fixed charge coverage slightly.

Profitability Ratios: Overall Efficiency and Performance

Gross Profit Margin

	19X9	19X8
$\dfrac{\text{Gross profit}}{\text{Net sales}}$	$\dfrac{86{,}236}{215{,}600} = 40.0\%$	$\dfrac{61{,}121}{153{,}000} = 39.9\%$

Operating Profit Margin

	19X9	19X8
$\dfrac{\text{Operating profit}}{\text{Net sales}}$	$\dfrac{19{,}243}{215{,}600} = 8.9\%$	$\dfrac{11{,}806}{153{,}000} = 7.7\%$

Net Profit Margin

	19X9	19X8
$\dfrac{\text{Net earnings}}{\text{Net sales}}$	$\dfrac{9{,}394}{215{,}600} = 4.4\%$	$\dfrac{5{,}910}{153{,}000} = 3.9\%$

Gross profit margin, operating profit margin, and net profit margin represent the firm's ability to translate sales dollars into profits at different stages of measurement. The gross profit margin, which shows the relationship between sales and the cost of products sold, measures the ability of a company both to control costs of inventories or manufacturing of products and to pass along price increases through sales to customers. The operating profit margin, a measure of overall operating efficiency, incorporates all of the expenses associated with ordinary business activities. The net profit margin measures profitability after considering all revenue and expense, including interest, taxes, and non-operating items.

There was little change in the R.E.C., Inc. gross profit margin, but the company improved its operating margin. Apparently, the firm was able to control the growth of operating expenses while sharply increasing sales. There was also a slight increase in net profit margin, a flow-through from operating margin, but it will be necessary to look at these ratios over a longer term and in conjunction with other parts of the analysis to explain the changes.

Cash Flow Margin

	19X9	19X8

$$\frac{\text{Cash flow from operating activities}}{\text{Net sales}} \qquad \frac{10,024}{215,600} = 4.6\% \qquad \frac{(3,767)}{153,000} = (2.5\%)$$

Another important perspective on operating performance the relationship between cash generated from operations and net sales. As pointed out in Chapter 4, it is cash, not accrual-measured earnings, that a firm needs to service debt, pay dividends, and invest in new capital assets. The cash flow margin measures the ability of the firm to translate sales into cash.

In 19X9 R.E.C., Inc. had a cash flow margin that was greater than its operating profit margin, the result of a strongly positive generation of cash. The performance in 19X9 represents a solid improvement over 19X8 when the firm failed to generate cash from operations and had a negative cash flow margin.

Return on Investment (ROI)

	19X9	19X8

$$\frac{\text{Net earnings}}{\text{Total assets}} \qquad \frac{9,394}{95,298} = 9.9\% \qquad \frac{5,910}{75,909} = 7.8\%$$

Return on Equity (ROE)

	19X9	19X8

$$\frac{\text{Net earnings}}{\text{Stockholders' equity}} \qquad \frac{9,394}{45,935} = 20.5\% \qquad \frac{5,910}{37,867} = 15.6\%$$

Return on investment and return on equity are two ratios that measure the overall efficiency of the firm in managing its total investment in assets and in generating return to shareholders. Return on investment or return on assets indicates the amount of profit earned relative to the level of investment in total assets. Return on equity measures the return to common shareholders; this ratio is also calculated as return on common equity if a firm has preferred stock outstanding. R.E.C., Inc. registered a solid improvement in 19X9 of both return ratios.

Figure 5.1 shows the use of key financial ratios discussed in the chapter.

ANALYZING THE DATA

Would you as a bank loan officer extend $1.5 million in new credit to R.E.C., Inc.? Would you as an investor purchase R.E.C., Inc. common shares at the current market price of $30 per share? Would you as a wholesaler of running shoes sell your products on credit to R.E.C., Inc.? Would you as a recent college graduate accept a position as manager-trainee with R.E.C., Inc.? Would you as the chief financial officer of R.E.C., Inc. authorize the opening of 25 new retail stores during the next two years?

To answer such questions, it is necessary to complete the analysis of R.E.C., Inc.'s financial statements, using the common size financial statements and key financial ratios as well as other information presented throughout the book. Ordinarily, the analysis would deal with only one of the above questions, and the perspective of the financial statement user would determine the focus of the analysis. However, since the purpose of the chapter is to

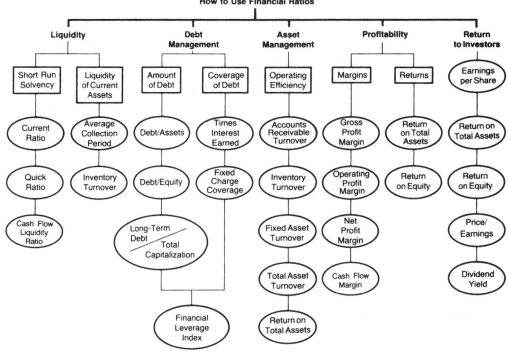

Figure 5.1

present a general approach to financial statement analysis, the evaluation covers each of four broad areas that would typically constitute a fundamental analysis of financial statements: (1) background on firm, industry, economy, and outlook; (2) short-term liquidity; (3) capital structure and long-term solvency; and (4) operating efficiency and profitability. Using this general approach, each analytical situation can be tailored to meet specific user objectives.

The following table shows the steps of financial statement analysis:

Steps of a Financial Statement Analysis

1. Establish objectives of the analysis.
2. Study the industry in which firm operates and relate industry climate to current and projected economic developments.
3. Develop knowledge of the firm and the quality of management.
4. Evaluate financial statements.
   - Tools: Common size financial statements, key financial ratios, trend analysis, structural analysis, and comparison with industry competitors.
   - Major Areas: Short-term liquidity, capital structure and long-term solvency, operating efficiency and profitibility, market ratios, and segmental analysis (when relevant).
5. Summarize findings based on analysis and reach conclusions about firm relevant to the established objectives.

Background: Economy, Industry, and Firm

An individual company does not operate in a vacuum. Economic developments and the actions of competitors affect the ability of any business enterprise to perform successfully. It is therefore necessary to preface the analysis of a firm's financial statements with an evaluation of the environment in which the firm conducts business. This process involves blending hard facts with guesses and estimates. Reference to the "Other Sources" listed earlier in this chapter may be beneficial for this part of the analysis. A brief discussion of the business climate of R.E.C., Inc. follows.[4]

Recreational Equipment and Clothing Incorporated (R.E.C., Inc.) is the third largest retailer of recreational products in the U.S. The firm offers a broad line of medium-to-high price sporting goods and equipment and active sports apparel. R.E.C., Inc. sells equipment used in running, aerobics, walking, basketball, golf, tennis, skiing, football, SCUBA diving, and other sports; merchandise for camping, hiking, fishing, and hunting; men's and women's sporting apparel; gift items; games; and consumer electronic products. The firm also sells sporting goods directly to institutional customers such as schools and athletic teams.

The general and executive offices of the company are in Dime Box, Texas. These facilities were expanded in 19X9. Most of the retail stores occupy leased space in major regional or suburban shopping districts throughout the southeastern United States. Eighteen new retail outlets were added in late 19X8, and 25 new stores were opened in 19X9. The firm owns distribution warehouses in Alabama, Florida, Georgia, Louisiana, and Texas.

The recreational products industry is affected by current trends in consumer preferences, a cyclical sales demand, and weather conditions. The running boom has shifted to walking and aerobics; golf, once on the downswing, is increasing in popularity; by winning the Tour de France three times, Greg LeMond revolutionized and revitalized the cycling industry in the U.S., aided by the craze for fat-tire bikes. Recreational product retailers also rely heavily on sales of sportswear for their profits, since the markup on sportswear is generally higher than on sports equipment. These products are also affected by consumer preference shifts. Most retail sales occur in November, December, May, and June. Sales to institutions are highest in August and September. Weather also influences sales volume, especially of winter sports equipment.

Competition within the recreational products industry is based on price, quality, and variety of goods offered as well as on the location of outlets and the quality of service. R.E.C., Inc.'s two major competitors are also full-line sporting goods companies. One operates in the northwest and the other primarily in the western and southwestern U.S., reducing direct competition among the three firms.

The current outlook for the sporting goods industry is promising, following a recessionary year in 19X8. Americans have become increasingly aware of the importance of physical fitness and have become more actively involved in recreational activities. The 25 to 44 age group is the most athletically active and is projected to be the largest age group in the U.S. during the next decade. The southeastern U.S. is expected to provide a rapidly expanding market because of its population growth and excellent weather conditions for year-round recreational participation.

---

[4] The background section of R.E.C., Inc. is based on an unpublished paper by Kimberly Ann Davis, "A Financial Analysis of Oshman's Sporting Goods, Inc."

Short-Term Liquidity

Short-term liquidity analysis is especially important to creditors, suppliers, management, and others concerned with the ability of a firm to meet near-term demands for cash. The evaluation of R.E.C., Inc.'s short-term liquidity position began with the preparation and interpretation of the firm's common size balance sheet presented earlier in the chapter. From that assessment, it was evident that inventories have increased relative to cash and marketable securities in the current asset section; and there has been an increase in the proportion of debt, both short-and long-term. These developments were traced primarily to policies and financing needs related to new store openings. Additional evidence useful to short-term liquidity analysis is provided by a five-year trend of selected financial ratios and a comparison with industry averages. Sources of comparative industry ratios include: Dun and Bradstreet, *Industry Norms and Key Business Ratios*, Murray Hill, NJ; Robert Morris Associates, *Annual Statement Studies*, Philadelphia, PA; and Standard and Poor's Corporation, *Industry Surveys*, New York, NY. As a source of industry comparative ratios, the analyst may prefer to develop a set of financial ratios for one or more major competitors.

R.E.C., Inc	19X9	19X8	19X7	19X6	19X5	Industry Average 19X9
Current ratio	2.40	2.75	2.26	2.18	2.83	2.53
Quick Ratio	.68	.95	.87	1.22	1.20	.97
Cash-flow liquidity	.70	.32	.85	.78	.68	*
Average collection period	15 days	20 days	13 days	11 days	10 days	17 days
Inventory turnover	2.75	2.50	2.74	2.99	3.20	3.12
Cash flow from operating activities ($ thousands)	10,024	(3,767)	5,629	4,925	3,430	*

*Not available

Liquidity analysis is something of an impossible task: to predict the *future* ability of the firm to meet prospective needs for cash. This prediction is made from the historical record of the firm, and no one financial ratio or set of financial ratios or other financial data can serve as a proxy for future developments. For R.E.C., Inc. the financial ratios are somewhat contradictory.

The current and quick ratios have trended downward over the five-year period, indicating a deterioration of short-term liquidity. However, the cash-flow liquidity ratio improved strongly in 19X9 after a year of negative cash generation in 19X8. The average collection period for accounts receivable and the inventory turnover ratio after worsening between 19X5 and 19X8—also improved in 19X9. These ratios measure the quality or liquidity of accounts receivable and inventory. The average collection period increased to a high of 20 days in 19X8, which was a recessionary year, then decreased to a more acceptable 15-day level in 19X9.

The common size balance sheet for R.E.C., Inc. revealed that inventories now comprise about half of the firm's total assets. The growth in inventories has been necessary to satisfy the requirements associated with the opening of new retail outlets but has been accomplished by reducing holdings of cash and cash equivalents. This represents a trade-off of highly liquid assets for potentially less liquid assets. The efficient management of inventories is critical for the firm's ongoing liquidity. In 19X9 inventory turnover improved in spite of the buildups necessary to stock new stores. Sales demand in 19X9 was more than adequate to absorb the 28% increase in inventories recorded for the year.

The major question in the outlook for liquidity is the ability of the firm to produce cash from operations. Problems in 19X8 resulted partly from the depressed state of the economy and poor ski conditions which reduced sales. The easing of sales hit the company in a year that marked the beginning of a major market expansion. Inventories and receivables increased too fast for the limited sales growth of a recessionary year, and R.E.C. also experienced some reduction of credit availability from suppliers who also felt the economic pinch. The consequence was a cash "crunch" and negative cash flow from operations.

In 19X9 R.E.C., Inc. has enjoyed considerable improvement, generating over $10 million in cash from operations. It has also improved its managment of inventories and receivables. Presently, there appears to be no major problem with the firm's short-term liquidity position. Another poor year, however, might well cause problems similar to those experienced in 19X8. The timing of further expansion of retail outlets will be critical to the ongoing success of the firm.

Net Trade Cycle

One additional tool in the assessment of liquidity is the net trade cycle or cash conversion cycle. The normal operating cycle of a firm consists of buying or manufacturing inventory, with some purchases on credit and the creation of accounts payable; selling inventory, with some sales on credit and the creation of accounts receivable; and collecting the cash. The net trade cycle measures this process in number of days and is calculated as follows for R.E.C., Inc.:

	19X9	*19X8*
Accounts receivable Average daily sales	15 days	20 days
plus		
Inventory Average daily sales*	79 days	87 days
minus		
Accounts payable Average daily sales*	(24 days)	(18 days)
equals		
Cash conversion cycle	70 days	89 days

*Net sales divided by 360 days

As with other ratios, there are alternative calculations, such as cost of sales in the denominator of the ratio.

By reducing and thus improving the net trade cycle by 19 days between 19X8 and 19X9, R.E.C., Inc. has increased cash flow by over $11 million: 19X9 average daily sales of $598,889 X 19 days = $11,378,891. The net trade cycle helps the analyst understand why cash-flow generation has improved or deteriorated by analyzing the key balance sheet accounts—accounts receivable, inventory, and accounts payable—which affect cash flow from operating activities.

Capital Structure and Long-Term Solvency

The analytical process includes an evaluation of the amount and proportion of debt in a firm's capital structure as well as the firm's ability to service debt. Debt implies risk because debt involves the satisfaction of fixed financial obligations. The disadvantage of debt financing is that the fixed commitments must be met in order for the firm to continue operations. The major advantage of debt financing is that, when used successfully, shareholder returns are magnified through financial leverage. The concept of financial leverage can best be illustrated with an example.

Example of Financial Leverage

Sockee Sock Company has $100,000 in total assets, and the firm's capital structure consists of 50% debt and 50% equity:

Debt	$50,000
Equity	50,000
Total Assets	$100,000

Cost of debt = 10%
Average tax rate = 40%

If Sockee has $20,000 in operating earnings, the return to shareholders as measured by the return on equity ratio would be 18%:

Operating earnings	$20,000
Interest expense	5,000
Earnings before tax	15,000
Tax expense	6,000
Net earnings	$ 9,000

Return on equity: 9,000/50,000 = 18%

If Sockee is able to double operating earnings from $20,000 to $40,000, the return on equity will more than double, increasing from 18% to 42%:

Operating earnings	$40,000
Interest expense	5,000
Earnings before tax	35,000
Tax expense	14,000
Net earnings	$21,000

Return on equity: 21,000/50,000 = 42%

The magnified return on equity results from *financial leverage*.   Unfortunately, leverage has a double edge.   If operating earnings are cut in half from $20,000 to $10,000, the return on equity is more than halved, declining from 18% to 6%:

Operating earnings	$10,000
Interest expense	5,000
Earnings before tax	5,000
Tax expense	2,000
Net earnings	3,000

Return on equity: 3,000/50,000 = 6%

The amount of interest expense is fixed, regardless of the level of operating earnings.   When operating earnings rise or fall, financial leverage produces positive or negative effects on shareholder returns.   In evaluating a firm's capital structure and solvency, the analyst must constantly weigh the potential benefits of debt against the risks inherent in its use.

R.E.C., Inc	19X9	19X8	19X7	19X6	19X5	Industry Average 19X9
Debt to total assets	51.8	50.1	49.2	40.8	39.7	48.7
Long-term debt to total capitalization	31.4	31.0	24.1	19.6	19.8	30.4
Debt to equity	107.5	100.5	96.5	68.2	65.8	97.7

The debt ratios for R.E.C., Inc. reveal a steady increase in the use of borrowed funds.   Total debt has risen relative to total assets, long-term debt has increased as a proportion of the firm's permanent financing, and external or debt financing has increased relative to internal financing.   Given the greater degree of risk implied by borrowing, it is important to determine: (1) why debt has increased; (2) whether the firm is using debt successfully; and (3) how well the firm is covering its fixed charges.

Why has debt increased? The Summary Statement of Cash Flows, discussed in Chapter 4 and repeated here (Exhibit 5.4) provides an explanation.   Exhibit 5.4 shows the inflows and outflows of cash both in dollars and percentages.

Exhibit 5.4 shows that R.E.C., Inc. has substantially increased its investment in capital assets, particularly in 19X9 when additions to property, plant, and equipment accounted for 82% of the total cash outflows.   These investments have been financed largely by borrowing, especially in 19X8 when the firm had a sluggish operating performance and no internal cash generation.   Operations supplied 73% of R.E.C., Inc.'s cash in 19X7 and 62% in 19X9, but the firm had to borrow heavily in 19X8 (98% of cash inflows).   The impact of this borrowing is seen in the firm's debt ratios.

EXHIBIT 5.4 R.E.C., Inc.
          Summary Analysis Statement of Cash Flows
          (in thousnds)

	19X9	19X8	19X7
Inflows (thousands)			
Operations	$10,024	$0	$5,629
Sales of other assets	295	0	0
Sales of common stock	256	183	124
Additions of short-term debt	0	1,854	1,326
Additions of long-term debt	5,600	7,882	629
Total	$16,175	$9,919	$7,708
Outflows (thousands)			
Operations	$ 0	$ 3,767	$ 0
Purchase of property, plant and equipment	14,100	4,773	3,982
Reductions of short-term debt	30	0	0
Reductions of long-term debt	1,516	1,593	127
Dividends paid	1,582	1,862	1,841
Total	$17,228	$11,995	$5,950
Change in cash and marketable securities	($1,053)	($2,076)	$1,758
Inflows (percent total)			
Operations	62.0%	0.0%	73.0%
Sales of other assets	1.8	0.0	0.0
Sales of common stock	1.6	1.8	1.6
Additions of short-term debt	0.0	18.7	17.2
Additions of long-term debt	34.6	79.5	8.2
Total	100.0%	100.0%	100.0%
Outflows (percent of total)			
Operations	0.0%	31.4%	0.0%
Purchase of property, plant and equipment	81.8	40.0	66.9
Reuctions of short-term debt	0.2	0.0	0.0
Reductions of long-term debt	8.8	13.2	2.1
Dividends paid	9.2	15.4	31.0
Total	100.0%	100.0%	100.0%

How effectively is R.E.C., Inc. using financial leverage? The answer is determined by calculating the *Financial Leverage Index*, as follows:

$$\frac{\text{Return on equity}}{\text{Adjusted return on assets*}} = \text{Financial Leverage Index}$$

$$\frac{\text{*Net earnings} + \text{interest expense } (1 - \text{tax rate})}{\text{Total assets}} = \text{Adjusted return on assets}$$

When the Financial Leverage Index (FLI) is greater than 1, indicating that return on equity exceeds return on assets, the firm is using debt beneficially.   A FLI of less than 1 means the firm is not using debt successfully.   For R.E.C., Inc., the FLI is calculated as follows:

Financial Leverage Index	*19X9*	*19X8*	*19X7*
$\dfrac{\text{Return on equity}}{\text{Adjusted return on assets*}}$	$\dfrac{20.45}{11.35} = 1.8$	$\dfrac{15.61}{9.50} = 1.6$	$\dfrac{17.53}{9.57} = 1.8$

*ROA Adjusted: $\dfrac{9,394 + 2,585\,(.55)}{95,298} = 11.35\%$ $\quad \dfrac{5,910 + 2,277(.57)}{75,909} = 9.50\%$ $\quad \dfrac{5,896 + 1,274\,(.55)}{66,146} = 9.97\%$

Average tax rate: $\qquad\qquad\qquad \dfrac{7,686}{17,080} = 45.0\%$ $\qquad \dfrac{4,457}{10,367} = 43.0\%$ $\qquad \dfrac{4,824}{10,720} = 45.0\%$
Income tax/earnings before tax

The FLI for R.E.C., Inc. of 1.8 in 19X9, 1.6 in 19X8, and 1.8 in 19X7 indicates a successful use of financial leverage for the three-year period when borrowing has increased.   The firm has generated sufficient operating returns to more than cover the interest payments on borrowed funds.

How well is R.E.C., Inc. covering fixed charges? The answer requires a review of the coverage ratios.

R.E.C., Inc	*19X9*	*19X8*	*19X7*	*19X6*	*19X5*	*Industry Average 19X9*
Times interest earned	7.44	5.18	8.84	13.34	12.60	7.2
Fixed charge coverage	2.09	2.01	2.27	2.98	3.07	2.5

Given the increased level of borrowing, the times interest earned ratio has declined over the 5-year period but remains above the industry average.   R.E.C., Inc. leases most of its retail outlets so the fixed charge coverage ratio, which considers lease payments as well as interest expense, is the more relevant ratio.   This ratio has also decreased, as a result of store expansion and higher payments for leases and interest.   Although below the industry average, the firm is still covering all fixed charges by more than two times out of operating earnings, and coverage does not at this point appear to be a problem.   The fixed charge coverage ratio should be monitored closely in the future, however, particularly if R.E.C., Inc. continues to expand.

Operating Efficiency and Profitability

The analysis now considers of how well the firm has performed in overall operating efficiency and profitability, beginning with the evaluation of several key ratios.

R.E.C., Inc	19X9	19X8	19X7	19X6	19X5	Industry Average 19X9
Fixed asset turnover	7.41	8.06	8.19	10.01	10.11	8.72
Total asset turnover	2.26	2.02	2.13	2.87	2.95	2.43

As noted earlier, R.E.C., Inc. has increased its investment in fixed assets as a result of home office and store expansion. The asset turnover ratios reveal a downward trend in the efficiency with which the firm is generating sales from investments in fixed and total assets. The total asset turnover rose in 19X9, the progress traceable to improved management of inventories and receivables. The fixed asset turnover ratio is still declining, a result of expanding offices and retail outlets, but should improve if the expansion is successful.

R.E.C., Inc	19X9	19X8	19X7	19X6	19X5	Industry Average 19X9
Gross profit margin	40.00	39.95	42.00	41.80	41.76	37.25
Operating profit margin	8.93	7.72	8.00	10.98	11.63	7.07
Net profit margin	4.36	3.86	4.19	5.00	5.20	3.74
Cash flow margin	4.65	(2.46)	4.00	4.39	3.92	*

* Not available

Profitability—after a relatively poor year in 19X8 because of the recession, adverse ski conditions, and the costs of new store openings—now looks more promising. Management adopted a growth strategy reflected in aggressive marketing and the opening of 18 new stores in 19X8 and 25 in 19X9. With the exception of the cash-flow margin, the profit margins are all below their 19X5 and 19X6 levels but have improved in 19X9 and are above industry average. The cash-flow margin, as a result of strong cash generation from operations in 19X9, was at its highest level of the 5-year period.

The gross profit margin was stable, a positive sign in light of new store openings featuring many "sale" and discounted items to attract customers; and the firm managed to improve its operating profit margin in 19X9. The increase in operating profit margin is especially noteworthy since it occurred during an expansionary period with sizable increases in operating expenses, especially lease payments required for new stores. The net profit margin also improved despite increased interest and tax expenses and a reduction in interest revenue from marketable security investments.

R.E.C., Inc	19X9	19X8	19X7	19X6	19X5	Industry Average 19X9
Return on assets	9.86	7.79	8.91	14.35	15.34	9.09
Return on equity	20.45	15.61	17.53	24.25	25.46	17.72

After declining steadily through 19X8, both return on assets and return on equity rebounded strongly in 19X9. These ratios measure the overall success of the firm in generating profits from its investment and management strategies. It appears that R.E.C., Inc. is well positioned for future growth. It will be important to monitor the firm's management of inventories (which account for half of total assets), because of past problems. The expansion will necessitate a continuation of advertising expenditures, at least at the current level, to attract customers to both new and old areas. R.E.C., Inc. has financed much of its expansion with debt, and thus far its shareholders have benefited from the use of debt through financial leverage.

R.E.C., Inc. experienced a negative cash flow from operations in 19X8, another problem that bears watching in the future. The negative cash flow occurred in a year of only modest sales and earnings growth:

R.E.C., Inc	19X9	19X8	19X7	19X6	19X5
Sales growth	40.9%	8.7%	25.5%	21.6%	27.5%
Earnings growth	59.0%	.2%	5.2%	16.9%	19.2%

Sales expanded rapidly in 19X9 as the economy recovered and the expansion of retail outlets began to pay off. The outlook is for continued economic recovery.

Ratio Analysis Summary

A good summary of ratio analysis is provided by the DuPont system, which helps explain how the financial ratios interrelate to produce the overall return to shareholders, return on equity:

$$\underset{\text{Net Profit Margin}}{(1)} \quad \text{X} \quad \underset{\text{Total Asset Turnover}}{(2)} \quad = \quad \underset{\text{Return on Investment}}{(3)}$$

$$\frac{\text{Net income}}{\text{Sales}} \quad \text{X} \quad \frac{\text{Sales}}{\text{Assets}} \quad = \quad \frac{\text{Net income}}{\text{Assets}}$$

$$\underset{\text{Return on Investment}}{(3)} \quad \text{X} \quad \underset{\text{Financial Leverage}}{(4)} \quad = \quad \underset{\text{Return on Equity}}{(5)}$$

$$\frac{\text{Net income}}{\text{Assets}} \quad \text{X} \quad \frac{\text{Assets}}{\text{Equity}} \quad = \quad \frac{\text{Net income}}{\text{Equity}}$$

This series of relationships enables the analyst to identify and trace potential strengths and weaknesses in the financial performance of a firm.

The (3) return on investment is a product of the (1) net profit margin (profit generated from sales) and the (2) asset turnover (ability to produce sales from assets). The (5) return on equity (profit relative to ownership interest) is a product of (3) return on investment and (4) financial leverage (proportion of debt in the capital structure).

For R.E.C., Inc. this system of analysis would show the following for the period 19X5 to 19X9:

	(1) NPM	X	(2) TAT	=	(3) ROI	X	(4) FL	=	(5) ROE
19X5	5.20	X	2.95	=	15.34	X	1.66	=	25.46
19X6	5.00	X	2.87	=	14.35	X	1.69	=	24.25
19X7	4.19	X	2.13	=	8.91	X	1.97	=	17.60
19X8	3.86	X	2.02	=	7.79	X	2.00	=	15.60
19X9	4.36	X	2.26	=	9.86	X	2.07	=	20.40

Return on equity in 19X9 is below the 19X5 and 19X6 levels because both the profit margin and the asset turnover are lower. The combination of increased debt and the improvement in profitability and asset utilization has produced an improved overall return in 19X9 relative to the two previous years. Specifically, the firm has added debt to finance capital asset expansion. While debt carries risk and added cost in the form of interest expense, debt also has the positive benefit of financial leverage, which R.E.C., Inc. is using successfully. The 19X9 improvement in inventory management has had a favorable impact on asset turnover, and the firm's ability to control operating costs while increasing sales during expansion has improved the net profit margin, combining to boost return on investment.

Projections, Pro Formas, and Market Ratios

There are some additional analytical tools and financial ratios that are relevant to financial statement analysis, particularly for investment decisions and long-range planning. What follows is an introductory treatment of projections, pro forma financial statements, and several investment-related financial ratios.

The investment analyst, in valuing securities for investment decisions, must project the future earnings stream of a business. Techniques of earnings forecasting are beyond the scope of this book. The reader should refer to the resources listed under "Other Sources" earlier in the chapter for references which provide earnings forecasts.

Pro forma financial statements are projections of financial statements based on a set of assumptions regarding future revenues, expenses, level of investment in assets, financing methods and costs, and working capital management. Pro forma financial statements are used primarily for long-range planning and long-term credit decisions. A bank considering $1.5 million in new credit to R.E.C., Inc. would want to look at the firm's pro forma statements, assuming the loan is granted, and determine—using different scenarios regarding the firm's performance—whether cash flow from operations would be sufficient to service the debt. R.E.C., Inc.'s CEO, who is making a decision about new store expansion, would develop pro formas based on varying estimates of performance outcomes and financing alternatives.

Four market ratios of particular interest to the investor are earnings per common share, the price to earnings ratio, the dividend payout ratio, and dividend yield. Earnings per common share is net income for the period divided by the weighted average number of common shares outstanding. One million dollars in earnings will look different to the investor if there are 1,000,000 shares of stock outstanding or 100,000 shares. The earnings per share ratio provides the investor with a common denominator by which to gauge investment returns.

The *earnings per share* computations for R.E.C., Inc. are made as follows:

	19X9	19X8	19X7
$\dfrac{\text{Net earnings}}{\text{Avg. shares outstanding}}$	$\dfrac{9,394,000}{4,792,857} = 1.96$	$\dfrac{5,910,000}{4,581,395} = 1.29$	$\dfrac{5,896,000}{4,433,083} = 1.33$

The price to earnings ratio (P/E ratio) relates earnings per common share to the market price at which the stock trades, expressing the "multiple" which the stock market places on a firm's earnings. For instance, if two competing firms had annual earnings of $2.00 per share, and Company 1 shares sold for $10.00 each while Company 2 shares sold for $20.00 each, the market is placing a different value on the same $2.00 earnings: a multiple of 5 for Company 1 and 10 for Company 2. The P/E ratio is the combination of a myriad of factors which include the quality of earnings, future earnings potential, and the performance history of the company.

The *price to earnings ratio* for R.E.C., Inc. is determined as follows:

	19X9	19X8	19X7
$\dfrac{\text{Market price of common stock}}{\text{Earnings per share}}$	$\dfrac{30.00}{1.96} = 15.3$	$\dfrac{17.00}{1.29} = 13.2$	$\dfrac{25.00}{1.33} = 18.8$

The P/E ratio is higher in 19X9 than 19X8 but below the 19X7 level. This could be because of developments in the market generally and/or because the market is reacting cautiously to the firm's good year. Another factor could be the reduction of cash dividend payments.

The *dividend payout ratio* is determined by the formula cash dividends per share divided by earnings per share:

	19X9	19X8	19X7
$\dfrac{\text{Dividends per share}}{\text{Earnings per share}}$	$\dfrac{.33}{1.96} = 16.8\%.$	$\dfrac{.41}{1.29} = 31.8\%.$	$\dfrac{.41}{1.33} = 30.8\%$

R.E.C., Inc. reduced its cash dividend payment in 19X9. It is unusual for a company to reduce cash dividends because this decision can be interpeted as a negative signal regarding the firm's future. It is particularly uncommon for a firm to reduce dividends during a good year. The explanation provided by management is that the firm has adopted a new policy that will result in lower dividend payments in order to increase the availability of internal funds for expansion. Management expects the overall long-term impact to be extremely favorable to shareholders and has committed to maintaining the $.33 per share annual cash dividend.

The *dividend yield* shows the relationship between cash dividends and market price:

	19X9	19X8	19X7
$\dfrac{\text{Dividends per share}}{\text{Market price of common stock}}$	$\dfrac{.33}{30.00} = 1.1\%$	$\dfrac{.41}{17.00} = 2.4\%$	$\dfrac{.41}{25.00} = 1.6\%$

The R.E.C., Inc. shares are yielding a 1.1% return based on the market price at year-end 19X9. An investor would likely choose R.E.C., Inc. as an investment more for its long-term capital appreciation than for its dividend yield.

Summary of Analysis

The analysis of any firm's financial statements is a mixture of steps and pieces that inter-relate and affect each other. The analysis must always be interpreted with this in mind. Short-term liquidity impacts profitability; profitability begins with sales, which relate to the liquidity of assets. The efficiency of asset management influences the cost and avail-ability of credit, and that shapes the capital structure. Every aspect of a firm's financial condition, performance, and outlook affects the share price. The last step of financial statement analysis is to integrate the separate pieces into a whole, leading to conclusions about the business. The specific conclusions drawn will be affected by the original objec-tives established at the begining of the analytsis.

A summary of the major findings from the analysis of R.E.C., Inc.'s financial state-ments is listed below.

Strengths
1. Favorable economic and industry outlook; firm well-positioned geographically to benefit from expected economic and industry growth.
2. Aggressive marketing and expansion strategies.
3. Recent improvement in management of accounts receivable and inventory.
4. Successful use of financial leverage and solid coverage of debt service requirements.
5. Effective control of operating costs.
6. Substantial sales growth, partially resulting from market expansion, suggesting future performance potential.
7. Increased profitability in 19X9; strong, positive generation of cash flow from operations.

Weaknesses
1. Highly sensitive to economic fluctuations and weather conditions.
2. Negative cash flow from operating activities in 19X8.
3. Historical problems with inventory management and some weakness in overall asset management efficiency.
4. Increased risk associated with debt financing.

The answers to specific questions regarding R.E.C., Inc. are determined by the values placed on each of the strengths and weaknesses. In general, the outlook for the firm is promising. R.E.C., Inc. appears to be a sound credit risk with attractive investment potential. The management of inventories, a continuation of effective cost controls, and careful timing of further expansion will be critically important to the firm's future success.

Map

This book began with the notion that financial statements should serve as a map to successful business decision-making, even though the user of financial statement data would confront maze-like challenges in seeking to find and interpret the necessary information. The chapters have covered the enormous volume of material found in corporate financial reporting; the complexities and confusions created by accounting rules and choices; the potential for management manipulation of financial statement results; the distortions caused by inflation; and the difficulty in finding necessary information. The exploration of financial statements has required a close examination of the form and content of each financial statement presented as well as the development of tools and techniques for analyzing the data. The author hopes that readers will be able to use financial statements as a map, leading to sound and profitable business decisions.

Figure 5.2

SELF-TEST SOLUTIONS ARE PROVIDED IN APPENDIX D

____ **1.** What is the first step in an analysis of financial statements?
  (a) Check the auditor's report.
  (b) Check references containing financial information.
  (c) Specify the objectives of the analysis.
  (d) Do a common size analysis.

____ **2.** What is a creditor's objective in performing an analysis of financial statements?
  (a) To decide whether the borrower has the ability to repay interest and principal on borrowed funds.
  (b) To determine the firm's capital structure.
  (c) To determine the company's future earnings stream.
  (d) To decide whether the firm has operated profitably in the past.

___ **3.** What is an investor's objective in financial statement analysis?

   (a) To determine if the firm is risky.
   (b) To determine the stability of earnings.
   (c) To determine changes necessary to improve future performance.
   (d) To determine whether an investment is warranted by estimating a company's future earnings stream.

___ **4.** What information does the auditor's report contain?

   (a) The results of operations.
   (b) An unqualified opinion.
   (c) An opinion as to the fairness of the financial statements.
   (d) A detailed coverage of the firm s liquidity, capital resources, and operations.

___ **5.** Which of the following would not result in a "qualified" auditor's report?

   (a) The failure to use generally accepted accounting principles.
   (b) Financial statements that present fairly the financial position, results of operations, and changes in financial position.
   (c) The inconsistent application of accounting principles.
   (d) Uncertainties regarding the outcome of significant factors affecting the ongoing operations of the firm.

___ **6.** Which of the following is not required to be discussed in Management's Discussion and Analysis of the Financial Condition and Results of Operations?

   (a) Liquidity.
   (b) Capital resources.
   (c) Operations.
   (d) Earnings projections.

___ **7.** What type of information found in supplementary schedules is required for inclusion in an annual report?

   (a) Segmental data.
   (b) Inflation data.
   (c) Material litigation and management photographs.
   (d) Management remuneration and segmental data.

___ **8.** What is Form 10-K?

   (a) A document filed with the AICPA, containing supplementary schedules showing management remuneration and elaborations of financial statement disclosures.
   (b) A document filed with the Securities and Exchange Commission by companies selling securities to the public, containing much of the same information as the annual report as well as additional detail.
   (c) A document filed with the Securities and Exchange Commission containing key business ratios and forecasts of earnings.
   (d) A document filed with the Securities and Exchange Commission containing nonpublic information.

___ **9.** What information can be gained from sources such as *Industry Norms and Key Business Ratios, Annual Statement Studies, Analyst's Handbook*, and *Industry Surveys?*
   (a) The general economic condition.
   (b) Forecasts of earnings.
   (c) Elaborations of financial statement disclosures.
   (d) A company's relative position within its industry.

___ **10.** Which of the following is not a tool or technique used by a financial statement analyst?
   (a) Common size financial statements.
   (b) Trend analysis.
   (c) Random sampling analysis.
   (d) Industry comparisons.

___ **11.** What are common size financial statements?
   (a) Statements that express each account on the balance sheet as a percentage of total assets and each account on the income statement as a percentage of net sales.
   (b) Statements that standardize financial data in terms of trends.
   (c) Statements that relate the firm to the industry in which it operates.
   (d) Statements based on common sense and judgment.

___ **12.** Which of the following is not revealed on a common size balance sheet?
   (a) The debt structure of a firm.
   (b) The capital structure of a firm.
   (c) The dollar amount of assets and liabilities.
   (d) The distribution of assets in which funds are invested.

___ **13.** What is a serious limitation of financial ratios?
   (a) Ratios are screening devices.
   (b) Ratios can be used only by themselves.
   (c) Ratios indicate weaknesses only.
   (d) Ratios are not predictive.

___ **14.** What is the most widely used liquidity ratio?
   (a) Quick ratio.
   (b) Current ratio.
   (c) Inventory turnover.
   (d) Debt ratio.

___ **15.** What is a limitation common to both the current and the quick ratio?
   (a) Accounts receivable may not be truly liquid.
   (b) Inventories may not be truly liquid.
   (c) Marketable securities are not liquid.
   (d) Prepaid expenses are potential sources of cash.

___ **16.** Why is the quick ratio a more rigorous test of short-run solvency than the current ratio?
   (a) The quick ratio considers only cash and marketable securities as current assets.

(b) The quick ratio eliminates prepaid expenses for the numerator.

(c) The quick ratio eliminates prepaid expenses for the denominator.

(d) The quick ratio eliminates inventories from the numerator.

____ **17.** What does an increasing collection period for accounts receivable suggest about a firm s credit policy?

(a) The credit policy is too restrictive.

(b) The firm is probably losing qualified customers.

(c) The credit policy may be too lenient.

(d) The collection period has no relationship to a firm's credit policy.

____ **18.** Which of the following statements about inventory turnover is false?

(a) Inventory turnover measures the efficiency of the firm in managing and selling inventory.

(b) Inventory turnover is a gauge of the liquidity of a firm's inventory.

(c) Inventory turnover is calculated with either cost of goods sold or net sales in the numerator.

(d) A low inventory turnover is generally a sign of efficient inventory management.

____ **19.** Which of the following is not a reason for a high inventory turnover ratio?

(a) Stockpiling inventory.

(b) Decrease in prices.

(c) Understocking inventory.

(d) Shortage of materials.

____ **20.** What do the asset turnover ratios measure?

(a) The liquidity of the firm s current assets.

(b) Management's effectiveness in generating sales from investments in assets.

(c) The overall efficiency and profitability of the firm.

(d) The distribution of assets in which funds are invested.

____ **21.** Which of the following ratios would not be used to measure the extent of a firm's debt financing?

(a) Debt ratio.

(b) Debt to equity.

(c) Times interest earned.

(d) Long-term debt to total capitalization.

____ **22.** Why is the amount of debt in a company's capital structure important to the financial analyst?

(a) Debt implies risk.

(b) Debt is less costly than equity.

(c) Equity is riskier than debt.

(d) Debt is equal to total assets.

____ **23.** Why is the fixed charge coverage ratio a broader measure of a firm's coverage capabilities than the times interest earned ratio?

(a) The fixed charge ratio indicates how many times the firm can cover interest payments.

(b) The times interest earned ratio does not consider the possibility of higher interest rates.

    (c) The fixed charge ratio includes lease payments as well as interest payments.

    (d) The fixed charge ratio includes both operating and capital leases while the times interest earned ratio includes only operating leases.

____ **24.** Which profit margin measures the overall operating efficiency of the firm?

    (a) Gross profit margin.

    (b) Operating profit margin.

    (c) Net profit margin.

    (d) Return on equity.

____ **25.** Which ratio(s) measures the overall efficiency of the firm in managing its investment in assets and in generating return to shareholders?

    (a) Gross profit margin and net profit margin.

    (b) Return on investment.

    (c) Total asset turnover and operating profit margin.

    (d) Return on investment and return on equity.

____ **26.** What does a financial leverage index greater than "1" indicate about a firm?

    (a) The unsuccessful use of financial leverage.

    (b) Operating returns more than sufficient to cover interest payments on borrowed funds.

    (c) More debt financing than equity financing.

    (d) An increased level of borrowing.

____ **27.** What does the price to earnings ratio measure?

    (a) The "multiple" which the stock market places on a firm's earnings.

    (b) The relationship between dividends and market prices.

    (c) The earnings for one share of common stock.

    (d) The percentage of dividends paid to net earnings of the firm.

28. Match the following ratios to the corresponding calculations.

____   **(a)** Current ratio   **(1)** $\dfrac{\text{Accounts receivable}}{\text{Average daily sales}}$

____   **(b)** Quick ratio   **(2)** $\dfrac{\text{Net Sales}}{\text{Net property, plant, and equipment}}$

____   **(c)** Average collection period   **(3)** $\dfrac{\text{Total liabilities}}{\text{Total assets}}$

____   **(d)** Accounts receivable turnover   **(4)** $\dfrac{\text{Operating profit}}{\text{Interest expense}}$

____   **(e)** Inventory turnover   **(5)** $\dfrac{\text{Gross profit}}{\text{Net sales}}$

____   **(f)** Fixed asset turnover   **(6)** $\dfrac{\text{Current assets}}{\text{Current liabilities}}$

____   **(g)** Total asset turnover   **(7)** $\dfrac{\text{Net earnings}}{\text{Average shares outstanding}}$

____ **(h)** Debt ratio

(8) $\dfrac{\text{Net earnings}}{\text{Net sales}}$

____ **(i)** Long-term debt to total capitalization

(9) $\dfrac{\text{Net earnings}}{\text{Stockholders' equity}}$

____ **(j)** Debt to equity

(10) $\dfrac{\text{Cost of goods sold}}{\text{Inventories}}$

____ **(k)** Times interest earned

(11) $\dfrac{\text{Market price}}{\text{Earnings per share}}$

____ **(l)** Fixed charge coverage

(12) $\dfrac{\text{Net sales}}{\text{Total assets}}$

____ **(m)** Cash-flow liquidity ratio

(13) $\dfrac{\text{Cash flow from operating activities}}{\text{Net sales}}$

____ **(n)** Cash-flow margin

(14) $\dfrac{\text{Cash and marketable securities} + \text{cash flow from operating activities}}{\text{Current liabilities}}$

____ **(o)** Gross profit margin

(15) $\dfrac{\text{Long-term debt}}{\text{Long-term debt} + \text{Stockholders' equity}}$

____ **(p)** Operating profit margin

(16) $\dfrac{\text{Dividends per share}}{\text{Earnings per share}}$

____ **(q)** Net profit margin

(17) $\dfrac{\text{Current assets - inventory}}{\text{Current liabilities}}$

____ **(r)** Return on investment

(18) $\dfrac{\text{Operating profit} + \text{Lease payments}}{\text{Interest expense} + \text{Lease payments}}$

____ **(s)** Return on equity

(19) $\dfrac{\text{Total liabilities}}{\text{Stockholders' equity}}$

____ **(t)** Earnings per common share

(20) $\dfrac{\text{Net earnings}}{\text{Total assets}}$

____ **(u)** Price to earnings ratio

(21) $\dfrac{\text{Net sales}}{\text{Accounts receivable}}$

____ **(v)** Dividend payout ratio

(22) $\dfrac{\text{Operating profit}}{\text{Net sales}}$

_____ **(w)** Dividend yield   **(23)** $\dfrac{\text{Dividend per share}}{\substack{\text{Market price of} \\ \text{common stock}}}$

Use the following data to answer questions 29 through 32.

JDL Corporation Selected Financial Data
December 31, 19X9

Current assets	$150,000
Current liabilities	100,000
Inventories	50,000
Accounts receivable	40,000
Net sales	900,000
Cost of goods sold	675,000

_____ **29.** JDL's current ratio is:
  (a) 1.0 to 1.
  (b) 0.7 to 1.
  (c) 1.5 to 1.
  (d) 2.4 to 1.

_____ **30.** JDL's quick ratio is:
  (a) 1.0 to 1.
  (b) 0.7 to 1.
  (c) 1.5 to 1.
  (d) 2.4 to 1.

_____ **31.** JDL's average collection period is:
  (a) 6 days.
  (b) 11 days.
  (c) 16 days.
  (d) 22 days.

_____ **32.** JDL's inventory turnover is:
  (a) 1.25 times.
  (b) 13.5 times.
  (c) 3.0 times.
  (d) 37.5 times.

Use the following data to answer questions 33 through 36.

RQM Corporation Selected Financial Data
December 31, 19X9

Net sales	$1,800,000
Cost of goods sold	1,080,000
Operating expenses	315,000
Net operating income	405,000
Net income	195,000
Total stockholders equity	750,000
Total assets	1,000,000
Cash flow from operating activities	25,000

___ **33.** RQM's gross profit margin, operating profit margin, and net profit margin, respectively are:
    (a) 40.00%, 22.50%, 19.50%
    (b) 60.00%, 19.50%, 10.83%
    (c) 60.00%, 22.50%, 19.50%
    (d) 40.00%, 22.50%, 10.83%

___ **34.** RQM's return on equity is:
    (a) 26%
    (b) 54%
    (c) 42%
    (d) 19%

___ **35.** RQM's return on investment is:
    (a) 22.5%
    (b) 26.5%
    (c) 19.5%
    (d) 40.5%

___ **36.** RQM's cash flow margin is:
    (a) 1.4%
    (b) 2.5%
    (c) 10.8%
    (d) 12.8%

STUDY QUESTIONS AND PROBLEMS

5.1 Eleanor's Computers is a retailer of computer products. Using the financial data provided, complete the financial ratio calculations for 19X7. Advise management of any ratios that indicate potential problems and provide an explanation of possible causes of the problems.

	19X5	19X6	19X7	Industry Averages 19X7
Current Ratio	1.71X	1.65X		1.70X
Quick Ratio	.92X	.89X		.95X
Average collection period	60 days	60 days		65 days
Inventory turnover	4.20X	3.90X		4.50X
Fixed asset turnover	3.20X	3.33X		3.00X
Total asset turnover	1.40X	1.35X		1.37X
Debt ratio	59.20%	61.00%		60.00%
Times interest earned	4.20X	3.70X		4.75X
Gross profit margin	25.00%	23.00%		22.50%
Operating profit margin	12.50%	12.70%		12.50%
Net profit margin	6.10%	6.00%		6.50%
Return on total sales	8.54%	8.10%		8.91%
Return on equity	20.93%	20.74%		22.28%

	Balance Sheet at 12/31/X7		Income Statement for Year Ended 12/31/X7	
Cash	$ 125,000	Sales		$1,500,000
Accounts receivable	275,000	Cost of goods sold		1,200,000
Inventory	325,000	Gross profit		$ 300,000
Current assets	$ 725,000	Operating expenses		100,000
Fixed assets (Net)	$ 420,000	Operating profit		$ 200,000
Total Assets	$1,145,000	Interest expense		72,000
		Earnings before tax		128,000
Accounts payable	$ 150,000	Income tax (0.4)		51,200
Notes payable	225,000	Net income		$ 76,800
Accrued liabilities	100,000			
Current liabilities	475,000			
Long-term debt	400,000			
Total Liabilities	$ 875,000			
Equity	270,000			
Total Liabilities and Equity	$1,145,000			

5.2 Luna Lighting, a retail firm, has experienced modest sales growth over the past 3 years but has had difficulty translating the expansion of sales into improved profitability. Using 3 years financial statements, you have developed the following ratio calculations and industry comparisons. Based on this information, suggest possible reasons for Luna's profitability problems.

	X9	X8	X7	Industry X9
Current	2.3X	2.3X	2.2X	2.1X
Average collection period	45d	46d	47d	50d
Inventory turnover	8.3X	8.2X	8.1X	8.3X
Fixed asset turnover	2.7X	3.0X	3.3X	3.5X
Total asset turnover	1.1X	1.2X	1.3X	1.5X
Debt ratio	50%	50%	50%	54%
Times interest earned	8.1X	8.2X	8.1X	7.2X
Fixed charge covered	4.0X	4.5X	5.5X	5.1X
Gross profit margin	43%	43%	43%	40%
Operating profit margin	6.3%	7.2%	8.0%	7.5%
Net profit margin	3.5%	4.0%	4.3%	4.2%
Return on assets	3.7%	5.0%	5.7%	6.4%
Return on equity	7.4%	9.9%	11.4%	11.8%

5.3 Aggieland Autos is an automobile dealership. Using the financial data presented in the next pages, complete the problems listed next.

Required:

(a) Calculate figures for the common size income statement and balance sheet for 19X9.

(b) Calculate cash flow from operating activities for 19X9.

(c) Calculate the relevant financial ratios for 19X9.

(d) Analyze the data, and list the strengths and weaknesses of the company. What recommendations would you make to Aggie Al for improving the company?

Aggieland Autos
Background

Aggieland Autos is celebrating its tenth anniversary as a profitable company. Aggie Al, the owner and business manager, has guided the company from a small used car lot to the second largest car dealer in the community. Bob Cole (sales manager), who has been with the company for three years, oversees two salespersons. The firm also employs a mechanic and a bookkeeper.

Aggieland Autos sells new and used cars, trucks, and vans. A service center generates a minor portion of profits for the company; the main purpose of the service center is to meet warranty requirements set by the auto manufacturer. The building that houses the service center is currently leased for $1,000 per month. This has increased from $950 per month in 19X8 and 19X7. Accounts receivable are typically sold to a finance company within three weeks of the sale of a vehicle.

Aggie Al has hired you as a consultant because of your expertise in financial statement analysis. (He heard about the well-known course you took in that subject at an undisclosed university.) Al would like an assessment of the financial strengths and weaknesses of the business and has provided you with the last 3 years balance sheets and income statements.

Aggieland Autos
Balance Sheet at December 31,

	19X9	19X8	19X7
Cash	$ 88,531	$ 104,287	$ 117,910
Accounts receivable	117,793	107,009	106,500
Inventory	675,550	564,450	427,526
Total Current Assets	$ 881,874	$ 775,746	$ 651,936
Gross property, plant, and equipment	$ 430,000	$ 420,000	$ 420,000
Accumulated depreciation	(130,000)	(97,000)	(65,000)
Net property, plant, and equipment	300,000	323,000	355,000
Total Assets	$1,181,874	$1,098,746	$1,006,936
Notes Payable	$ 192,632	$ 155,000	$ 103,500
Current maturities of long-term debt	30,000	30,000	30,000
Accounts payable	180,000	160,550	157,000
Accrued expenses	45,400	58,804	71,436
Total Current Liabilities	$ 448,032	$ 404,354	$ 361,936
Long-term debt	370,000	400,000	430,000
Total Liabilities	$ 818,032	$ 804,354	$ 791,936
Equity	363,842	294,392	215,000
Total Liabilities and Equity	$1,181,874	$1,098,746	$1,006,936

Aggieland Autos
Income Statement For Years Ending December 31,

	19X9	19X8	19X7
Sales	$1,650,000	$1,452,000	$1,304,000
Cost of goods sold	1,344,750	1,161,600	1,043,200
Gross Profit	$ 305,250	$ 290,400	$ 260,800
Depreciation	33,000	32,000	35,000
Lease payments	12,000	11,400	11,400
Other operating expenses	60,500	56,600	53,600
Operating profit	$ 199,750	$ 190,400	$ 160,800
Interest expense	84,000	58,080	39,120
Earnings before Tax	$ 115,750	$ 132,320	$ 121,680
Income tax	46,300	52,928	48,672
Net Income	$ 69,450	$ 79,392	$ 73,008

Aggieland Autos
Common Size Balance Sheet
(%)

	19X9	19X8	19X7
Cash		9.49	11.71
Accounts receivable		9.74	10.58
Inventory		51.37	42.46
Total Current Assets		70.60	64.74
Gross property, plant, and equipment		38.23	41.71
Accumulated depreciation		(8.83)	(6.46)
Net property, plant, and equipment		29.40	35.26
Total Assets		100.00	100.00
Notes Payable		14.11	10.28
Current maturities of long-term debt		2.73	2.98
Accounts payable		14.61	15.59
Accrued expenses		5.35	7.09
Total Current Liabilities		36.80	35.94
Long-term debt		36.41	42.70
Total Liabilities		73.21	78.65
Equity		26.79	21.35
Total Liabilities and Equity		100.00	100.00

Aggieland Autos
Common Size Income Statement
(%)

	19X9	19X8	19X7
Sales		100.00	100.00
Cost of goods sold		80.00	80.00
Gross Profit		20.00	20.00
Depreciation		2.20	2.68
Lease payments		0.79	0.87
Other Operating Expenses		3.90	4.11
Operating Profit		13.11	12.33
Interest expense		4.00	3.00
Earnings before Tax		9.11	9.33
Income tax		3.65	3.73
Net Income		5.47	5.60

Aggieland Autos
Ratio Analysis

	19X9	19X8	19X7	Industry Average
Current ratio		1.92X	1.80X	1.70X
Quick ratio		0.52X	0.62X	0.40X
Cash-flow liquidity ratio		0.17X	0.54	0.61X
Average collection period		26.53 days	29.40 days	14.00 days
Inventory turnover		2.06X	2.44X	4.50X
Total asset turnover		1.32X	1.30X	3.70X
Fixed asset turnover		4.50X	3.67X	6.50X
Debt ratio		73.21%	78.65%	68.80%
Debt to equity		2.73X	3.68X	2.20X
Long-term debt to total capitalization		57.60%	66.67%	34.09%
Times interest earned		3.28X	4.11X	2.40X
Fixed charge coverage		2.90X	3.41X	2.50X
Gross profit margin		20.00%	20.00%	15.20%
Operating profit margin		13.11%	12.33%	9.00%
Net profit margin		5.47%	5.60%	3.00%
Cash-flow margin		(2.42%)	6.08%	7.12%
Return on equity		26.97%	33.96%	35.58%
Return on investment		7.23%	7.25%	11.10%

Aggieland Autos
Cash Flow from Operating Activities

	19X9	19X8	19X7
Net income		$ 79,392	$73,008
Depreciation		32,000	35,000
Accounts receivable		(509)	(7,900)
Inventories		(136,924)	(27,500)
Accounts payable		3,550	2,400
Accrued expenses		(12,632)	4,300
Cash Flow from Operating Activities		($35,123)	$79,308

5.4 Friendly Frank's Mobile Homes is a retailer of new and used mobile homes. Frank started his company 7 years ago and has been very pleased with its rapid growth. There have been a few cash-flow problems associated with the growth. The problems got so bad during 19X7 that Frank put $20,300 of additional capital into the company. Frank realizes that some financial problems still exist. Having heard of your expertise in the financial statement analysis, he would like you to provide a financial analysis of the firm.

Required:

(a) Calculate figures for the common size balance sheet and income statement for 19X7.

(b) Calculate the relevant financial ratios for 19X7.

(c) Calculate cash flow from operating activities for 19X7.

(d) Calculate the net trade cycle for 19X7.

(e) Analyze the data and list the strengths and weaknesses of the company. Discuss recommendations you would make to Frank to improve the company.

Friendly Frank's Mobile Homes
Balance Sheets

	19X7	19X6	19X5
Assets			
Cash	$ 71,000	$ 67,000	$ 63,800
Accounts receivable (net)	73,000	54,000	32,000
Inventory	927,000	678,000	475,700
Prepaid expenses	25,000	24,000	15,000
Current Assets	$1,096,000	$ 823,000	$586,500
Gross fixed assets	$ 412,000	$ 310,000	$232,500
Accumulated depreciation	($ 49,000)	($ 27,000)	($ 15,000)
Net Fixed Assets	363,000	283,000	217,500
Total Assets	$1,459,000	$1,106,000	$804,000
Liabilities			
Accounts payable	$ 90,000	$ 81,000	$ 42,100
Notes payable	685,000	498,000	321,800
Current maturities of long-term debt	30,000	25,000	15,000
Accrued expenses	121,000	82,000	54,300
Current Liabilities	$ 926,000	$ 686,000	$433,200
Long-term debt	219,000	155,000	131,000
Total Liabilities	$1,145,000	$841,000	$564,200
Equity	314,000	265,000	239,800
Total Liabilities and Equity	$1,459,000	$1,106,000	$804,000

Friendly Frank's Mobile Homes
Income Statements

	19X7	19X6	19X5
Net sales	$3,210,000	$2,515,000	$1,947,000
Cost of goods sold	2,529,000	1,952,000	1,489,000
Gross Profit	681,000	563,000	458,000
Depreciation expense	22,000	12,000	9,000
Lease expense	12,000	10,800	9,600
Other operating expenses	549,000	468,200	390,400
Operating Profit	$ 98,000	$ 72,000	$ 49,000
Interest expense	57,000	36,000	22,000
Earnings before Tax	41,000	36,000	27,000
Income Tax (.3)	12,300	10,800	8,100
Net Income	$ 28,700	$ 25,200	$ 18,900

Friendly Frank's Mobile Homes
Common Size Balance Sheet
(As a Percentage of Total Assets)

	19X7	19X6	19X5
Assets			
Cash		6.06	7.93
Accounts receivable (net)		4.88	3.98
Inventory		61.30	59.17
Prepaid expenses		2.17	1.87
Current Assets		74.41	72.95
Gross fixed assets		28.03	28.92
Accumulated depreciation		(2.44)	(1.87)
Net Fixed Assets		25.59	27.05
Total Assets		100.00	100.00
Liabilities			
Accounts payable		7.32	5.24
Notes payable		45.03	40.02
Current maturities of long-term debt		2.26	1.87
Accrued liabilities		7.41	6.75
Current Liabilities		62.03	53.88
Long-term debt		14.01	16.29
Total Liabilities		76.04	70.17
Equity		23.96	29.83
Total Liabilities and Equity		100.00	100.00

Friendly Frank's Mobile Homes
Common Size Income Statements
(As a Percentage of Net Sales)

	19X7	19X6	19X5
Net Sales		100.00	100.00
Cost of Goods Sold		77.61	76.48
Gross Profit		22.39	23.52
Depreciation expense		.48	.46
Lease expense		.43	.49
Other operating expenses		18.62	20.05
Operating Profit		2.86	2.52
Interest expense		1.43	1.13
Earnings Before Tax		1.43	1.39
Income tax		.43	.42
Net Income		1.00	.97

Friendly Frank's Mobile Homes
Ratio Analysis

Ratio	19X7	19X6	19X5	Industry Average for 19X7
Current		1.20X	1.35X	1.20X
Quick		0.21X	0.26X	0.20X
Cash-flow liquidity		(0.09X)	(0.05X)	0.50X
Average collection period		7.72 days	5.92 days	4.19 days
Inventory turnover		2.88X	3.13X	3.30X
Fixed asset turnover		8.89X	8.95X	11.30X
Total asset turnover		2.27X	2.42X	2.50X
Debt ratio		76.04%	70.17%	75.10%
Long-term debt to total capitalization		36.91%	35.33%	29.30%
Debt to equity		3.17X	2.35X	3.50X
Times interest earned		2.00X	2.23X	2.40X
Fixed charge coverage		1.77X	1.85X	1.50X
Gross profit margin		22.39%	23.52%	23.10%
Operating profit margin		2.86%	2.52%	2.00%
Net profit margin		1.00%	0.97%	1.10%
Cash-flow margin		(5.15%)	(4.48%)	4.30%
Return on investment		2.28%	2.35%	2.75%
Return on equity		9.51%	7.88%	11.04%

Friendly Frank's Mobile Homes
Cash Flow from Operating Activities

	19X7	19X6	19X5
Net Income		$25,200	$18,900
+Deprecistion expense		12,000	9,000
		37,200	27,900
Change in accounts receivable		(22,000)	(15,000)
Change in inventory		(202,300)	(122,300)
Change in prepaid expenses		(9,000)	1,000
Change in accounts payable		38,900	7,100
Change in accrued expenses		27,700	14,100
Cash Flow from Operating Activities		($129,500)	($87,200)

Friendly Frank's Mobile Homes
Net Trade Cycle

	19X7	19X6	19X5
Accounts Receivable		7.73 days	5.92 days
Average daily sales			
PLUS			
Inventory		97.05 days	87.96 days
Average daily sales			
MINUS			
Accounts payable		(11.59) days	(7.78) days
Average daily sales			
EQUALS			
Cash conversion cycle		93.19 days	86.10 days

5.5 In this problem we return to R.E.C., Inc. To find the data needed to solve the problem, refer to the R.E.C., Inc. financial statements and common size financial statements used earlier in this chapter.

Required: Based on the following assumptions, prepare a pro forma income statement for R.E.C., Inc. for the year ended 12/31/X0 and a forecast of the stock price range.

    (a) Sales increase by 30%.

    (b) Cost of goods sold percentage same as 19X9.

    (c) Selling and administrative expenses as a percentage of sales representing the average percent of sales for 19X7 to 19X9.

    (d) Advertising expense at 7% of sales.

    (e) Lease payments increase by 20%.

    (f) Depreciation and amortization increase of $500,000.

    (g) Repairs and maintenance increase by 25%.

    (h) Interest income: 12% of marketable securities, which will remain at year end 19X9 level.

    (i) Interest expense increase by 10%.

    (j) Income tax rate same as 19X9.

    (k) Number of shares outstanding will increase by the same number that they increased from 19X8 to 19X9. (Note G to R.E.C., Inc. financial statements, Chapter 1.)

    (l) Price to earnings ratio will fluctuate in a range between the average price/earnings ratio for 19X8–19X9 and 19X7–19X9.

5.6 Determine the effect on the current ratio, the quick ratio, net working capital (current assets less current liabilities), and the debt ratio (total liabilities to total assets) of each of the following transactions. Consider each transaction separately and assume that prior to each transaction the current ratio is 2X, the quick ratio is 1X, and the debt ratio is 50%. The company uses an allowance for doubtful accounts.

  Use I for increase, D for decrease, and N for no change.

	Current Ratio	Quick Ratio	Net Working Capital	Debt Ratio
(a) Borrows $10,000 from bank on short-trem note				
(b) Writes off a $5,000 customer account				
(c) Issues $25,000 in new common stock for cash				
(d) Purchases for cash $7,000 of new equipment				
(e) $5,000 inventory is destroyed by fire				
(f) Invests $3,000 in short-term marketable securities				
(g) Issues $10,000 long-term bonds				
(h) Sells equipment with book value of $6,000 for $7,000				
(i) Issues $10,000 stock in exchange for land				
(j) Purchases $3,000 inventory for cash				
(k) Purchases $5,000 inventory on credit				
(l) Pays $2,000 to supplier to reduce account payable				

5.7 Laurel Street, president of Uvalde Manufacturing, Inc. is preparing a proposal to her board of directors regarding a planned plant expansion which will cost $10,000,000. At issue is whether the expansion should be financed with debt (a long-term note at First National Bank of Uvalde with an interest rate of 15%) or through the issuance of common stock (200,000 shares at $50 per share).

Uvalde Manufacturing currently has a capital structure of:

Debt (12% interest)	40,000,000
Equity	50,000,000

The firm's most recent income statement is presented next:

Sales	$ 100,000,000
Cost of goods sold	65,000,000
Gross profit	35,000,000
Operating expenses	20,000,000
Operating profit	15,000,000
Interest expense	4,800,000
Earnings before tax	10,200,000
Income tax expense (40%)	4,080,000
Net Income	$ 6,120,000
Earnings per share (800,000 shares)	$ 7.65

Laurel Street is aware that financing the expansion with debt will increase risk but could also benefit shareholders through financial leverage. Estimates are that the plant expansion will increase operating profit by 20%. The tax rate is expected to stay at 40%. Assume a 100 percent dividend payout ratio.

> *Required:*
> **(a)** Calculate the debt ratio, time interest earned, earnings per share, and the financial leverage index under each alternative, assuming the expected increase in operating profit is realized.
> **(b)** Discuss factors the board should consider in making a decision.

5.8 Country Creamery Credit Analysis Case. C. Alexander, president of Country Creamery, has approached your bank to discuss the firm's credit needs for 19X5. Country Creamery currently has a $120,000 line of credit ($100,000 outstanding at year end) and would like to increase the line by the amount necessary to support its borrowing requirement. C. Alexander has provided the bank with Country Creamery's balance sheet at 12/31/X4 and income statement for 19X4.

Balance Sheet at 12/13/X4

Cash	$ 30,000	Accounts payable	$270,000
Accounts receivable	250,000	Notes payable	100,000
Inventory	200,000	Accrued wages payable	50,000
Fixed assets (net)	320,000	Long-term debt	220,000
	$800,000	Equity	160,000
			$800,000

Income Statement for Year Ending 12/31/X4

Sales		$2,650,000
Cost of goods sold		1,974,250
Gross profit		675,750
Operating expenses		
Depreciation	$ 50,000	
Other	519,750	569,750
Operating profit		106,000
Interest expense		38,400
Earnings before tax		67,600
Income tax (25%)		16,900
Net Income		$ 50,700

Country Creamery has made the following projections for 19X5: sales increase 20%; cost of goods sold percentage 75%; depreciation expense increase by $18,500; other operating expenses increase 15%; interest expense increase 20%; tax rate will remain at 25%. Country Creamery plans to invest $92,500 in new cheese-making equipment and will retire $30,000 of long-term debt.   Country Creamery has provided a partial pro forma balance sheet at 12/31/X5.

Cash	$ 40,000	Accounts payable	$315,000
Accounts receivable	290,000	Notes payable	?
Inventory	274,000	Accrued wages payable	40,000
Fixed assets (net)	344,000	Long-term debt	190,000
	$948,000	Equity	?
			$948,000

Required:
   (a) Prepare a pro forma 19X5 income statement.
   (b) Prepare a schedule of cash inflows and cash outflows for 19X5. Assuming Country Creamery must maintain a cash balance of $40,000, what is the firm's estimated total borrowing requirement for the line of credit? (To prepare the schedule of cash inflows and outflows you must convert the revenue and expenses on the income statement to a cash basis.)
   (c) Complete the pro forma balance sheet.
   (d) Determine cash flow from operating activities for 19X5, and prepare a statement of cash flows.
   (e) To help assess Country Creamery's credit potential, calculate the company's net trade cycle for 19X4 and 19X5 and analyze the change in the trade cycle.
   (f) Compute the following ratios for 19X4 and 19X5: current, quick, average, collection period, inventory turnover, debt, times interest earned.
   (g) Analyze the preceding data and make a recommendation regarding the credit request.   Explain the reasons for your decision.

5.9 C. Parker Incorporated Credit Analysis Case. C. Parker Incorporated, a manufacturer of refrigeration equipment in the local community, has approached your bank for a loan. C.P.I. currently has a line of credit with the bank; it wishes to increase this line by an amount necessary to support its borrowing needs for the upcoming year. Currently the line is at $150,000 with $135,000 outstanding.

I. M. Cold, president of C.P.I., has provided the bank with historical data (19X5 balance sheet and income statement) and future projections for the company.
Required:
   (a) Prepare a pro forma income statement for 19X6.
   (b) Prepare a full pro forma balance sheet for year end 19X6.
   (c) Prepare a schedule of cash inflows and cash outflows for 19X6. Assuming C.P.I. must maintain a cash balance of at least $35,000, what is the estimated total borrowing requirement for the line of credit?   (To prepare this schedule, it is necessary to convert the revenue and expenses on the income statement to cash basis.)

(d) Determine cash flow from operating activities for 19X6.

(e) Prepare a statement of cash flows for 19X6.

(f) Calculate the net trade cycle for 19X5 and 19X6. Analyze the change in the trade cycle.

(g) Compute the following ratios for 19X5 and 19X6: current, quick, average collection period, inventory turnover, debt ratio, and times interest earned.

(h) Analyze the data given in order to make a recommendation regarding the credit request. Include the reasons for your decision.

Projections for 19X6

- Sales increase by 22%.
- Cost of goods sold percentage at 77%.
- Depreciation expense increase by $22,500.
- Other operating expense increase 5%.
- Interest expense increase 20%.
- Tax rate remains at 39%.
- New equipment costing $90,000 will be purchased.
- C.P.I. will pay cash dividends of $26,800.
- $30,000 of long-term debt will be retired.
- A partial pro forma balance sheet at year end 19X6 follows:

Cash	$ 35,000	Accounts payable	$ 327,000
Accounts receivable	326,000	Notes payable	?
Inventory	305,000	Accrued wages	55,000
Fixed assets (net)	349,500	Long-term debt	207,000
	$1,015,500	Equity	?
			$1,015,500

C. Parker Incorporated
Balance Sheet for 19X5

Assets		Liabilities and Equity	
Cash	$ 39,000	Accounts payable	$285,000
Accounts receivable	265,000	Notes payable	135,000
Inventory	257,000	Accrued wages	65,000
Fixed assets (net)	344,000	Long-term debt	237,000
	$905,000	Equity	183,000
			$905,000

Income Statement for 19X5

Sales		$2,745,000
Cost of goods sold		2,050,700
Gross profit		694,300
Operating expenses		
Depreciation	$ 62,000	
Other	509,740	571,740
Operating profit		122,560
Interest expense		41,000
Earnings before tax		81,560
Income tax (39%)		31,808
Net income		$ 49,752

5.10 Dandy Corporation Comprehensive Ratio Analysis Case. Dandy Corporation manufactures and markets electronics for the home and office. Distribution is through 5,928 company-owned stores and 3,090 dealer/franchise locations in approximately one hundred countries. Dandy has the largest number of retail electronics outlets in the world.

Products offered include: telephone equipment; radios; scanners; citizens band radios; security devices; electronic kits and games; clocks and parts; and audio, video, and computer parts.

Dandy plays a major role in the computer marketplace and the firm has recently begun to emphasize its telephone products. Their newest type of store is the Ding-a-ling Telephone Center, which specializes in business telephone system sales, leasing, and installation. A number of Ding-a-ling Telephone Centers are combined with or adjacent to the Computer Centers. About 36% of the products in the Dandy catalog are manufactured, assembled, or packaged in its plants.

In the 19X7 fiscal year, Dandy made three substantial cash expenditures. The acquisition of Cosman Industries required cash of $91,500,000. (Cosman is a manufacturer/wholesaler of consumer electronic stands, racks, desks, and accessories.) Open market purchases of 2,785,000 shares for the treasury totaled $92,535,000. Also, the company used $150,000,000 of cash to finance part of its $355,000,000 purchase and retirement of 10,000,000 shares of common stock. The remainder was financed through long-term debt.

Required:
   (a) Calculate the 19X7 ratios and cash flow from operating activities for Dandy Corporation.
   (b) Analyze the following:
   Short-term liquidity
   Capital structure and long-term solvency
   Operating efficiency and profitability
   (c) Discuss possible reasons for the trend in return on equity.

Dandy Corporation
Distribution of Sales

Class of Product	19X3	19X4	19X5	19X6	19X7
Radios, phonographs, TVs	12.1%	11.6%	9.4%	8.6%	8.6%
CB radios, walkie-talkies, scanners, PA systems	9.3	6.8	6.0	4.9	5.5
Audio equipment, tape recorders	29.5	25.4	21.5	18.2	17.8
Electronic parts, batteries, test equipment	15.8	14.5	13.9	13.2	13.7
Toys, antenna, security devices, timers, calculators	12.6	14.1	12.0	12.5	11.9
Telephones and intercoms	5.6	5.8	6.5	8.0	8.9
Microcomputers, software, and peripherals	15.1	21.8	30.7	34.6	33.6
	100.0	100.0	100.0	100.0	100.0

Ratio Analysis

Ratio	19X7	19X6	19X5	19X4	19X3	Industry Average*
Current		4.42	4.07	3.48	3.15	2.50
Quick		1.47	1.19	0.96	0.57	0.80
Cash-flow liquidity		1.45	1.09	1.35	0.70	N/A
Average collection period (days)		15.64	14.81	8.96	6.69	11.06
Inventory turnover		1.19	1.23	1.37	1.37	2.30
Fixed asset turnover		9.76	9.03	8.88	8.38	17.50
Total asset turnover		1.59	1.66	1.81	1.95	2.80
Debt		0.29	0.34	0.39	0.60	0.62
Long-term debt to total capitalization		0.14	0.18	0.22	0.48	0.25
Debt to equity		0.41	0.51	0.64	1.51	2.90
Times interest earned		22.30	19.20	14.85	8.69	9.93
Fixed charge coverage		4.91	4.60	4.25	3.37	8.69
Gross profit margin		0.59	0.59	0.58	0.57	0.31
Operating profit margin		0.22	0.21	0.20	0.17	0.08
Net profit margin		0.11	0.11	0.10	0.08	0.04
Cash-flow margin		0.05	0.04	0.08	0.08	N/A
Return on Investment		17.60	18.04	18.10	15.60	9.20
Return on equity		24.85	27.24	29.68	39.00	11.30
Cash flow from operating activities		$136,061	85,877	134,127	108,330	N/A

*Retail specialty stores for 19X7

Consolidated Income Statements
(In thousands except per share amounts)
Three Years Ended June 30

	19X7	*19X6*	*19X5*
Net Sales	$2,784,479	$2,513,297	$2,061,212
Costs and expenses			
Cost of products sold	1,184,531	1,008,187	826,842
Selling, general, and administrative	899,885	823,274	690,646
Rent	114,942	106,970	89,732
Depreciation and amortization	46,079	38,679	29,437
Earnings before interest and tax	539,042	536,187	424,555
Interest expense	(27,905)	(24,044)	(22,114)
Interest income	23,542	15,139	20,946
Income from continuing operations			
before interest and tax	534,679	527,282	423,387
Provision for income taxes	242,808	248,761	199,302
Net Income	$ 281,871	$ 278,521	$ 224,085
Income per share	$ 2.75	$ 2.67	$ 2.17

Dandy Corporation Consolidated Balance Sheets
(In thousands)

	6/30/X7	6/30/X6
Assets		
Cash and short-term investments	$ 154,655	$ 279,743
Accounts receivable	122,910	107,530
Inventories	910,530	844,097
Other current assets	40,456	31,928
Total current assets	1,228,551	1,263,298
Property and equipment, net of		
accumulated depreciation	288,854	257,620
Other assets	135,039	60,990
Total Assets	$1,652,444	$1,581,908
Liabilities and Stockholders' Equity		
Notes payable	$ 51,036	$ 55,737
Accounts payable	88,961	64,640
Accrued expenses	130,386	115,054
Income taxes payable	5,003	50,668
Total current liabilities	275,386	286,099
Long-term debt	347,548	138,420
Deferred income taxes	22,502	17,682
Other noncurrent liabilities	18,312	18,835
Total other liabilities	388,362	174,937
Stockholders' Equity		
Common stock, $1 par	95, 645	105,645
Additional paid-in capital	75,413	68,111
Retained earnings	914,297	969,626
Foreign currency translation effects	(21,672)	(16,297)
Treasury stock at cost	(74,987)	(6,213)
Total stockholders' equity	$988,696	$1,120,872
Total liabilities and equity	$1,652,444	$1,581,908

5.11 The following financial statements were reported by Go Go Grocers in 19X9:

Go Go Grocers
Balance Sheet at 12/31/X9

	19X9	19X8
Assets	$ 18,200	$ 12,500
Accounts receivable	148,000	132,000
Inventories	226,800	175,500
Plant and equipment	1,557,000	1,516,000
Accumulated depreciation	(108,000)	(95,500)
Plant and equipment (net)	1,449,000	1,420,500
Total assets	1,842,000	1,740,500
Liabilities and equity		
Accounts payable	69,000	91,000
Notes payable	136,000	61,500
Accrued liabilities	9,000	6,000
Common stock	300,000	300,000
Additional paid-in capital	1,000,000	1,000,000
Retained earnings	328,000	282,000
Total liabilities and equity	$1,842,000	$1,740,500

Go Go Grocers
Income Statement for Year Ending 12/31/X9

	19X9	19X8
Sales	$3,000,000	$2,700,000
Cost of goods sold	1,527,500	1,425,000
Gross profit	1,472,500	1,275,000
Depreciation	12,500	10,000
Other operating expenses	1,050,000	970,000
Operating profit	410,000	295,000
Income tax expense	164,000	118,000
Net income	$ 246,000	$ 177,000
Cash dividends	$ 200,000	$ 130,000

(a) Calculate the following ratios for 19X9 and 19X8:
- (1) Current
- (2) Quick
- (3) Average collection period
- (4) Inventory turnover
- (5) Fixed asset turnover
- (6) Total asset turnover
- (7) Debt ratio
- (8) Gross profit margin
- (9) Operating profit margin
- (10) Net profit margin

(11) Return on assets

(12) Return on equity

(b) Prepare a statement of cash flows for 19X9; use the indirect method to calculate cash flow from operating activities.

(c) Analyze the data and discuss any apparent strengths and weaknesses in the financial condition and performance of Go Go.

(d) As an officer at Farmers' State Bank, what additional information would you like in order to make a decision regarding Go Go's request for a time extension on the notes payable?

L.A. GEAR, INC.
MINI-CASE

L.A. Gear, Inc. designs, develops and markets athletic and casual footwear. All of the Company's footwear products are manufactured by independent producers located primarily in South Korea, Indonesia, Taiwan and the People's Republic of China.

The Company's products are sold domestically and internationally. Domestic sales account for approximately 80% of total net sales. Advertising and promotion activities are principal elements in the Company's marketing strategies. The Company maintains an "open stock" inventory which permits it to ship to retailers on an "at once" basis, but requires the Company to maintain large levels of inventory.

The athletic footwear industry is highly competitive. L.A. Gear's primary competitors are Nike, Reebok and Adidas.

L.A. Gear provides the following table of financial highlights on page 1 of its 1990 annual report:

FINANCIAL HIGHLIGHTS

In thousands, except per share data

For the Years Ended November 30,	1990	1989	1988	1987	1986
Net sales	$902,225	$617,080	$223,713	$70,575	$36,299
Net earnings	31,338	55,059	22,030	4,371	1,745
Net earnings per common share	$ 1.56	$ 3.01	$ 1.29	$ .27	$ .14
Working capital	180,281	158,879	37,180	20,482	17,028
Total assets	363,955	266,558	128,833	36,794	28,741
Total liabilities	158,078	98,335	87,524	14,675	10,993
Shareholders' equity	205,877	168,223	41,309	22,119	17,748
Net book value per common share	10.61	8.80	2.53	1.37	1.10

As a prospective investor, you are encouraged by the firm's performance. Although earnings have declined in 1990, they are above the levels reported in 1986, 1987, and 1988. Sales are booming, working capital has steadily increased, and the asset base is growing. Net book value per share (assets less liabilities divided by common shares outstanding at year-end) has also risen each year.

The letter to shareholders from the L.A. Gear Chairman and President on page 2 of the 1990 annual report summarizes the firm's strengths and weaknesses:

"For those of us at L.A. Gear, 1990 will be remembered as a year that brought great accomplishments, and with them, great challenges. Our goals for the period were by no means modest, yet we were able to achieve a great many of them. Sales grew significantly; our international business tripled in volume; and we added key members to our management team to help guide us through the coming decade. In spite of the high points, we definitely experienced growing pains. Changes in business and product mix, price discounting, and national economic pressures all played a part in lowering our profitability . . . ."

"Like you, we are disappointed with our earnings. As the company's single largest shareholder, I share your profound concerns. It was inevitable that our company would face obstacles, but never have we moved forward with a greater urgency of mission. We are fully committed to taking steps necessary in 1991 to increase long-term profitability.

"These include expanding product sourcing, decreasing inventory levels and reducing operating expenses. While the short-term impact of these actions remains uncertain, we believe these measures will strengthen our Company and solidify the base from which to move forward and prosper."

Inspired and confident, you prepare to contact your broker. Before calling however, you decide to review the L.A. Gear financial statements and develop your own set of financial highlights and company strengths and weaknesses.

REQUIRED:

1. Analyze the firm's financial statements and supplementary information. Your analysis should include the preparation of common size financial statements, key financial ratios with industry comparisons, and an evaluation of short-term solvency, capital structure and long-term solvency, operating performance and efficiency, and market measures.

2. Identify the strengths and weaknesses of the Company.

3. Compare your evaluation with the 5-year financial highlights and shareholder's letter presented by the company.

Ratio	Industry Average
Current ratio	3.03 X
Quick ratio	1.90 X
Cash-flow liquidity ratio	1.15 X
Average collection period	57.2 days
A/R turnover	6.47 X
Inventory turnover	4.30 X
Fixed asset turnover	16.77 X
Total asset turnover	2.04 X
Debt ratio	33.28%
Long-term debt to total capitalization	8.58%
Debt to equity	50.53%
Times interest earned	19.16 X
Fixed charge coverage	10.60 X
Gross profit margin	39.40%
Operating profit margin	14.87%
Net profit margin	6.74%
Cash-flow margin	8.76%

Return on investment	13.06%
Return on equity	19.21%
PE ratio	11.00
Net trade cycle	83 days

L.A. GEAR, INC. AND SUBSIDIARIES
Consolidated Balance Sheets

	November 30,	
	1990	**1989**
ASSETS		
Current assets:		
Cash	$ 3,291,000	$353,000
Accounts receivable, net of allowance for doubtful accounts and merchandise returns (notes 3 and 4)	156,391,000	100,290,000
Inventory (note 4)	160,668,000	139,516,000
Prepaid expenses and other current assets	16,912,000	12,466,000
Deferred tax charges (note 6)	1,097,000	4,589,000
Total current assets	338,359,000	257,214,000
Property and equipment, at cost, net of accumulated depreciation and amortization of $4,975,000 and $1,809,000 in 1990 and 1989, respecitvely (note 4)	23,624,000	8,079,000
Other assets	1,972,000	1,265,000
	$363,955,000	$266,558,000
LIABILITIES AND SHAREHOLDERS' EQUITY		
Current liabilities:		
Line of credit (note 4)	$94,000,000	$37,400,000
Accounts payable	22,056,000	25,619,000
Accrued expenses and other current liabilities	39,672,000	17,627,000
Accrued compensation (note 5)	2,350,000	16,906,000
Income taxes payable (notes 3 and 6)	—	783,000
Total current liabilities	158,078,000	98,335,000
Shareholders' equity (note 5):		
Common stock, no par value. Authorized 80,000,000 shares; issued and outstanding 19,395,170 shares at November 30, 1990 and 19,108,753 shares at November 30, 1989	91,179,000	84,863,000
Perferred stock, no stated value. Authorized 3,000,000 shares; no shares issued	—	—
Retained earnings	114,698,000	83,360,000
Total shareholders' equity	205,877,000	168,223,000
Commitments and contingencies (notes 3, 4, 7 and 8)		
	$363,955,000	$266,558,000

L.A. GEAR, INC. AND SUBSIDIARIES
Consolidated Statements of Cash Flows

	Year Ended November 30,		
	1990	1989	1988
Cash flows from operating activities:			
Net earnings	$31,338,000	$55,059,000	$22,030,000
Adjustments to reconcile net			
cash used in operating activities:			
Depreciation and amortization	3,394,000	1,199,000	446,000
Issuance of stock to employee			
as compensation	—	558,000	—
(Increase) decrease in:			
Accounts receivable	(56,101,000)	(50,764,000)	(34,378,000)
Inventory	(21,152,000)	(72,960,000)	(50,743,000)
Prepaids and other current assets	(4,446,000)	(9,083,000)	(2,432,000)
Deferred taxes	3,492,000	(3,555,000)	(1,020,000)
Increase (decrease) in:			
Accounts payable	(3,563,000)	17,871,000	7,197,000
Accrued expenses, accrued compensation			
and other current liabilities	7,489,000	16,204,000	8,319,000
Income taxes payable	(783,000)	(3,434,000)	3,894,000
Net cash used in operating activities	(40,332,000)	(48,905,000)	(46,687,000)
Cash flows from investing activities:			
Capital expenditures	(18,939,000)	(6,168,000)	(2,546,000)
Other assets	(707,000)	(246,000)	(406,000)
Net cash used in investing activities	(19,646,000)	(6,414,000)	(2,952,000)
Cash flows from financing activities:			
Exercise of stock options and warrants	908,000	1,309,000	495,000
Tax benefit arising from the exercise			
of incentive stock options	5,408,000	1,372,000	—
Proceeds from issuance of common stock	—	68,616,000	—
Borrowings under credit agreements	56,600,000	(19,830,000)	50,104,000
Net cash provided by financing activities	62,916,000	51,467,000	50,599,000
Net cash flow	2,938,000	(3,852,000)	960,000
Cash at beginning of year	353,000	4,205,000	3,245,000
Cash at end of year	$ 3,291,000	$ 353,000	$ 4,205,000

L.A. GEAR, INC. AND SUBSIDIARIES
Consolidated Statements of Earnings

	Year Ended November 30,		
	1990	**1989**	**1988**
Net sales	$902,225,000	$617,080,000	$223,713,000
Cost of sales	591,740,000	358,482,000	129,103,000
Gross profit	310,485,000	258,598,000	94,610,000
Selling, general and administrative expenses	240,596,000	154,449,000	53,168,000
Interest expense, net (notes 3 and 4)	18,515,000	12,304,000	4,102,000
Earnings before income taxes	51,374,000	91,845,000	37,340,000
Income tax expense (note 6)	20,036,000	36,786,000	15,310,000
Net earnings	$ 31,338,000	$ 55,059,000	$ 22,030,000
Earnings per common share	$ 1.56	$ 3.01	$ 1.29
Weighted average shares outstanding	20,041,000	18,308,000	17,110,000

COMMITMENTS AND CONTINGENCIES

The Company occupies certain facilities, including the home office and distribution centers, and uses certain equipment under operating leases. Rental expense for 1990, 1989 and 1988 amounted to approximately $10,603,000, $3,296,000 and $1,752,000, respectively.

COMMON STOCK, DIVIDEND POLICY

The Company's stock is traded on the New York Stock Exchange. To date, the Company has not paid dividends on its Common Stock. Under the terms of the bank agreement, as amended, the Company is prohibited from declaring dividends on its Common Stock. At January 31, 1991, there were 3,294 shareholders of record.

	February 28,		May 31,		August 31,		November 30,	
	1990	**1989**	**1990**	**1989**	**1990**	**1989**	**1990**	**1989**
Price range of common stock:								
High	$ 35.38	$ 17.56	$ 50.13	$ 26.32	$ 31.25	$ 33.75	$ 16.88	$ 45.75
Low	$ 23.38	$ 10.00	$ 26.88	$ 15.07	$ 12.88	$ 25.75	$ 10.63	$ 29.94

Appendices

Appendix A

A Guide to Earnings Quality

The assessment of earnings quality is critical in the analysis of financial statements. The earnings statement encompasses many areas that provide management with opportunites to influence the outcome of reported earnings in ways that may not best represent economic reality or the future operating potential of a firm. These include:

Accounting choices, estimates, and judgments.
Changes in accounting methods and assumptions.
Discretionary expenditures.
Nonrecurring transactions.
Nonoperating gains and losses.
Revenue and expense recognitions that do not match cash flow.

In evaluating a business firm, it is essential that the financial statement analyst consider the *qualitative* as well as the *quantitative* components of earnings for an accounting period. The higher the quality of financial reporting, the more useful the information for business decision-making. The analyst should develop an earnings figure which reflects the future ongoing potential of the firm. This process requires consideration of qualitative factors and necessitates, in some cases, an actual adjustment of the reported earnings figure.

The purpose of this Appendix is to provide the financial statement user with a step-by-step guide which links the items on an earnings statement with the key areas in the financial statement data that affect earnings quality. (See Exhibit A.1).

EXHIBIT A.1 A Checklist for Earnings Quality

I. Sales
   1. Allowance for doubtful accounts
   2. Price vs. volume changes
   3. Real vs. nominal growth

II. Cost of Goods Sold
   4. Cost-flow assumption for inventory
   5. Base LIFO layer reductions
   6. Loss recognitions on write downs of inventory (also see item 13)

III. Operating Expenses
   7. Discretionary expenses
      Research and development
      Repair and maintenence
      Advertising and marketing
   8. Depreciation (depletion, amortization)
      Methods
      Estimates
   9. Pension accounting—interest rate assumptions

IV. Nonoperating Revenue and Expense
   10. Gains (losses) from sales of assets
   11. Interest income
   12. Equity income
   13. Loss recognitions on write downs of assets (also see item 6)
   14. Accounting changes
   15. Extraordinary items

V. Other Issues
   16. Acquisitions and dispositions
   17. Material changes in number of shares outstanding

The list does not, by any means, include all of the items which affect earnings quality. Rather, the examples illustrate some of the qualitative issues which are most commonly encountered in financial statement data. Another purpose of this Appendix is to provide the financial statement user with an approach to analyzing and interpreting the qualitative factors. The checklist attempts to provide a framework for the analysis of earnings quality rather than a complete list of its components.

Although the examples in this book deal primarily with the financial reporting of wholesale, retail, and manufacturing firms, the concepts and techniques presented can also apply to other types of industries. For instance, there is a discussion of the provision for doubtful accounts as it impacts earnings quality. The same principles would apply to the provision for loan loss reserves for financial institutions. Almost all of the items on the checklist—other than those directly related to cost of goods sold—would apply to most types of business firms, including service-oriented companies.

USING THE CHECKLIST

Each item on the checklist in Exhibit A.1 is discussed and illustrated with examples from the 19X9 ABC Corporation Annual Report. ABC Corporation, a manufacturer of steel products, has diversified its operations through the acquisition of an oil and gas company.

I. SALES

1. Allowance for Doubtful Accounts. Most companies sell products on credit. Revenue is recognized on the income statement when the sales are made, and accounts receivable are carried on the balance sheet until the cash is collected. Because some customer accounts are never satisfied, the balance sheet includes an allowance for doubtful accounts. A discussion of sales, accounts receivable, and the allowance for doubtful accounts is provided in Chapters 2 and 3.

The allowance account, which is deducted from the balance sheet accounts receivable account, should reflect the volume of credit sales, the firm's past experience with customers, the customer base, the firm's credit policies, the firm's collection practices, economic conditions, and changes in any of these. There should be a consistent relationship between the rate of change in sales, accounts receivable, and the allowance for doubtful accounts. If the amounts are changing at different rates or in different directions, for example, if sales and accounts receivable are increasing, but the allowance account is decreasing or is increasing at a much smaller rate, the analyst should be alert to the potential for manipulation using the allowance account. Of course, there could also be a plausible reason for such a change.

The relevant items needed to relate sales growth with accounts receivable and the allowance for doubtful accounts are found on the income statement (sales) and balance sheet (accounts receivable and allowance for doubtful accounts.)[1]

The following is an excerpt from the 19X9 ABC Corporation Consolidated Statement of Income and Consolidated Balance Sheet.

(In millions)	19X9	19X8	% Change
Sales	$19,283	$19,104	00.9
Receivables	1,570	1,650	(04.8)
Less allowance for doubtful accounts	(12)	(39)	(69.2)
Receivables (net)	1,558	1,611	

Between 19X8 and 19X9 sales for ABC increased slightly (by .9%) while accounts receivable decreased slightly (by 4.8%). During the same period, the allowance for doubtful accounts decreased considerably (by 69.2%). Since the allowance account involves estimations by management of accounts that will not be collected during the next accounting period, the analyst would want to determine whether the firm is justified in reducing the

[1] The underlying liquidity of accounts receivable is also extremely important in assessing earnings quality. This topic is covered in Chapter 4 and 5.

account by such a large percentage relative to gross receivables and sales since this reduction has a positive impact on pretax earnings (of $27 million). If the account is manipulated to increase earnings, then the quality of reported earnings is lessened. On the other hand, there may be a reasonable explanation for the large reduction—such as a change in customer base or economic conditions.

2. Price vs. Volume Changes. If a company's sales are increasing (or decreasing), it is important to determine whether the change is a result of price, volume, or a combination of both. Are sales growing because the firm is increasing prices or because more units are being sold, or both? It would seem that, in general, higher quality earnings would be the product of both volume and price increases (during inflation). The firm would want to sell more units and keep prices increasing at least in line with the rate of inflation.

The reasons for sales growth (or decline) are covered in a firm's Management Discussion and Analysis section of the annual or 10-K report, (Chapter 1). To relate sales growth to reasons for sales growth, use sales data from the income statement and the volume/price discussion from the management discussion and analysis section.

From the ABC Consolidated Statement of Income:

	19X9	19X8	19X7
Sales (millions)	$19,283	$19,104	$17,539

The following is an excerpt from the ABC Management Discussion and Analysis of Financial Condition and Results of Operations:

> Sales increased to $19.3 billion in 19X9 from $19.1 billion in 19X8 and $17.5 billion in 19X7. The increase from 19X8 reflects higher steel shipment levels, increased refined hydrocarbon liftings, partially offset by lower selling prices for steel, crude oil, natural gas and refined products. The increase in sales in 19X8 from 19X7 reflected higher steel shipment levels and net selling prices, increased volumes of liquid hydrocarbon liftings from the South Brazos field and increased shipments and prices for most chemical products.

From this information it can be determined that the slight sales growth in 19X9 was the result of volume increases, offset by a price decline; and in 19X8, the sales growth resulted from both price and volume increases.

3. Real vs. Nominal Growth. A related issue is whether sales are growing in "real" (inflation-adjusted) as well as "nominal" (as reported) terms. Disclosures regarding inflation accounting, no longer required, as discussed in Chapter 1. The change in sales in nominal terms can be readily calculated from the figures reported on the income statement. An adjustment of the reported sales figure with the Consumer Price Index (or some other measure of general inflation) will enable the analyst to make a comparison of the changes in real and nominal terms. To make the calculation to compare real with nominal sales, begin with the sales figures reported in the income statement, and adjust years prior to the current year with the CPI or some other price index.

Sales (millions)	19X9	19X8	Percentage Change
As reported (nominal)	$19,283	$19,104	0.937
Adjusted (real)	19,283	19,786	(2.542)
Using Average CPI (1967 = 100).			
(19X9 CPI/19X8 CPI) X 19X8 Sales = Adjusted Sales			
(322.2/311.1) X $19,104 = $19,786			

Sales, when adjusted for general inflation, actually decreased in 19X9. An alternative approach would be to compare the growth in nominal sales—an increase of .9%—with the change in the CPI—an increase from 311.1 to 322.2 of 3.6%. Either way, it is apparent that ABC sales growth did not keep pace with the rate of general inflation. The point made in the previous section is that prices actually decreased for many product lines.

II. COST OF GOODS SOLD

4. Cost-flow Assumption for Inventory. During periods of inflation, the LIFO cost-flow assumption for inventory accounting, described in Chapter 2, produces lower earnings than FIFO or average cost. But LIFO results in the matching of current costs with current revenues and therefore produces higher quality earnings than either FIFO or average cost unless the firm operates in an industry with volatile or falling prices. The inventory accounting system used by the company is described in the note to the financial statement which details accounting policies or the note discussing inventory. The following excerpt is from Note 1, Summary of Principal Accounting Policies from the ABC Corporation annual report:

> Inventories. The cost of inventories is determined primarily under the last-in, first-out (LIFO) method . . . .

The quality of ABC's earnings is enhanced by the LIFO choice. Cash flow is also helped because LIFO ordinarily produces lower taxable earnings and thus lower tax payments. The LIFO system, however, generally results in undervalued inventory on the balance sheet during inflation because the ending inventory balance is determined by the older, lowest cost items. Companies using LIFO disclose the current value of the inventory or the amount by which inventory is undervalued in a note to the financial statements, such as the following for ABC Corporation:

> Current acquisition costs are estimated to exceed inventory values at December 31 by approximately $1.05 billion in 19X9 and $1.18 billion in 19X8.

5. Base LIFO Layer Reductions. If a company using the LIFO method reduces inventory during the accounting period and liquidates the base LIFO layer, as discussed in Chapter 2, there will be an increase in earnings as a result. When this situation occurs, LIFO has the opposite earnings effect from that described in item 4. When LIFO liquidations occur, earnings are enhanced. A base LIFO layer reduction reduces the quality of earnings in the sense that there is an improvement in operating profit from what would generally be considered a negative occurrence: inventory reductions. The base LIFO layer reduction and its effect on earnings is quantified in a note to the financial statements.

> Cost of sales has been reduced and operating income increased by $143 million in 19X9, $180 million in 19X8, and $402 million in 19X7 as a result of liquidations of LIFO inventories.

In considering the future, ongoing potential of the company, it would be appropriate to exclude from earnings the effect of LIFO liquidations because a firm would not want to continue benefiting from inventory shrinkages.

6. Loss Recognitions on Write-downs of Inventories. The principle of conservatism in accounting requires that firms carry inventory in the accounting records at the lower of cost (as determined by the cost-flow assumption such as LIFO, FIFO, average cost) or market. If the value of inventory falls below its original cost, the inventory is written down to market value. Market generally is determined by the cost to replace or reproduce the inventory but should not exceed the net realizable amount (selling price less completion and disposal costs) the company could generate from selling the item. The amount of the write-down will affect comparability, and thus quality, of the profit margins from period to period.

Firms also write down the carrying cost of property, plant, and equipment when there is a permanent impairment in value; and certain investments in marketable equity securities (according to the provisions of FASB No. 115 discussed in Chapter 2) are carried at market value.

When the write-down of inventory is included in cost of goods sold, the gross profit margin is affected in the year of the write-down. The following is an example from one of ABC's competitors, XYZ Corporation:

> Gross profit as a percent of sales and operating revenues was 54.5% in fiscal 19X9 compared to 57.3% in 19X8. During the past two years, the percentage has been adversely impacted by the unsettled conditions in the foreign steel market which created heavy discounting. During the third quarter of fiscal 19X9, the company determined that certain products needed to be permanently reduced in price because of changes in pricing structure within the industry and sharp declines in material prices. The cost of goods sold included inventory write-downs of approximately $33 million in recognition of these changes.

In comparing the gross profit margin between periods, the analyst should be aware of the impact on the margin that occurs from such write-downs.

III. OPERATING EXPENSES

7. Discretionary Expenses. A company can increase earnings by reducing variable operating expenses in a number of areas, for example repair and maintenance of capital assets, research and development, and advertising and marketing. If such discretionary expenses are reduced primarily to benefit the current year's reported earnings, the long-term

impact on the firm's operating profit may be detrimental and thus the quality lowered.   The analyst should review the trends of these discretionary expenses and compare them to the firm's volume of activity and level of capital investment.   Amounts of discretionary expenditures are disclosed in notes, such as the following for ABC Corporation:

(In millions)	19X9	19X8	19X7
Repairs and maintenance	$1,158	$1,176	$1,281
Research and development	54	61	84

ABC reduced expenditures both for the maintenance and repair of plant and equipment and for research and development.   These reductions occurred during a period of growing sales and increased investments in capital assets:

(In millions)	19X9	19X8	19X7
Sales	$19,283	$19,104	$17,539
Property, plant, equipment	23,735	23,670	21,807

The analyst would want to determine the reasons for such reductions in discretionary expenses and assess the long-term effect of these policies on profitability.

8. Depreciation.   The amount of annual depreciation expense recognized for an accounting period, as discussed in Chapter 1, depends on the choice of depreciation method and estimates of the useful life and salvage value of the asset being depreciated. Most companies use the straight-line method rather than an accelerated method for reporting purposes because it produces a smoother earnings stream and higher earnings in the early years of the depreciation period.   The straight-line method, however, is lower in quality in most cases because it does not reflect the fact that most machinery and equipment does not wear evenly over the depreciation period.   Depreciation policy is explained in notes to the financial statements:

> Property, plant and equipment.   Depreciation is generally computed on the straight-line method, based upon the estimated life of assets.

Similarly, the analyst would want to review depletion for firms operating in the extractive industries and amortization for intangible assets.   Depletion of the cost of mineral properties, other than oil and gas, is based on rates which are expected to amortize the cost over the estimated tonnage of materials to be removed.   ABC reports the following:

> Depreciation and depletion of oil and gas producing properties are computed at rates applied to the units of production on the basis of proved oil and gas reserves as determined by the corporation geologists and engineers.[2]

---

[2] It is also important to note that ABC uses the successful efforts method of accounting for oil and gas exploration and development.   This means that the firm carries as a balance sheet asset only the cost of successful exploration and development.   Costs of unsuccessful efforts are expensed in the year they occur.   The other acceptable method, but one which is lower in quality, is the full-cost method, by which companies capitalize— carry on the balance sheet—all costs, whether or not they resulted in productive operations.

> ... The purchase price exceeded the value of the net tangible assets acquired by $60 million. This intangible asset is being amortized on a straight-line basis over 15 years.

The intangible asset being amortized by ABC is goodwill, discussed in Chapter 2, which arises in business combinations when the acquiring company pays more than the fair market value for the net tangible assets acquired. Goodwill is carried on the balance sheet as a noncurrent asset. Other intangible assets which are amortized include patents, trademarks, copyrights, and leasehold improvements.

9. Pension Accounting—Interest Rate Assumptions.

Although a detailed explanation of pension accounting is beyond the scope of this book, it is important to be aware of some basic pension accounting principles as they impact earnings quality. Related to pension accounting, the reader is referred to the discussion of disclosure requirements for postretirement benefits other than pensions in Chapter 2.

Pension accounting is based on expectations regarding the benefits which will be paid when employees retire and on the interest that pension assets will earn over time. The provisions for pension accounting are specified in Statement of Financial Accounting Standards No. 87, "Employers' Accounting for Pensions."[3]

If, based on actuarial estimates, a company changes the interest rate assumptions used in pension accounting, this change affects the amount of annual pension expense and the present value of the pension benefits. If the assumed rate of interest is increased, pension cost is reduced and earnings increased. For example, if you need $5,000 in 20 years, the amount you would have to invest today would be different if your investment earned 6% or 8%. At 6% you would have to invest $1,560 to accumulate $5,000 at annual compound interest in 20 years; if the interest rate were increased to 8%, you would only have to contribute $1,075.[4] Also, the present value of the benefits to be paid in the future is affected by increasing the interest rate. The present value of $5,000 to be paid in 20 years is $1,560 at a 6% discount rate and $1,075 at an 8% rate.

To summarize the effects of a change in the pension interest rate assumption, if the assumed interest rate is lowered, the annual pension cost will increase and the present value of the benefits will also increase; if the assumed interest rate is increased, pension cost and the present value of the benefits are reduced.

FASB Statement No. 87 requires companies with a defined benefit pension plan—a plan that states the benefits to be received by employees after retirement or the method of determining such benefits—to disclose the following:

1. A description of the plan, including employee groups covered, type of benefit formula, funding policy, and types of assets held.

---

[3] For a detailed discussion of FASB Statement 87, see Revsine, L. "Understanding Financial Accounting Standard 87," *Financial Analysts Journal*, January-February 1989.

[4] $5,000 X .312 = $1,560; $5,000 X .215 = $1,075. (Factors for present value of single sum for 20 periods, 6% and 85%).

2. The amount of pension expense showing separately the service cost, the interest cost, the actual return on assets for the period, and the net total of other components.[5]

3. A schedule reconciling the funded status of the plan with amounts reported in the company's balance sheet.

4. The weighted average discount rate and rate of compensation increase used to measure the projected benefit obligation and the weighted average expected long-term rate of return on plan assets.

5. The amounts and types of securities included in plan assets.

A *liability* is recognized if the pension expense recognized to date is greater than the amount funded; an *asset* is reported if the pension expense to date is less than the amount funded. An *additional liability* is recognized if the accumulated benefit obligation is greater than the fair market value of plan assets less the balance in the accrued pension liability account or plus the balance in the deferred pension asset account.

A portion of the footnote disclosure relating to employees' benefit plans from the ABC Annual Report is provided:

The company and certain of its subsidiaries have defined benefit plans for regular full-time employees. Cost for the company's defined benefit plans includes the following components:

(In millions)	19X9	19X8	19X7
Service cost (benefits earned during period)	$11.9	$ 9.7	$ 7.7
Interest cost on projected benefit obligation	10.0	8.9	7.2
Investment loss (gain) on plan assets	(9.9)	(19.7)	6.1
Net amortization and deferral	(.2)	10.9	(14.1)
Net pension cost	$11.8	$ 9.8	$ 6.9

The plans' assets are diversified in stocks, bonds, real estate, short-term and other investments. The plans' funded status was as follows:

	19X9	19X8
Plan assets at market value	$117.2	$107.7
Projected benefit obligation	(133.0)	(119.1)
Total projected obligation (in excess of) plan assets	(15.8)	(11.3)
Unamortized transitional net assets	(2.3)	(2.5)
Unamortized net (gain) loss	6.6	12.0
Unrecognized prior service cost	.5	.5
Net pension liability	(11.0)	(1.2)

[5] The service cost represents the increase during the year in the discounted present value of payable benefits, resulting from employees' working an additional year; interest cost arises from the passage of time and increases interest expense; return on plan assets reduces pension expense; other components include net amortization and deferrals and are related to the choice of discount and interest rates. The same rate must be used to compute service cost and interest cost, but a different rate can be used to compute the expected rate of return on pension plan assets.

The discount rate and rate of future compensation increased used in determining the projected benefit obligation and costs were 9% and 6%, respectively, and the expected long-term rate of return on plan assets was 9% at December 31, 19X9, 19X8, and 19X7.

For ABC, the net pension cost is calculated as service cost, plus interest cost, plus or minus the investment gain or loss, less the net amortization and deferral. The net pension liability is the amount by which the projected benefit obligation exceeds the plan assets at fair value, plus the unamortized transitional net assets, less the unrecognized net gain and the unrecognized prior service cost.

FASB Statement No. 87 has substantially improved the accounting methods and disclosure requirements for pension accounting, but pension accounting remains an important qualitative issue. A change in interest rate assumptions is important because it represents an accounting estimate which affects annual pension cost and the relationship between pension assets and the present value of pension benefits. When a firm changes its interest rate assumptions, there is an impact on pension expense as well as the status of the plan. While FASB No. 87 included explicit criteria for selecting interest rates, it still allows some management discretion.[6] ABC Corporation had no changes in interest rate assumptions over the three year period.

IV. NONOPERATING REVENUE AND EXPENSE

10. Gains (Losses) from Sales of Assets. As discussed in Chapter 1, when a company sells a capital asset, such as property or equipment, the gain or loss is included in net income for the period. The sale of a major asset is sometimes made to increase earnings and/or to generate needed cash during a period when the firm is performing poorly. Such transactions are not part of the normal operations of the firm and should be excluded from net income when considering the future operating potential of the company.

Gains and losses on asset sales are disclosed in a financial statement note, such as the following from ABC Corporation:

(In millions)	19X9	19X8
Other income includes:		
Gain on disposal of assets	$55	$265

The total income before taxes, extraordinary gains, and accounting changes for ABC was $797 million in 19X9 and $980 million in 19X8. The nonoperating gains from sales of assets thus accounted for 7% and 27% of pretax ordinary income.

11. Interest Income. Interest income is also nonoperating except for certain types of firms such as financial institutions. Interest income results primarily from short-term temporary investments in marketable securities to earn a return on cash not immediately

---

[6] An interesting article on the effect of interest rate assumptions is Susan Pulliam, "Hopeful Assumptions Let Firms Minimize Pension Contributions," *The Wall Street Journal*, September 2, 1993.

needed in the business. These security investments were explained in Chapter 2. In the assessment of earnings quality, the analyst should be alert to the materiality and variability in the amount of interest income because it is not part of operating income. Interest income is disclosed on the face of the income statement or in notes to the financial statements. An excerpt from ABC's notes:

(In millions)	19X9	19X8
Interest income	$59	$91

Using the pretax, ordinary income figures from item 10 for ABC, it can be determined that interest income contributed 7% in 19X9 and 9% in 19X8 to earnings before taxes, extraordinary items, and accounting changes. The two nonoperating sources combined—asset sales and interest income—accounted for 14% in 19X9 and 36% in 19X8. Because these income items are material to the financial statements as a whole and fluctuate significantly between periods, they are important in analyzing earnings quality. A large and varying proportion of ABC income is the result of nonoperating sources.

12. Equity Income. Use of the equity method to account for investments in unconsolidated subsidiaries, discussed and illustrated in Chapter 3, permits the investor to recognize as investment income the investor's percentage ownership share of the investee's reported income rather than recognizing income only to the extent of cash dividends actually received. The net effect is that the investor, in most cases, records more income than is received in cash. Detail on such investments is provided in the notes, such as the following for ABC:

(In millions)	19X9	19X8
Net income (loss) from ABC's share in equity method entities	$63	$35
Dividends received from equity method entities	$31	$30

In each year, ABC reported more earnings on the earnings statement than were received in dividends. Cash flow from operations, discussed in Chapter 4, excludes the amount by which investment income recognized exceeds cash received: $32 million in 19X9 and $5 million in 19X8 for ABC. It would also be appropriate to eliminate this noncash portion of earnings for comparative purposes.

13. Loss Recognition on Write-downs of Assets. As was discussed in item 6, the write-down of asset values, following the principle of carrying assets at the lower of cost or market value, affects the comparability and thus the quality of financial data. (Also note the provisions of FASB Statement No. 115, discussed in Chapter 2, for *unrealized gains and losses* on investments in debt and equity securities.) The reasons for the write-downs would also be important in assessing the quality of the financial data. Information on asset write-downs is presented in notes to the financial statements.

ABC reported the following:

The following unusual items resulted in favorable (unfavorable) effects on income:

(In millions)	19X9	19X8
Provisions for estimated shutdown costs	$15	$ 0
Adjustment to provision for occupational		
disease claims	$24	$ 0
Revaluation of assets	$ 0	($47)
	$39	($47)

ABC got a positive earnings boost in 19X9 from the upward revaluation of provisions made in earlier periods to recognize the shutdown of plant facilities and the provision for potential black lung disease claims; and recorded a loss in 19X8 from the write-down of assets. These amounts should be reviewed and excluded from earnings to make comparisons with other years when assessing future operating potential.

14. Accounting Changes.   Accounting changes are explained and quantified in financial statement notes.   ABC reported the following change in accounting principles:

> In 19X9, the Corporation adopted a change in accounting for petroleum revenue tax payable to the United Kingdom. The newly adopted method of accounting for this income tax is based on the estimated effective tax rate over the life of the Brazos field. This method recognizes certain unique tax allowances proportionally over the income from the field rather than when realized for tax return purposes. Management considers the new method to be a preferred accounting practice under the circumstances, resulting in a better matching of expense with revenue and a better measurement of the deferred tax liability. The cumulative effect of the change on prior years is $45 million, net of United States income tax. The effect on the income for the year 19X9 is as follows:

(In millions except per share data)	19X9
Total income before extraordinary gain	$ 15
Per share—primary	.14
—fully diluted	.12
Net income	$ 60
Per share—primary	.54
—fully diluted	.47

The cumulative effect of the change, net of tax—$45 million—is shown separately on the income statement and should be eliminated in making comparisons with future and prior years' earnings because prior years' earnings were computed using a different accounting method.

15. Extraordinary Items.   Extraordinary items are gains and losses which are both unusual and infrequent. They are shown separately, net of tax, on the income statement. Because very few transactions meet the definition of extraordinary, it is rare to see such items on an earnings statement.   Most of those that do appear are the result of early debt extinguishments.

In-substance defeasance, a common type of early debt extinguishment, is of particular importance in the analysis of earnings quality because of the gain which is included in income and also because debt, which is still outstanding, is removed from the books. FASB Statement No. 76, "Extinguishment of Debt," permits firms to purchase at a discount[7] riskless securities (U.S. government securities or securities backed by the U.S. government), place the securities in an irrevocable trust designated to meet the interest and principal payments on the outstanding debt, to recognize a gain for the difference between the principal amount of the debt and the price paid for the riskless securities in the open market, and to eliminate the original liability.

For example, assume that on January 1, 1995 Topco Corporation issues $100,000 principal amount of 10-year, 8% bonds, with interest payable semiannually on June 30 and December 31.   On January 1, 1999, Topco executes an in-substance defeasance by purchasing at a discount for $75,000 (because market rates of interest have risen and bond prices have fallen) U.S. government securities which match in maturity, interest, and principal the Topco bonds.   Topco places the U.S. government securities in an irrevocable trust to meet the interest payment on the bonds and the principal amount at maturity. Topco recognizes an extraordinary gain of $25,000 (net of tax) and eliminates the $100,000 as a liability, even though it is still a legal liability.

Defeasance transactions are explained in notes to the financial statements, such as the following for ABC in 19X9:

> In 19X9 the Corporation extinguished $399 million principal amount of debt, resulting in a net extraordinary gain of $51 million, after income tax of $43 million.   The debt securities extinguished included all outstanding 4-5/8% Sinking Fund Debentures due 20X6—$168 million, all outstanding 7-3/4% Sinking Fund Debentures due 20X9—$34 million and $59 million principal amount of Environmental Improvement Bonds.   All of these securities, which were still outstanding at December 31, 19X9, were extinguished by placing securities into separate irrevocable trusts that will make the scheduled principal and interest payments.   Other extinguishments of debt in 19X9 included the repurchase of $85 million principal amount of Environmental Improvement Bonds and $53 million principal amount of various other debt securities.
>
> In 19X8 the Corporation repurchased debt securities with a total principal amount of $242 million, resulting in an extraordinary gain of $79 million, net of income tax of $6 million.

ABC eliminated $339 million debt from the balance sheet and recorded a gain in the earnings statement of $51 million in 19X9; the firm eliminated $242 million debt and posted a $79 million gain in 19X8.   In the process ABC has tied up enormous sums of liquid assets which will be unavailable for other purposes for many years.   It is also possible that the trustee holding the securities could default and the original liability would be reinstated on the balance sheet.[8]   The gain recognized from an in-substance defeasance should be eliminated from earnings when evaluating a firm's future operating potential.

---

[7] During a period when market rates of interest have risen and bond prices have fallen.

[8] For more reading on this topic, see Guamnitz, B.R. and Thompson, J.E. "In-Substance Defeasance: Costs, Yes; Benefits, No," *Journal of Accountancy*, March 1987.

V. OTHER ISSUES

There are other issues which an analyst should consider in assessing earnings quality. Among these are material changes in the number of shares outstanding and acquisitions and dispositions.

The number of common stock shares outstanding and thus the computation of earnings per share can change materially from one accounting period to the next. These changes result from such transactions as treasury stock purchases and the purchase and retirement of a firm's own common stock. Acquisitions and dispositions of other companies and/or major lines of business can have a significant impact on the comparability of financial reporting. The treatment of goodwill, discussed in item 8, is one of the qualitative factors that results from acquisitions. Ongoing restructuring of a company can also be a signal of underlying problems.

In assessing the quality of a company's reported earnings, it is helpful to consider not only the issues presented in the Checklist but also any other factors which the analyst believes may cause the reported earnings figure to misrepresent the future operating potential of the firm.

WHAT ARE THE "REAL" EARNINGS?

What is the appropriate earnings figure for ABC in 19X9? There are numerous possible answers to this question—perhaps as many as there are readers. ABC reported a bottom line net income figure of $409 million in 19X9. At a minimum, the following adjustments should be considered:

(In millions)	
1. Start with total income before taxes, extraordinary gain, and cumulative effect of the change in accounting principle (from the income statement)	$797
2. Deduct:	
Base LIFO layer reductions (Item 5)	(143)
Gain on disposal of assets (Item 10)	(55)
Amount by which equity income exceeds cash received (Item 12)	(32)
Unusual items (Item 13)	(39)
Provision for taxes[9] (from income statement)	(484)
Adjusted income	$ 44

[9] It would also be appropriate to adjust the tax provision for the tax effect of items excluded from income; this information is not available for ABC.

In addition, consider other items discussed in the Appendix, for example, the following reductions between 19X8 and 19X9:

$27 million in the allowance for doubtful accounts;
$ 7 million in research and development expenditures;
$18 million in maintenance and repair of plant and equipment;
$32 million in interest income.

Comparable adjustments would also be required for previous years' earnings figures in order to make relevant comparisons. The ultimate objective in the analysis of earnings quality is to arrive at a performance measure which best reflects both financial reality and the future operating potential of the firm.

STUDY PROBLEM

A.1   Qualico Products, Inc.—An Earnings Quality Case.   Given are the 19X9 and 19X8 income statements, balance sheets, selected notes to the financial statements, and a partial management discussion and analysis section for Qualico Products, Inc.   Using the information provided,

(a)   Discuss each item on the Checklist for Earnings Quality (Exhibit A.1) as it relates to the quality of earnings reported by Qualico, Inc. in 19X9.

(b)   Recommend any adjustments to 19X9 earnings you think would be necessary to develop a more relevant earnings figure that would reflect Qualico's future earnings potential.

Income Statement
Qualico Products, Inc.
(Millions of dollars, except per share amounts)

For year ending	19X9	19X8
Sales	$18,637	$18,272
Operating Costs		
Cost of sales	13,476	12,948
Selling, general, and administratve expenses	838	818
Pension, insurance, and other employee benefits	414	458
Depreciation and amoritization	2,272	2,228
State, local and miscellaneous taxes	1,135	1,125
Total Operating Costs	18,135	17,577
Operating income	502	695
Equity income	61	33
Other income	288	43
Total Income from Operations	851	771
Interest income	62	23
Interest expense	(715)	(777)
Unusual items	(15)	—
Total income before Tax, Extraordinary Gain, and Cumulative Effect of Accounting Change	183	17
Less income tax	(55)	(5)
	128	12
Extraordinary gain on exinguishment of debt, net of tax	49	—
Cumulative effect on prior years of a change in accounting principles, net of tax	44	—
Net income	$ 221	$ 12
Earnings per Share (number of shares outstanding was 157 million and 172 million in 19X9 and 19X8, respectively)	$ 1.41	$ 0.07
Dividends per share	$ 0.50	$ 0.75

Qualico Products, Inc.
Balance Sheet
(In millions)

	19X9	19X8
Assets at year end		
Current Assets		
Cash and marketable securities	$ 722	$ 425
Receivables, less allowance for doubtful accounts of $14 in 19X9 and $40 in 19X8	1,629	1,523
Inventories	1,837	2,362
Other current assets	48	57
Total Current Assets	4,236	4,367
Long-term receivables and other investments	721	733
Property, plant, and equipment (gross)	26,318	21,630
Less: accumulated depreciation, amoritization	(11,743)	(9,601)
Property, plant, and equipment (net)	14,575	12,029
Goodwill, net of amortization	52	
Total Assets	$19,584	$17,129
Liabilities and Stockholders' Equity at year end		
Current Liabilities		
Notes payable	$ 1,083	$ 950
Accounts payable	2,076	1,802
Accrued expenses	1,175	1,118
Current portion of long-term debt	207	117
Total current liabilities	4,541	3,987
Long-Term Debt	8,191	6,532
Deferred Taxes	692	537
Stockholder's Equity		
Common Stock	160	150
Additional paid-in capital	2,323	1,973
Cumulative foreign currently translation adjustment	(89)	(120)
Treasury stock (65 million shares and 50 million shares, respectively)	(625)	(100)
Retained earnings	4,391	4,170
Total stockholder's equity	6,160	6,073
Total Liabilities and Stockholders' Equity	$19,584	$17,129

Qualico Products, Inc.
Selected Notes to the Finacial Statements

Note 1.   Summary of Accounting Policies

Principles of Consolidation. The financial statements include the accounts of the Corporation and its majority-owned subsidiaries. Investments in other entities in which the Corporation has significant influence in the management and control are accounted for using the equity method of accounting. They are carried in the investment account at the Corporation's share of the entity's net assets. The proportionate share of income from equity investments is included in income from affiliates.

Property, Plant, and Equipment. Depreciation is generally computed on the straight-line method based on the estimated life of the asset for financial reporting purposes (See Note 2.)

Inventories. The cost of inventories is determined primarily under the last-in, first out (LIFO) method. If the FIFO (first-in, first-out) method had been in use, inventories would have been $1,203 and $1,345 million higher than reported at December 31, 19X9 and 19X8, respectively.

Income Taxes. Deferred income taxes result from recognizing items of income and expense in consolidated financial statements in different years than income tax returns, primarily in the accounting for depreciation expense.

Note 2.   Change in Accounting Principle

Results for 19X9 include the effect of an accounting change adopted as of January 1, 19X9. This change, which does not affect income tax payments or cash flow, is described below.

As explained in Note 1, the staight-line method has been used to account for depreciation for financial reporting purposes. Effective January 1, 19X9, the Corporation changed to the straight-line method from an accelerated method, double declining balance, in order to achieve greater comparability with the accounting practices of most industrial concerns. This change in accounting principle increased 19X9 net income for credits earned during the year by approximately $15 million or $0.09 per share. In addition, the cumulative effect for the period through December 31, 19X8 amounted to $44 million or $0.28 per share in the income statement under "Cumulative effect on prior years of a change in accounting principle."

Note 3.   Supplemental Cost Information

(in Millions)	19X9	19X8	19X7
Advertising and marketing	$ 90	97	109
Research and development	1,057	1,104	1,133
Maintenace and repairs	47	54	75

Note 4.   Other Income

For 19X9, other income includes a gain on the disposal of solar energy operations of $181 million and a $107 million and a gain on the sale of various other properties.

Note 5. Inventories

The classification of inventories at December 31 follows:

(in Millions)	19X9	19X8
Raw materials	526.9	777.9
Work-in-progress	660.5	947.3
Finished Goods	649.6	636.8
Total	1,837.0	2,362.0

Cost of sales has been reduced and operating income increased by $140 mllion in 19X9 and $152 million in 19X8 as a result of liquidations of LIFO inventories.

Earnings for 19X9 include pretax charges of $8.7 million to write down the value of merchandise inventory. These changes have been included in 19X9 cost of goods sold.

Note 6. Investment in Unconsolidated Subsidiaries

The following financial data summarizes the corporation's share in equity method entities.

Income data-year	19X9	19X8
Net sales	$3,050	$1,650
Gross profit	845	481
Net income	61	33
Dividends received	0	0

Note 7. Extinguishment of Debt

In 19X9, the Corporation extinguished $350 million principal amount of debt through an in-substance defeasance resulting in a net extraordinary gain of $49 million, after income tax of $37 million.

Note 8. Unusual Items

The following item resulted in an unfavorable effect on net income in 19X9.

(In millions)	
Revaluation of assets	($15)

Note 9. Pension and Other Retirement Benefit Plans

The Company has pension plans covering substantially all employees. During 19X9, the Corporation increased the actuarially assumed rate of return used to determine the present value of benefits for these plan participants to reflect more current expectations of future economic conditions. This had the net effect of reducing 19X9 pension expense approximately $47 million.

Information on the pension plan's accumulated benefits and net assets at the end of the year is as follows:

	19X9	19X8
Actual present value of accumulated plan		
Benefits		
Vested	$7,168	$6,167
Nonvested	404	397
	$7,572	$6,564
Market value of net assets available for benefits	$9,874	$7,273

The interest rates used in determining the actuarial present value were 10.7% in 19X9 and 9.3% in 19X8.

Note 10. Goodwill

Goodwill on the Balance Sheet resulted from the excess purchase price over the net tangible assets of a business acquired during 19X9. This amount, net of amortization, was $52 million as of year end 19X9. Amortization is recorded over a forty year period using the straight-line method.

Qualico Products, Inc.
Management Discussion and Analysis
(Partial)

Net Sales in 19X9 increased 2 % over those for 19X8. The increase was due to increased volume.

Other information	19X9	19X8
Average Consumer Price Index	343.4	329.4

Appendix B

The Analysis of Segmental Data

Diversified companies that operate in different industries are required by the provisions of Financial Accounting Standards Board Statement No. 14, "Financial Reporting for Segments of a Business Enterprise," to disclose supplementary financial data for each reportable segment. FASB Statement No. 14 also covers reporting requirements for foreign operations, export sales, and sales to major customers. Segmental disclosures are valuable to the financial analyst in identifying areas of strength and weakness within a company; proportionate contribution to revenue and profit by each division; the relationship between capital expenditures and rates of return for operating areas; and segments that should be de-emphasized or eliminated. The information on segments is presented as a supplementary section in the notes to the financial statements, as part of the basic financial statements, or in a separate schedule that is referenced to and incorporated into the financial statements.

An *industry segment* is defined by FASB Statement No. 14 as a component of a business enterprise that sells primarily to outside markets and for which information about revenue and profit is accumulated. *Segment revenue* includes sales of products and services to unaffiliated customers and intersegment sales, with company transfer prices used to determine sales between segments. *Operating profit or* loss is segment revenue less all operating expenses. *Segment operating expense* includes expenses relating to unaffiliated customers and segment revenue; expenses not directly traceable to segments are allocated to segments on a reasonable basis. Operating expenses exclude general corporate revenue and expenses, income taxes, extraordinary items, and interest expense. *Identifiable assets* are tangible and intangible assets associated with or used by a segment and include an allocated portion of jointly used assets.

A segment is considered to be reportable if any one of three criteria is met:

Revenue is 10% or more of combined revenue, including intersegment revenue.

Operating profit or loss is 10% or more of the greater of combined profit of all segments with profit or combined loss of all segments with loss.

Identifiable assets exceed 10% or more of combined identifiable assets of all segments.

The following information is to be presented for each reportable segment and in the aggregate for remaining segments not reported separately:

Segment revenue.
Operating profit (loss).
Carrying amount of identifiable assets.
Aggregate depreciation, depletion, and amortization.
Capital expenditures.

EXHIBIT B.1 Multico Incorporated
Revenue and Operating Profit by
Product Category (Continuing Operations)
(in thousands of dollars)

	19X9	19X8	19X7
Revenue			
Automated Process Equipment	$ 114,805	$113,160	$ 137,377
Electronic Controls and Systems	165,132	189,390	191,448
Energy Services and Products	286,223	306,704	200,521
Speciality Materials	69,937	82,048	74,356
Total Industrial Technology	636,097	691,302	603,702
Bowling Products	155,577	158,610	145,426
Marine Products	64,755	88,967	69,452
Sports Products	197,789	212,925	231,202
Total Leisure Products	418,121	460,502	446,080
Total Revenue	$1,054,218	$1,151,804	$1,049,782
Operating Profit			
Automated Process Equipment	$ 14,569	$ 18,680	$ 20,399
Electronic Controls and Systems	10,655	15,435	16,341
Energy Services and Products	40,166	63,181	39,699
Specialty Materials	6,913	16,553	13,703
Total Industrial Technology	72,303	113,849	90,142
Bowling Products	39,042	44,699	42,460
Marine Products	(4,737)	4,784	2,478
Sports Products	8,678	18,703	16,328
Total Leisure Products	42,984	68,186	61,266
Product Category Totals	115,587	182,035	151,408
Corporate Expenses	(59,889)	(65,882)	(69,347)
Income Before Income Taxes	$ 55,398	$ 116,153	$ 82,061

Sales between product categories are insignificant and have been eliminated in arriving at total revenue.
Operating profit is total revenue less cost of sales and expenses (excluding corporate expenses) plus interest and other income to the extent specifically related to product categories.

EXHIBIT B.2 Multico Incorporated
Product Categories
Assets, Depreciation & Capital Expenditures
(in thousands of dollars)

The Company's operations are included in seven principal product categories. Automated process Equipment includes labor saving machinery for industrial use by the apparel, bakery, food, food service, tire and tobacco industries. Electronic Contols and Systems include relays, switches, timing devices, controls, control systems, circuit breakers and motors. Energy Services and Products are electronic inspection and coating services for oil field tubulars, directional drilling instruments and services, and instruments to obtain seismic data, while Specialty Materials include liquid fiftration, and medical diagnostic products. Bowling Products include automatic pinspotters and scoring systems, lanes, bowling balls, pins, bags, and shoes, while Marine Products include yachts and sailboats. Sports Products include sporting goods equipment used for golf, tennis and other racquet sports, snow skiing and various team sports.

	Identifiable Assets			Depreciation & Amortization			Capital Expenditures		
	19X9	19X8	19X7	**19X9**	19X8	19X7	**19X9**	19X8	19X7
Automated Process Equipment	**$ 57,076**	$ 63,635	$ 82,439	**$ 3,540**	$ 3,616	$ 3,358	**$ 5,556**	$ 3,899	$ 3,509
Electronic Controls & Systems	**84,802**	96,476	98,899	**5,795**	5,187	4,099	**8,343**	7,683	10,010
Energy Services & Products	**286,450**	255,690	148,359	**24,686**	17,120	11,869	**84,060**	83,531	41,554
Specialty Materials	**52,777**	55,025	50,434	**3,102**	2,834	2,458	**3,702**	6,495	6,832
Total Industrial Technology	**481,105**	470,826	380,131	**37,123**	28,757	21,784	**101,661**	101,608	61,905
Bowling Products	**150,357**	168,046	170,354	**5,333**	6,111	6,795	**7,724**	7,181	7,310
Marine Products	**41,678**	41,528	38,009	**2,234**	2,201	1,849	**4,211**	2,902	3,936
Sports Products	**123,059**	124,438	135,583	**4,985**	4,952	5,028	**5,971**	6,583	6,507
Total Leisure Products	**315,094**	334,012	343,946	**12,552**	13,264	13,672	**17,906**	16,666	17,753
Product Category Totals	**796,199**	804,838	724,077	**49,675**	42,021	35,456	**119,567**	118,274	79,658
Corporate amounts	**93,870**	86,706	69,492	**1,568**	2,283	1,768	**1,176**	1,052	671
Total Continuing Operations	**890,069**	891,544	793,569	**$51,243**	$44,304	$37,224	**$120,743**	$119,326	$80,329
Net Assets of Discontinued Operations	**—**	39,827	136,470						
Total Assets	**$890,069**	$931,371	$930,039						

Identifiable assets include both assets directly related to product categories and an allocable share of jointly used assests. Corporate assets consist primarily of cash and short term investments, future income tax benefits and corporate administrative facilities. Capital expenditures include additions to machines leased to customers.

Exhibits B.1 and B.2 illustrate the segmental disclosures for Multico Incorporated from the 19X9 annual report. Multico has seven reportable segments: Automated Process Equipment, Electronic Controls and Systems, Energy Services and Products, Specialty Materials, Bowling Products, Marine Products, and Sports Products. Segmental reporting does not include complete financial statements, but it is feasible to perform an analysis of the key financial data presented.

Refer first to Exhibit B.1. 19X9 has been a generally poor year for Multico with total revenue declining by 8 % and operating profit by 52 percent. Revenue decreased for every segment except Automated Process Equipment.   Profit was lower in 19X9 for all seven segments.

In order to analyze the performance for each segment, six tables have been prepared from computations based on the figures provided in Exhibits B.1 and B.2.   Table B.1 shows the percentage contribution to total revenue by segment.

TABLE B.1

	(Percentages)		
	19X9	19X8	19X7
Contribution by Segment to Revenue			
Automated Process Equipment	10.89	9.83	13.09
Electronic Controls Systems	15.66	16.44	18.24
Energy Services and Products	27.15	26.63	19.10
Speciality Materials	6.64	7.12	7.08
Bowling Products	14.76	13.77	13.85
Marine Products	6.14	7.72	6.62
Sports Products	18.76	18.49	22.02
Total Revenue	100%	100%	100%

Note the change in trends over the three-year period.   In 19X7 the major producer of revenue was Sports Products; by 19X9 Energy Services and Products was clearly dominant, increasing revenue share from 19 to 27%. Energy Services and Products are operations related to oil field service activities, while Sports Products include sporting goods equipment used for golf, racquet sports, snow skiing, and team sports.   Electronic Controls and Equipment remains the third largest contributor to revenue at 15.7%. Bowling products generated 14.8% of Multico's total revenue in 19X9, followed by Automated Process Equipment (industrial machinery), Specialty Materials (liquid filtration and medical diagnostic products) and Marine Products (yachts and sailboats).

TABLE B.2

	(Percentages)		
	19X9	19X8	19X7
Contribution by Segment to Operating Income			
Automated Process Equipment	12.64	10.26	13.47
Electronic Controls and Systems	9.24	8.48	10.79
Energy Services and Products	34.84	34.71	26.22
Specialty Materials	5.99	9.09	9.05
Bowling Products	33.87	24.56	28.04
Marine Products	(4.11)	2.63	1.64
Sports Products	7.53	10.27	10.79
Total Operating Profit	100%	100%	100%

TABLE B.3

	(Percentages)		
	19X9	*19X8*	*19X7*
Operating Profit Margin by Segment			
Automated Process Equipment	12.69	16.51	14.85
Electronic Controls and Systems	6.45	8.15	8.54
Energy Services and Products	14.03	20.60	19.80
Specialty Materials	9.88	20.17	18.43
Bowling Products	25.10	28.18	29.20
Marine Products	(7.32)	5.38	3.57
Sports Products	4.39	8.78	7.06

Table B.2 reveals the contribution by segment to operating income and provides a basis for assessing the ability of a segment to translate revenue into profit. Energy Products and Services was the leading contributor to operating profit in 19X9 at 35%; Bowling Products was a very close second at 34% up from a 28 % share in 19X7. Sports Products, which was ranked second in terms of revenue in 19X9, fell behind in profit contribution, with a 7.5% share. Marine Products registered an operating loss.

Operating Profit Margin (operating profit divided by revenue) is presented for each segment in Table B.3. The operating profit margin shows the percentage of every sales dollar that is converted to (before-tax) profit. The profit margin is highest in 19X9 for Bowling Products, with Energy Services and Products second, and Automated Process Equipment third. Operating profit margins declined for all seven segments between 19X8 and 19X9 and were especially sharp for Specialty Materials and Marine Products.

TABLE B.4

	(Percentages)		
	19X9	*19X8*	*19X7*
Capital Expenditures by Segments			
Automated Process Equipment	4.65	3.30	4.40
Electronic Controls and Systems	6.98	6.50	12.56
Energy Services and Products	70.30	70.62	52.17
Specialty Materials	3.10	5.49	8.58
Bowling Products	6.46	6.07	9.18
Marine Products	3.52	2.45	4.94
Sports Products	4.99	5.57	8.17
Total Capital Expenditures	100%	100%	100%

TABLE B.5

	(Percentages)		
	19X9	*19X8*	*19X7*
Return on Investment by Segment			
Automated Process Equipment	25.53	29.35	24.74
Electronic Controls and Systems	12.56	16.00	16.52
Energy Services and Products	14.02	24.71	26.76
Specialty Materials	13.10	30.08	27.17
Bowling Products	25.97	26.60	24.92
Marine Products	(11.37)	11.52	6.52
Sports Products	7.05	15.03	12.04

Table B.4 is a percentage breakdown of capital expenditures by segment. It is obvious that the firm's management has elected to invest heavily in Energy Services and Products, with minimal expenditures elsewhere among the segments. Notice also in Exhibit B.2 that in 19X7 Bowling Products was the largest segment. By 19X9 Energy Services and Products had almost doubled in size and is now the dominant segment, with Bowling Products second and Sports Products third.

It is important to examine the relationship between investment and return, and this information is provided in Table B.5, which shows Return on Investment by segment (operating profit divided by identifiable assets). Bowling Products and Automated Process Equipment have consistently generated the highest returns. The return on assets fell sharply in 19X9 for Energy Services and Products, Specialty Materials, and Marine Products. While Energy contributes the highest percentage of operating profit at 35%, the deterioration of operating profit margin and return on investment are alarming developments. Clearly, the Marine Products division is in trouble, with negative returns in 19X9. This is an area in which the firm has been increasing investment. Management blamed softness in the boating industry for the decreased 19X9 revenue.

TABLE B.6

19X9	Percentage of Total Identifiable Assets	Percent Contribution to Operating Income	Operating Profit Margin	Return on Investment
Energy Services and Products	36.0	34.8	14.0	14.0
Bowling Products	18.9	33.9	25.1	26.0
Sports Products	15.5	7.5	4.4	7.1
Electronic Controls and Systems	10.6	9.2	6.5	12.6
Automated Process Equipment	7.2	12.6	12.7	25.5
Specialty Materials	6.6	6.0	9.9	13.1
Marine Products	5.2	(4.1)	(7.3)	(11.4)

Table B.6 compares a ranking of segments in 19X9 by identifiable assets with percentage contribution to operating income, operating profit margin, and return on investment. Overall, Bowling Products and Automated Process Equipment appear to be the strongest segments and have performed consistently well over the three-year period. Problem divisions are apparently Marine Products and to a lesser extent Sports Products. Given the large doses of capital investment in Energy and the recent decline in that segment's return ratios, it is another potential problem area.

SUMMARY

The analytical tools used to assess the segmental data of Multico are applicable to any company with segmental disclosures. Minor variations and/or additions to the tables prepared for Multico may be appropriate for a particular company, but the basic analysis should include, by segment and for at least a three-year period: (1) percentage contribution to revenue; (2) percentage contribution to operating income; (3) operating profit margin; (4) capital expenditures; (5) return on investment; and (6) an examination of the relationship between the size of a division and its relative contribution.

STUDY PROBLEM

B.1 Digital Instruments—Segmental Analysis. Digital Instruments (DI) as a whole has had increasing sales over the last four years, but decreasing profits. In 19X9, DI withdrew entirely from home computer products because of poor performance in this area.

The company is engaged in the development, manufacture, and sale of a variety of products in the electrical and electronics industry for industrial, consumer, and government markets. These products consist of components (semiconductors, such as integrated circuits, and electrical and electronic control devices); government electronics (such as radar, infrared surveillance systems and missile guidance and control systems); and digital products (such as minicomputers, professional personal computers, data terminals, industrial controls, electronic calculators, and learning aids).

The company also produces metallurgical materials (primarily clad metals) for use in a variety of applications such as automotive equipment, appliances, and telecommunications equipment, and provides services, primarily through the electronic collection and processing of seismic data in connection with petroleum exploration.

Industry segment profit is not equivalent to income before provision for income taxes due to exclusion of general corporate expenses, net interest, currency gains and losses, product phase-out, and employment reduction costs.

Identifiable assets are those associated with segment operations, excluding unallocated cash and short-term investments, internal company receivables, and tax related timing differences.

Required: Analyze each segment's performance based on contribution to sales, profit, and return on investment. Assess the capital expenditure strategy DI is using.

Net Sales Billed
(In millions)

	19X9	19X8	19X7	19X6
Components	$1,704	$1,349	$1,460	$1,767
Digital products	1,069	1,138	1,064	987
Government electronics	1,204	1,059	876	738
Metallurgical materials	152	136	146	138
Services	440	629	649	432
Total Net Sales Billed	$4,569	$4,311	$4,195	$4,062

Profit
(In millions)

	19X9	19X8	19X7	19X6
Components	$ 59	$ 34	$ 26	$263
Digital products	4	23	26	64
Government electronics	54	46	35	23
Metallurgical materials	20	12	19	27
Services	22	81	119	63
Income Before Provision for Income Taxes	$159	$196	$225	$440

Indentifiable Assets
(In millions)

	19X9	19X8	19X7	19X6
Components	$1,079	$918	$971	$1,113
Digital products	493	737	579	584
Government electronics	489	454	315	331
Metallurgical materials	93	85	92	92
Services	198	254	325	228
Total	$2,352	$2,448	$2,282	$2,348

Property, Plant and Equipment—Net Additions
(In millions)

	19X9	19X8	19X7	19X6
Components	$232	$140	$155	$300
Digital products	27	44	48	73
Governmental electronics	149	86	45	64
Metallurgical materials	10	4	10	18
Services	22	48	108	105
Total	$440	$322	$366	$560

Appendix C

Understanding Bank Financial Statements

Reading and interpreting the financial statements of commercial banking institutions[1] involves exposure to some financial statement accounts and analytical ratios that are different from those discussed in previous sections of this book. Banks generate profits, if they are successful, by earning more on their assets (loans and investments) than they pay in interest to depositors. Despite differences that result from the nature of a bank's operations, however, the underlying concepts of assessing a bank's financial condition and performance are essentially similar because—like their nonbank counterparts—banking institutions attempt to effectively manage the tradeoff between risk and return in order to improve the overall return on equity.

One major positive aspect about the evaluation of bank financial statements is that all insured commercial banking institutions in the U.S.—regardless of type and size of bank and whether or not the bank is privately held or publicly traded—prepare financial statements in a uniform reporting format, and this information is available to banks and to the general public on both a quarterly and an annual basis. Insured banks file required financial data on an established periodic basis with the appropriate regulatory authority: *Comptroller of the Currency* for national banks; *Federal Reserve Board* for state banks which are members of the Federal Reserve System; and the *Federal Deposit Insurance Corporation* for other state-chartered banks. The balance sheet and income statement for each bank are compiled and published in a standardized document that also includes financial ratios and other analytical data as well as peer group comparisons. This document, called the *Uniform Bank Performance Report,* is provided free to each banking

---

[1] For more information about this topic, see Donald R. Fraser and Lyn M. Fraser, *Evaluating Commercial Bank Performance, A Guide to Financial Analysis*, Bankers Publishing Company, Rolling Meadows, Illinois, 1990.

institution and can be purchased by other users for any insured commercial banks in the U.S. from the Federal Examinations Institution Council.[2]

The format and content of banking information provided in the *Uniform Bank Performance Report* forms the basis for the material presented here. Comparable data could also be developed from a bank's annual or 10-K report. Only the balance sheet and income statement are covered because they are the two statements presented in the report; the statement of cash flows is less important to the analysis of depository institutions, given the nature of there assets (loans and investments) and liabilities (deposits).

The chapter includes a discussion of the financial statements of Metrobank, a large urban bank. The reporting format is a condensed version of the statements presented in the *Uniform Bank Performance Reports*; the analytical ratios and peer group data are drawn from the report. The financial ratios and analytical approach used for Metrobank also apply to smaller banks and rural banks. Like the analysis of any business firm, however, the analyst needs to be aware of the characteristics of the bank in its particular operating environment, economic conditions, and and the issues—such as the quality of financial reporting and the need to consider intangible, unquantifiable information—that were discussed in Chapter 1.

The analyst should also be alert to any changes in accounting principles which affect banking institutions; for example FASB Statement No. 115 "Accounting for Certain Investments in Debt and Equity Securities" (discussed in Chapter 2) has major implications for the commercial banking industry because it requires banks to value many of their securities at current market prices, effective for fiscal years beginning after December 15, 1993. Specifically, the rule requires that trading securities—debt and equity securities held for current resale—be reported at fair value with unrealized gains and losses included in earnings. Securities classified as available for sale are also reported at fair value with unrealized gains and losses included as a separate component of stockholders' equity. Debt securities held to maturity continue to be reported at amortized cost. Banks also are affected by FASB Statement No. 107, which requires the disclosure of the fair value of financial instruments; and by FASB Statement No. 114, which requires banks to value impaired or troubled loans at current value.

BALANCE SHEET

The balance sheet for Metrobank, an urban bank in a peer group of banks with total assets in excess of ten billion dollars, is presented in Exhibit C.1.

---

[2] For ordering information, contact the FDIC Disclosure Group, UBPR, Department 4320, Chicago, IL 60673.

EXHIBIT C.1 Metrobank Balance Sheet*
Assets, Liabilities, and Capital ($Millions) at December 31,

	19X9	19X8
Assets		
Loans		
Real Estate	1,248	1,382
Commercial	3,244	4,088
Individual	489	270
Agricultural	40	50
Other Domestic Loans and Leases	271	493
Foreign Loans and Leases	683	622
Gross Loans and Leases	5,975	6,905
Less: Unearned Income	30	36
Loans and Leases Allowance	258	265
Net Loans and Leases	5,687	6,603
U.S. Treasury, Agency Securities	892	844
Municipal Securities	455	494
Other Securities	510	1,034
Fed Funds Sold	1,905	911
Trading Account Assets	25	3
Total Investments	3,789	3,387
Total Earning Assets	9,477	9,990
Cash Due from Banks	987	977
Premises, Fixed Assets	289	297
Other Real Estate Owned	135	134
Other Assets	265	239
Total Assets	11,154	11,638
Average Assets	11,675	11,509
Liabilities and Capital		
Demand Deposits	1,960	2,055
Now and ATS	394	350
MMDA, Other Savings	1,126	946
Nonbrokered Time < $100M	775	707
Core Deposits	4,255	4,057
Brokered Deposits	87	94
Nonbrokered Time > $100M	1,141	1,435
Foreign Deposits	892	930
Total Deposits	6,374	6,517
Fed Funds, Other Borrowings	3,834	4,235
Volatile Liabilities	5,954	6,694
Other Liabilities	256	229
Total Liabilities	10,464	10,980
Subordinated Notes, Debentures	35	35
Common and Preferred Capital	655	623
Total Liabilities and Capital	11,154	11,638

*Totals may not add due to rounding.

Assets

For most banks, loans are the largest asset category and would be the counterpart to inventory and accounts receivable for a retail firm. Loans are listed by type—real estate, commercial, individual, and agricultural. This section also includes leases because lease arrangements sometimes substitute for direct lending. From gross loans and leases, deductions are made for unearned income and the allowance account. Unearned income is income—for example, the amount deducted from a discounted note—that will be recognized on the income statement over the life of a loan. The loan and lease allowance account is comparable to a nonbank business firm's allowance for doubtful accounts but is generally much more significant for banks because loan losses are the major source of risk and loss at banking institutions. The adequacy of this account is directly relevant to any assessment of bank risk. Bank management, with certain guidelines from the regulatory authorities, estimates an amount for uncollectible loans and leases; losses are charged against this account, while any recoveries are added to it. This allowance account is counted as primary capital in meeting a bank's capital requirement for regulation.

Investments for banks consist primarily of debt securities because banks are generally prohibited from investing in equity securities. These investments consist of U.S. government securities, municipal (states and political subdivisions) securities, interest-bearing balances due from banks, federal funds (interbank loans of cash reserves), and trading account assets (securities that banks hold for resale and for underwriting municipal issues).

Net loans and leases and total investments together comprise a bank's earning assets.

The remaining assets include cash (currency and coin) and non-interest balances due from other depository institutions; premises, furniture, fixtures, and any other long-lived assets (net of depreciation); and other real estate, such as foreclosed property from problem loans.

In addition to total assets, a figure for average assets is provided in the report.

Liabilities

The major liabilities for banks are different types of deposit accounts which are used to fund lending and investing. These accounts vary according to interest-payment, maturity, check-writing, and insurability. A differentiation is made between core deposits, which are not highly sensitive to changes in interest rates and are expected to be relatively stable in amount over time; and volatile liabilities, which fluctuate in both volume and interest rate sensitivity. Volatile liabilities include brokered deposits (deposits sold through brokers on which banks pay a commission); large certificates of deposit that sell in an established, secondary market; foreign deposits, and federal funds purchased.

Capital

Subordinated notes and debentures, actually debt, are counted as capital because this type of long-term debt, with claims subordinated to the claims of depositors, have the maturity and permanence of capital and can qualify as capital in meeting regulatory requirements. One weakness of the *Uniform Bank Performance Report* is that the remaining capital accounts (common and preferred stock, additional paid-in capital, retained earnings, and other categories) are lumped together as one reported item, making it difficult to trace changes in the capital account from period to period. The income statement shows the amount of cash dividends declared and the change in the retained earnings account for the period.

INCOME STATEMENT

Exhibit C.2 shows the income statement for Metrobank for the three years ending December 31, 19X9. (*The Uniform Bank Performance Report* always provides five periods of data, and this longer period will be used for the analysis of Metrobank.)

EXHIBIT C.2 Metrobank Income Statement
Revenue and Expenses ($ Millions) at December 31

	19X9	19X8	19X7
Interest income:			
Income on loans & leases (TE)	590.4	550.4	574.5
Income on investments (TE)	154.4	149.6	144.5
Other interest income	269.4	134.4	162.0
Total interest income (TE)	1,014.2	834.4	881.1
Interest expense:			
Foreign deposits	60.3	74.3	67.2
CDs over $100M	117.8	102.4	114.0
Other deposits	143.8	124.4	121.0
Fed funds	396.6	237.6	271.2
Total interest expense	754.0	577.6	608.2
Net interest expense (TE)	260.2	256.8	272.8
Non-interest income	173.6	134.6	143.9
Adjusted operating income (TE)	433.8	391.4	416.7
Overhead expenses	285.6	245.0	262.9
Provision loan/lease loss	51.0	59.0	61.0
Pretax operating income (TE)	97.2	87.4	92.8
Securities gains/losses	15.6	1.9	1.4
Pretax net operating income	112.8	89.3	94.2
Income taxes (TE)	38.8	30.8	31.9
Net operating income	74.0	58.5	62.3
Net extraordinary items	0	0	0
Net income	74.0	58.5	62.3
Cash dividends declared	26.0	70.0	60.0
Retained earnings	48.0	−11.5	2.3
Memo: Net int'l income	10.0	3.8	5.9

Because loans are the largest category of assets for most banks, interest on loans is the major source of income. The reader will notice the designation "TE" next to the figure for "income for loans and leases" and other amounts on the income statement. Some bank income, for example interest on loans and investments relating to state and political subdivisions, is tax-exempt. A tax benefit is estimated, using a prescribed formula, and added to income in order to improve the comparability of interest income among banks.

Income on securities is the next revenue item, followed by other interest income—which includes interest on balances due from banks, income on federal funds, and income on assets held in trading accounts.

The various categories of interest expense reflect interest paid on designated types of liabilities—foreign deposits, large negotiable certificates of deposit, other deposits, fed funds, and other borrowings.

Net interest income is the difference between total interest income and total interest expense.

Non-interest income includes trust activities, service charges, gains/losses on trading account activities, and foreign transactions.

Other expenses are those for overhead (salaries and employee benefits, expenses of premises) and the provision for loan and lease losses.

Any gains or losses on the sale, exchange, redemption, or retirement of securities (other than trading account assets) are shown as a separate category on the income statement because they are not considered a part of normal banking operations.

Applicable income tax, includes the total estimated federal, state, local, and foreign income taxes on income.

The remainder of the income statement shows net income, cash dividends declared, the change in retained earnings for the period, and net international income (included as a memo item).

ANALYSIS

The reader should be aware that there are many more analytical tools available in *Uniform Bank Performance Report* and in banking textbooks than are covered in this appendix. An attempt has been made to select eighteen financial ratios that will be useful in evaluating the financial condition and performance of any commercial banking institution, with the understanding that other analytical information can be drawn upon to provide depth and detail in particular circumstances.   To the extent possible, the ratios selected are compatible with those used in Chapter 5 for nonbank business firms.

The reader should also be aware that there is no set of analytical tools that will accurately predict a bank's success or failure.   These ratios should be used in conjunction with the absolute dollar amounts shown in the financial statements as well as with considerable common sense and critical judgment.

Following a brief description of the financial ratios, a five year analysis of Metrobank is provided.   As the result of rounding in the financial data presented, the actual ratio calculations in the *Uniform Bank Performance Report* are somewhat different from those that would be calculated from the numbers on the Metrobank balance sheet and income statement.

Exhibit C.3 shows the eighteen financial ratios, based on the calculations as they are made in the Report, for Metrobank over the five year period, 19X5 to 19X9.   Comparable peer group averages, also from the Report, are presented for 19X9.

EXHIBIT C.3 Metrobank Financial Ratios

	19X9	19X8	19X7	19X6	19X5	Peer X9
Summary						
1 Net income/equity (ROE)	11.51	9.36	9.95	−12.4	8.14	18.5
2 Net income/avg assets (ROA)	.63	.51	.55	−.70	.49	.91
3 Equity capital/assets	5.87	5.36	5.42	5.63	5.48	5.40
Profitability						
Percent of average assets:						
4 Interest income	8.61	7.29	7.71	7.50	7.81	9.48
5 Interest expense	6.40	5.05	5.33	5.13	5.60	6.43
6 Net interest income	2.21	2.24	2.39	2.36	2.21	3.21
7 Non-interest income	1.47	1.18	1.26	1.00	.084	1.69
8 Overhead expense	2.43	2.14	2.30	2.81	2.46	3.05
9 Provision loan and lease loss	0.43	0.52	0.53	1.24	1.12	0.56
Risk						
10 Growth rate—assets	−4.16	5.95	4.36	−2.99	−1.00	4.47
11 Growth rate—capital	3.53	1.42	1.58	6.99	8.81	4.61
12 Cash dividends/net income	35.14	119.55	99.37	NA	39.71	40.70
13 Net loss/tot loans and leases	1.02	.42	.75	.82	1.15	.86
14 Earnings coverage net loss (X)	2.09	4.30	2.67	.73	1.61	3.46
15 Loss reserve/tot loans and leases	4.33	3.86	4.30	3.53	2.63	2.72
16 Temporary invest/volatile liab.	45.64	32.49	41.36	77.30	20.42	30.52
17 Net loans and leases/assets	50.99	56.74	50.12	61.26	61.00	60.41
18 Interest rate gap	−7.66					6.50

Summary Ratios

1. Net income/equity is return on equity (ROE), an overall measure of the bank's ability to generate return to its shareholders.

2. Net income/average assets is return on investment (ROI) or return on assets (ROA), revealing the bank's effectiveness in earning a profit from its lending, investing, and other income-generating activities.

3. Equity capital/assets is a summary measure of bank risk. The higher the proportion of capital relative to assets, the less is overall risk. Keep in mind that risk, in and of itself, is not necessarily bad and, in fact, can multiply overall return to shareholders, as discussed in Chapter 5. The objective of bank management is to manage risk effectively.

Profitability

4. Interest income/average assets,

5. Interest expense/ average assets,

6. Net interest income/average assets,

7. Non-interest income/average assets,

8. Overhead expense/average assets, and

9. Provision for loan and lease loss/average assets

are ratios that consider the proportion of a bank's major categories of revenue and expense relative to a common denominator.   They provide perspective on specific sources of revenue and expense over time and in comparison with the bank's peer group.

Risk

10. Growth rate of assets,

11. Growth rate of primary capital, and

12. Cash dividends/net operating income

help assess the relationship between assets and equity.   In general, the higher the proportion of assets relative to capital, the greater is a bank's risk.   Because of the importance of this relationship between assets and capital, it is helpful to compare the growth rate of assets and capital[3] over time.   If a bank's assets are growing rapidly, there is potential that growth may be coming from the extension of riskier loans.   Since core deposits generally increase at steady rates, volatile liabilities likely provide the funding sources for this asset growth, thus adding risk.   This increased risk is moderated by a comparable growth in capital.

The relationship between dividends and income provides information about how much capital will remain for the bank's internal growth; the higher the dividend payout, the lower is the potential for internal capital growth.

13. Net loss/total loans and leases,

14. Earnings coverage of net loss (expressed in "times"), and

15. Loss Reserves/total loans and leases

are all elements of credit risk.   Loan losses are a major cause of bank failures, underscoring the importance of assessing credit risk.

The net loss is gross loan and lease charge-offs, less gross recoveries.   Looking at net loss relative to total loans and leases shows the proportion of a bank's loan-lease portfolio that has been written off during the period.

Earnings coverage of net loss is a measure of the bank's ability to cover its loan losses from operating income.

Loss reserve relative to loans and leases considers the adequacy of the provision for potential losses.

---

[3] *The Uniform Bank Performance Report* uses primary capital, which includes common equity, the loan and lease loss reserve, permanent and convertible preferred stock, qualifying mandatory convertible debt and minority interest in consolidated subsidiaries, less intangible assets.

16. Temporary investments/volatile liabilities, and

17. Net loans and leases/assets

are measures of liquidity. Temporary investments include fed funds sold, trading account assets, short-term investment securities, and due from banks. Volatile liabilities are brokered deposits, large negotiable certificates of deposit, foreign deposits, and fed funds purchased and resold; these are funds that could "dry up" very quickly. The ratio thus looks at the relationship between the most liquid assets and the least stable liabilities; the higher this ratio, the greater is a bank's liquidity.

Since loans and leases hold the greatest potential for bank losses, their proportion relative to assets helps assess the degree of liquidity in the asset base (keep in mind that loans are also the primary source of bank profitability).

18. The interest rate gap

is a commonly used measure of interest rate risk, that indicates the effect on bank profitability of changes in interest rates. Banks earn interest on loans and investments; they pay interest to depositors. When interest rates change, there may be an effect on income if a bank holds rate-sensitive assets and liabilities. If, for example, a bank holds more rate-sensitive assets than liabilities when interest rates rise, profits will be improved because the bank will receive more in increased interest revenue than it will pay out in rising costs. The reverse is be true during a period of falling interest rates. The interest rate gap is the difference between rate-sensitive assets and liabilities; holding more rate-sensitive assets than liabilities is called a *positive gap,* and an excess of rate-sensitive liabilities over assets results in a *negative gap.*[4]

METROBANK

Exhibit C.3 presents a five-year summary of the eighteen ratios and a peer group comparison for all insured commercial banks having assets in excess of ten billion dollars.

Suggestion to the Reader: Before reading the remainder of the Appendix, look at the balance sheet (Exhibit C.1), income statement (Exhibit C.2), and financial ratios/peer group comparisons (Exhibit C.3) for Metrobank. Make a note of any significant trends in the figures presented and attempt to explain those trends. List Metrobank's strengths and weaknesses. Compare your analysis with the one provided here.

Analysis

Looking first at the three summary ratios, it appears that Metrobank, while still far below its peer group, has improved overall performance—both over the five-year period and in the most recent year—as measured by the return on equity and return on assets.

---

[4] The interest rate gap is estimated from data in the Uniform Bank Performance Report using the section on "Maturity and Repricing Distribution." The calculation is made by deducting the percent of interest bearing liabilities repriced within three months from the percent of interest bearing assets repriced within the last three months.

Metrobank accomplished the improvement in ROE while simultaneously reducing its overall level of risk, as indicated by the increase in equity/assets. This means that profitability has increased by relatively more than the reduction in risk. (See discussion of the leverage multiplier in Chapter 5.)

The gains in profitability are *not* the result of improvement in net interest income. Although interest income relative to average assets has risen, interest expense has risen more rapidly. 19X9 was a year of increasing interest rates in the economy. The interest rate gap (shown as the last ratio in Exhibit C.3) is negative for Metrobank, which means that the bank has more interest-rate sensitive liabilities than assets. A negative gap impairs profitability during a period of rising interest rates, and this was the case for Metrobank.

Metrobank accomplished its overall gains partly through an increase in non-interest income. For many banks, these traditionally less significant income sources—such as trust activities, various types of service charges, and trading account profits or losses—have become increasingly important during the era of deregulation. Banks have sought new sources of income as competition has increased pricing pressures on interest earning assets and liabilities. Apparently Metrobank is benefiting from such activities.

Another reason for the overall improvement in net income is a $15.6 million gain from securities transactions (see income statement). The analyst should bear in mind that this is a fluctuating source of income and is not part of normal banking operations.

Considering the various measures of risk, Metrobank has decreased its asset base (caused by a reduction in all categories of loans except loans to individuals), while accomplishing internal capital growth as the result of a reduction in the dividend payout ratio. Note that in 19X8 Metrobank paid more in dividends than it generated in income. The ratio in 19X7 was close to 100%, and the ratio in 19X6 does not compute because the bank reported a loss. The 19X9 dividend policy appears to be much more sensible from the standpoint of capital risk.

Credit risk measures indicate an increase in loan and lease losses relative to the loan-lease base and a reduction in earnings coverage of loan losses. The bank shows improvement in the loss allowance relative to the loan-lease base because gross loans and leases have decreased by more than the loan and lease loss allowance. Metrobank has reduced the provision for loan lease/average assets at a time when loan losses have increased. Credit risk appears to be a potential problem for Metrobank. From the information presented it is difficult to assess why the bank is experiencing the increased losses, but it is certainly an issue that warrants further scrutiny by the analyst. *The Uniform Bank Performance Report* shows net losses by type of loan. From this information (not presented here) it is evident that the major source of the losses is real estate loans, which may continue to be a problem for Metrobank since real estate loans comprise over 20% of the loan portfolio.

The bank appears to be improving its liquidity. Temporary investments/volatile liabilities have increased and are well above the peer group. The proportion of loans and leases to assets has declined and is substantially below the peer group. Given the problems associated with credit risk, this trend is probably a positive one.

The strengths for Metrobank are improved profitability, the reduction of overall risk achieved largely through internal capital growth, and improved liquidity.

The bank's weaknesses are credit risk, evidenced by problems with loan-lease losses; a negative interest rate gap in a period of increasing interest rates; and the fact that much of the improvement in income production was the result of securities gains, a potentially nonrecurring activity.

Appendix D

Solutions to Self-Tests

Chapter 1

1. (d)	**8.** (d)	**15.** (a)	(5) b
2. (d)	**9.** (c)	**16.** (c)	(6) a
3. (d)	**10.** (b)	**17.** (d)	(7) d
4. (b)	**11.** (c)	**18.** (1) c	(8) b
5. (a)	**12.** (b)	(2) b	(9) d
6. (d)	**13.** (c)	(3) a	(10) a
7. (b)	**14.** (d)	(4) c	

Chapter 2

1. (b)	**16.** (a)	(i) NC	(n) 6
2. (a)	**17.** (c)	(j) NC	(o) 8
3. (b)	**18.** (b)	**24.** (a) 4	**25.** (a) 7
4. (c)	**19.** (b)	(b) 5	(b) 1
5. (b)	**20.** (d)	(c) 8	(c) 5
6. (a)	**21.** (d)	(d) 7	(d) 9
7. (d)	**22.** (c)	(e) 1	(e) 4
8. (c)	**23.** (a) NC	(f) 2	(f) 6
9. (b)	(b) C	(g) 2	(g) 10
10. (c)	(c) C	(h) 5	(h) 2
11. (d)	(d) C	(i) 8	(i) 3
12. (a)	(e) NC	(j) 5	(j) 8
13. (c)	(f) C	(k) 3	
14. (b)	(g) C	(l) 2	
15. (d)	(h) C	(m) 1	

Chapter 3

1. (c)	**12.** (a)	(e) 5	(2) d
2. (b)	**13.** (a)	(f) 14	(3) a
3. (a)	**14.** (c)	(g) 1	(4) c
4. (c)	**15.** (d)	(h) 6	(5) d
5. (d)	**16.** (c)	(i) 11	(6) a
6. (a)	**17.** (b)	(j) 2	(7) e
7. (c)	**18.** (a)	(k) 10	(8) c
8. (d)	**19.** (a) 4	(l) 12	(9) c
9. (d)	(b) 9	(m) 3	(10) b
10. (b)	(c) 13	(n) 7	(11) d
11. (b)	(d) 8	**20.** (1) c	(12) c

Chapter 4

1. (d)	**10.** (b)	**19.** (b)	**28.** A
2. (a)	**11.** (b)	**20.** (d)	**29.** A
3. (b)	**12.** (c)	**21.** (c)	**30.** S
4. (a)	**13.** (a)	**22.** (b)	**31.** (a)
5. (c)	**14.** (d)	**23.** A	**32.** (b)
6. (d)	**15.** (d)	**24.** S	**33.** (a)
7. (b)	**16.** (c)	**25.** S	**34.** (d)
8. (c)	**17.** (d)	**26.** A	
9. (c)	**18.** (d)	**27.** S	

Chapter 5

1. (c)	**16.** (d)	(d) 21	(s) 9
2. (a)	**17.** (c)	(e) 10	(t) 7
3. (d)	**18.** (d)	(f) 2	(u) 11
4. (c)	**19.** (a)	(g) 12	(v) 16
5. (b)	**20.** (b)	(h) 3	(w) 23
6. (d)	**21.** (c)	(i) 15	**29.** (c)
7. (a)	**22.** (a)	(j) 19	**30.** (a)
8. (b)	**23.** (c)	(k) 4	**31.** (c)
9. (d)	**24.** (b)	(l) 18	**32.** (b)
10. (c)	**25.** (d)	(m) 14	**33.** (d)
11. (a)	**26.** (b)	(n) 13	**34.** (a)
12. (c)	**27.** (a)	(o) 5	**35.** (c)
13. (d)	**28.** (a) 6	(p) 22	**36.** (a)
14. (b)	(b) 17	(q) 8	
15. (a)	(c) 1	(r) 20	

Appendix E

Summary of Financial Ratios

Ratio	Method of Computation	Significance
Current	$$\frac{\text{Current assets}}{\text{Current liabilities}}$$	Measures short-term liquidity, the ability of a firm to meet needs for cash as they arise.
Quick or Acid-test	$$\frac{\text{Current assets - inventory}}{\text{Current liabilities}}$$	Measures short-term liquidity more rigorously than the current ratio by eliminating inventory, usually the least liquid current asset.
Cash-flow liquidity	$$\frac{\text{Cash + marketable securities + cash flow from operating activities}}{\text{Current liabilities}}$$	Measures short-term liquidity by considering as cash resources (numerator) cash plus cash equivalents plus cash flow from operating activities.
Average collection period	$$\frac{\text{Accounts receivable}}{\text{Net sales/ 360}}$$	Indicates days required to convert receivables into cash.

Accounts receivable turnover	$$\frac{\text{Net sales}}{\text{Accounts receivable}}$$	Indicates how many times receivables are collected during a year, on average.
Inventory turnover	$$\frac{\text{Cost of goods sold}}{\text{Inventories}}$$	Measures efficiency of the firm in managing and selling inventory.
Fixed asset turnover	$$\frac{\text{Net sales}}{\text{Net property, plant, and equipment}}$$	Measures efficiency of the firm in managing fixed assets.
Total asset turnover	$$\frac{\text{Net sales}}{\text{Total assets}}$$	Measures efficiency of the firm in managing all assets.
Debt ratio	$$\frac{\text{Total liabilities}}{\text{Total assets}}$$	Shows proportion of all assets that are financed with debt.
Long-term debt to total capitalization	$$\frac{\text{Long-term debt}}{\text{Long-term debt} + \text{stockholders' equity}}$$	Measures the extent to which long-term debt is used for permanent financing.
Debt to equity	$$\frac{\text{Total liabilities}}{\text{Stockholders' equity}}$$	Measure debt relative to equity base.
Times interest earned	$$\frac{\text{Operating profit}}{\text{Interest expense}}$$	Measures how many times interest expense is covered by operating earnings.
Fixed charge coverage	$$\frac{\text{Operating profit} + \text{lease payments}}{\text{Interest expense} + \text{Lease payments}}$$	Measures coverage capability more broadly than times interest earned by including lease payments as a fixed expense.
Gross profit margin	$$\frac{\text{Gross profit}}{\text{Net sales}}$$	Measures profit generated after consideration of cost of products sold.
Operating profit margin	$$\frac{\text{Operating profit}}{\text{Net sales}}$$	Measures profit generated after consideration of operating expenses.
Net profit margin	$$\frac{\text{Net profit}}{\text{Net sales}}$$	Measures profit generated after consideration of all expenses and revenues.
Cash-flow margin	$$\frac{\text{Cash flow from operating activities}}{\text{Net sales}}$$	Measures the ability of the firm to generate cash from sales.
Return on investment	$$\frac{\text{Net earnings}}{\text{Total assets}}$$	Measures overall efficiency of firm in managing assets and generating profits.

Return on equity	$\dfrac{\text{Net earnings}}{\text{Stockholders' equity}}$	Measures rate of return on stockholders' (owners') investment.
Earnings per common share	$\dfrac{\text{Net earnings}}{\text{Average common shares outstanding}}$	Shows return to common stock shareholder for each share owned.
Price to earnings	$\dfrac{\text{Market price of common stock}}{\text{Earnings per share}}$	Expresses a multiple that the stock market places on a firm's earnings.
Dividend payout	$\dfrac{\text{Dividends per share}}{\text{Earnings per share}}$	Shows percentage of earnings paid to shareholders.
Dividend yield	$\dfrac{\text{Dividends per share}}{\text{Market price of common stock}}$	Shows the rate earned by shareholders from dividends relative to current price of stock.

Appendix F

Glossary

Accelerated Cost Recovery System: The system established by the Economic Recovery Tax Act of 1981 to simplify depreciation methods for tax purposes and to encourage investment in capital by allowing rapid write-off of asset costs over predetermined periods, generally shorter than the estimated useful lives of the assets. The system remains in effect for assets placed in service between 1981 and 1986 but was modified by the Tax Reform Act of 1986 for assets placed in service after 1986. *See* Modified Accelerated Cost Recovery System.

Accelerated depreciation: An accounting procedure under which larger amounts of expense are apportioned to the earlier years of an asset's depreciable life and lesser amounts to the later years.

Accounting period: The length of time covered for reporting accounting information.

Accounting principles: The methods and procedures used in preparing financial statements.

Accounts payable: Amounts owed to creditors for items or services purchased from them.

Accounts receivable: Amounts owed to an entity, primarily by its trade customers.

Accounts receivable turnover: *See* Summary of financial ratios, Appendix E.

Accrual basis of accounting: A method of earnings determination under which revenues are recognized in the accounting period when earned, regardless of when cash is received; and expenses are recognized in the period incurred, regardless of when cash is paid.

Accrued liabilities: Obligations resulting from the recognition of an expense prior to the payment of cash.

Accumulated depreciation: A balance sheet account indicating the amount of depreciation expense taken on plant and equipment up to the balance sheet date.

Acid-test ratio: *See* Summary of financial ratios, Appendix E.

Activity ratio: A ratio that measures the liquidity of specific assets and the efficiency of the firm in managing assets.

Additional paid-in-capital: The amount by which the original sales price of stock shares sold exceeds the par value of the stock.

Adverse opinion: Opinion rendered by an independent auditor stating that the financial statements have not been presented fairly in accordance with generally accepted accounting principles.

Allowance for doubtful accounts: The balance sheet account that measures the amount of outstanding accounts receivable expected to be uncollectable.

Amortization: The process of expense allocation applied to the cost expiration of intangible assets.

Annual report: The report to shareholders published by a firm; contains information required by generally accepted accounting principles an/or by specific Securities and Exchange Commission requirements.

Assets: Items possessing service or use potential to owner.

Auditor's report: Report by independent auditor attesting to the fairness of the financial statements of a company.

Average collection period: *See* Summary of financial ratios, Appendix E.

Average cost method: A method of valuing inventory and cost of products sold; all costs, including those in beginning inventory, are added together and divided by the total number of units to arrive at a cost per unit.

Balance sheet: The financial statement that shows the financial condition of a company on a particular date.

Balancing Equation: Assets = Liabilities + Stockholders' Equity.

Book value: *See* Net book value of capital assets.

Calendar year: The year starting January 1 and ending December 31.

Capital assets: *See* Fixed assets.

Capital in excess of par value: See Additional paid-in-capital.

Capital lease: A leasing arrangement that is, in substance, a purchase by the lessee, who accounts for the lease as an acquisition of an asset and the incurrence of a liability.

Capital structure: The permanent long-term financing of a firm represented by long-term debt, preferred stock, common stock, and retained earnings.

Capitalize: The process in which initial expenditures are included in the cost of assets and allocated over the period of service.

Cash basis of accounting: A method of accounting under which revenues are recorded when cash is received and expenses are recognized when cash is paid.

Cash conversion cycle: The amount of time (expressed in days) required to sell inventory and collect accounts receivable, less the number of days credit extended by suppliers.

Cash equivalents: Security investments that are readily converted to cash.

Cash flow from financing activities: On the statement of cash flows, cash generated from/used by financing activities.

Cash flow from investing activities: On the statement of cash flows, cash generated from/used by investing activities.

Cash flow from operating activities: On the statement of cash flows, cash generated/used by operating activities.

Cash flow from operations: The amount of cash generated from/used by a business enterprise's normal, ongoing operations during an accounting period.

Cash flow liquidity ratio: *See* Summary of financial ratios, Appendix E.

Cash flow margin: *See* Summary of financial ratios, Appendix E.

Commercial paper: Unsecured promissory notes of large companies.

Common size financial statements: A form of financial ratio analysis that allows the comparison of firms with different levels of sales or total assets by introducing a common denominator. A common size balance sheet expresses each item on the balance sheet as a percentage of total assets, and a common size income statement expresses each item as a percentage of net sales.

Common stock: Shares of stock representing ownership in a company.

Complex capital structure: Capital structures including convertible securities, stock options, and warrants.

Conservatism: The accounting concept holding that in selecting among accounting methods the choice should be the one with the least favorable effect on the firm.

Consolidation: The combination of financial statements for two or more separate legal entities when one company, the parent, owns more than 50% of the voting stock of the other company or companies.

Constant dollar approach: An approach to adjust items for inflation by applying the change in a general price index; also called general price level.

Contra-asset account: An account shown as a deduction from the asset to which it relates in the balance sheet.

Convertible securities: Securities that can be converted or exchanged for another type of security, typically common stock.

Cost flow assumption: An assumption regarding the order in which inventory is sold; used to value cost of goods sold and ending inventory.

Cost method: A procedure to account for investments in the voting stock of other companies under which the investor recognizes investment income only to the extent of any cash dividends received.

Cost of goods sold: The cost to the seller of products sold to customers.

Cost of goods sold percentage: The percentage of cost of goods sold to net sales.

Cost of sales: *See* Cost of goods sold.

Cumulative effect of change in accounting principle: The difference in the actual amount of retained earnings at the beginning of the period in which a change in accounting principle is instituted and the amount of retained earnings that would have been reported at that date if the new accounting principle had been applied retroactively for all prior periods.

Cumulative translation adjustment: Adjustment to the equity section of the balance sheet resulting from the translation of foreign financial statements.

Current (assets/liabilities): Items expected to be converted into cash or paid out in cash in one year or one operating cycle, whichever is longer.

Current cost approach: An approach to adjusting items for inflation by applying the specific price change of each asset.

Current maturities of long-term debt: The portion of long-term debt that will be repaid during the upcoming year.

Current ratio: *See* Summary of financial ratios, Appendix E.

Debt ratio: *See* Summary of financial ratios, Appendix E.

Debt to equity ratio: *See* Summary of financial ratios, Appendix E.

Defeasance: An accounting technique for the early extinguishment of debt by which a firm purchases at a discount riskless securities (U.S. government securities or securities backed by the U.S. government), places the securities in an irrevocable trust to meet interest and principal payments on outstanding debt, recognizes a gain for the difference between the principal amount of the debt and the price paid for the riskless securities, and eliminates the original liability.

Deferred method (for investment tax credit): The accounting procedure under which the benefit of the tax credit is spread over the useful life of the asset that generated the credit.

Deferred taxes: The balance sheet account that results from temporary differences in the recognition of revenue and expense for taxable income and reported income.

Depletion: The accounting procedure used to allocate the cost of acquiring and developing natural resources.

Depreciation: The accounting procedure used to allocate the cost of an asset, which will benefit a business enterprise for more than a year, over the asset's service life.

Direct method: On the statement of cash flows, a method of calculating cash flow from operating activities that shows cash collections from customers; interest and dividends collected; other operating cash receipts; cash paid to suppliers and employees; interest paid; taxes paid; and other operating cash payments.

Disclaimer of opinion: Independent auditor could not evaluate the fairness of the financial statements and, as a result, expresses no opinion on them.

Discontinued operations: The financial results of selling a major business segment.

Discretionary items: Revenues and expenses under the control of management with respect to budget levels and timing.

Dividend payout ratio: *See* Summary of financial ratios, Appendix E.

Dividend yield: *See* Summary of financial ratios, Appendix E.

Double-declining balance method: An accounting procedure for depreciation under which the straight-line rate of depreciation is doubled and applied to the net book value of the asset.

Earnings before income taxes: The profit recognized before the deduction of income taxes.

Earnings before interest and taxes: The operating profit of a firm.

Earnings per common share: *See* summary of financial ratios, Appendix E.

Earnings statement: *See* Income statement.

Equity: *See* Stockholders' equity.

Equity method: The procedure used for an investment in common stock when the investor company can exercise significant influence over the investee company; the investor recognizes investment income of the investee's net income in proportion to the percent of stock owned.

Expenses: Cost incurred to produce revenue.

Extraordinary transactions: Items that are unusual and not expected to recur in the foreseeable future.

Financial leverage: The extent to which a firm finances with debt, measured by the relationship between total debt and total assets.

Financial leverage index: The ratio of return on equity to return on assets (adjusted to exclude the effect of the method used to finance assets) which indicates whether financial leverage is being used successfully by a firm. An index of greater than 1 indicates the successful use of financial leverage.

Financial ratios: Calculations made to standardize, analyze, and compare financial data; expressed in terms of mathematical relationships in the form of percentages or times.

Financial statements: Accounting information regarding the financial position of a firm, the results of operations, and the cash flows. Four statements comprise the basic set of financial statements: the balance sheet, the income statement, the statement of retained earnings (or the statement of shareholders' equity), and the statement of cash flows.

Financing activities: On the statement of cash flows, transactions that include borrowing from creditors and repaying the principal; and obtaining resources from owners and providing them with a return on the investment.

Finished goods: Products for which the manufacturing process is complete.

First-in-first-out (FIFO): A method of valuing inventory and cost of goods sold under which the items purchased are assumed to be sold first.

Fiscal year: A 12-month period starting on a date other than January 1 and ending 12 months later.

Fixed assets: Tangible, long-lived assets that are expected to provide service benefit for more than one year.

Fixed asset turnover: *See* Summary of financial ratios, Appendix E.

Fixed charge coverage: *See* Summary of financial ratios, Appendix E.

Flow-through method (for investment tax credit): The accounting procedure under which the benefit of the tax credit is taken in the year the asset is purchased.

Form 10-K: An annual document filed with the Securities and Exchange Commission by companies that sell securities to the public.

Fully diluted earnings per share: The earnings per share figure calculated using all potentially dilutive securities in the number of shares outstanding.

General price level adjustment: An approach used to adjust items for inflation by applying the change in a general price index; also called *constant dollar.*

Generally accepted accounting principles: The accounting methods and procedures used to prepare financial statements.

Goodwill: An intangible asset representing the unrecorded assets of a firm; appears in the accounting records only if the firm is acquired for a price in excess of the fair market value of its net assets.

Gross margin: *See* Gross profit.

Gross profit: The difference between net sales and cost of goods sold.

Gross profit margin: *See* Summary of financial ratios, Appendix E.

Historical cost: The amount of cash or value of other resources used to acquire an asset; for some assets, historical cost is subject to depreciation, amortization, or depletion.

Income statement: The financial statement presenting the revenues and expenses of a business for an accounting period.

Industry comparisons: Average financial ratios compiled for industry groups.

Industry segment: *See* segment.

In-substance defeasance: See Defeasance.

Intangible assets: Assets such as goodwill that possess no physical characteristics but have value for the company.

Integrated Disclosure System: A common body of information required by the Securities and Exchange Commission for both the 10-K Report filed with the Securities and Exchange Commission and the Annual Report provided to shareholders.

Interim statements: Financial statements issued for periods shorter than one year.

Inventories: Items held for sale or used in the manufacture of products that will be sold.

Inventory turnover: *See* Summary of financial ratios, Appendix E.

Investing activities: On the statement of cash flows, transactions that include acquiring and selling, or otherwise disposing of (a) securities that are not cash equivalents and (b) productive assets that are expected to benefit the firm for long periods of time; and lending money and collecting on loans.

Investment tax credit: A tax credit (direct reduction of taxes paid) provided by tax laws for investment in capital equipment.

Last-in-first-out (LIFO): A method of valuing inventory and cost of goods sold under which the items purchased last are assumed to be sold first.

Leasehold improvement: An addition or improvement made to a leased structure.

Leverage ratio: A ratio that measures the extent of a firm's financing with debt relative to equity and its ability to cover interest and other fixed charges.

Liabilities: Claims against asset.

Line of credit: A prearranged loan allowing borrowing up to a certain maximum dollar amount.

Liquidity: The ability of a firm to generate sufficient cash to meet cash needs.

Liquidity ratio: A ratio that measures a firm's ability to meet needs for cash as they arise.

Long-term debt: Obligations with maturities longer than one year.

Long-term debt to Total Capitalization: *See* Summary of financial ratios, Appendix E.

Lower of cost or market method: A method of valuing inventory under which cost or market, whichever is lower, is selected for each item, each group, or for the entire inventory.

Management's Discussion and Analysis of the Financial Condition and Results of Operation: A section of the annual and 10-K report that is required and monitored by the Securities and Exchange Commission in which management presents a detailed coverage of the firm's liquidity, capital resources, and operations.

Marketable securities: Cash not needed immediately in the business and temporarily invested to earn a return.

Matching principle: The accounting principle holding that expenses are to be matched with the generation of revenues in order to determine net income for an accounting period.

Merchandise inventories: Goods purchased for resale to the public.

Minority interest: Claims of shareholders other than the parent company against the net assets and net income of a subsidiary company.

Modified Accelerated Cost Recovery System (MACRS): A modification of the Accelerated Tax Recovery System (ACRS) in the Tax Reform Act of 1986 for assets placed in service after 1986.

Monetary assets/liabilities: Items that are stated in terms of current value and do not need to be adjusted for inflation; include cash, marketable securities, and all liabilities other than deferred income.

Multiple-step format: A format for presenting the income statement under which several intermediate profit measures are shown.

Net assets: Total assets less total liabilities.

Net book value of capital assets: The difference between original cost of property, plant, and equipment and any accumulated depreciation to date.

Net earnings: The firm's profit or loss after consideration of all revenue and expense reported during the accounting period.

Net income: *See* Net earnings.

Net profit margin: *See* Summary of financial ratios, Appendix E.

Net Sales: Total sales revenue less sales returns and sales allowances.

Net trade cycle: *See* Cash conversion cycle.

Noncurrent assets/liabilities: Items expected to benefit the firm for/with maturities of more than one year.

Notes payable: A short-term obligation in the form of a promissory note to suppliers or financial institutions.

Notes to the financial statements: Supplementary information to financial statements that explain the firm's accounting policies and provide detail about particular accounts and other information, for example, pension plans.

Off balance sheet financing: Financial techniques for raising funds that do not have to be recorded as liabilities on the balance sheet.

Operating activities: On the statement of cash flows, transactions that include delivering or producing goods for sale and providing services; the cash effects of transactions and other events that enter into the determination of income.

Operating cycle: The time required to purchase or manufacture inventory, sell the product, and collect the cash.

Operating expenses: Costs related to the normal functions of a business.

Operating lease: A rental agreement where no ownership rights are transferred to the lessee at the termination of the rental contract.

Operating profit: Sales revenue less the expenses associated with generating sales. Operating profit measures the overall performance of a company on its normal, on-going operations.

Operating profit margin: *See* Summary of financial ratios, Appendix E.

Options: *See* Stock options.

Par value: The floor price below which stock cannot be sold initially.

Plant and equipment: *See* Fixed assets.

Preferred stock: Capital stock of a company that carries certain privileges or rights not carried by all outstanding shares of stock.

Prepaid expenses: Expenditures made in the current or prior period that will benefit the firm at some future time.

Price-earnings ratio: *See* Summary of financial ratios, Appendix E.

Primary earnings per share: The earnings per share figure calculated on the assumption that only some of the potentially dilutive securities have been converted into common stock.

Principal: The original amount of a liability.

Prior period adjustment: A change in the retained earnings balance primarily resulting from the correction of errors made in previous accounting periods.

Pro forma financial statements: Projections of future financial statements based on a set of assumptions regarding future revenues, expenses, level of investment in assets, financing methods and costs, and working capital management.

Profitability ratio: A ratio that measures the overall performance of a firm and its efficiency in managing assets, liabilities, and equity.

Property, plant, and equipment: *See* Fixed assets.

Publicly held companies: Companies that operate to earn a profit and issue shares of stock to the public.

Qualified opinion: An opinion rendered by an independent auditor when the overall financial statements are fairly presented "except for" certain items (which the auditor discloses).

Quality of financial reporting: A subjective evaluation of the extent to which financial reporting is free of manipulation and accurately reflects the financial condition and operating success of a business.

Quick ratio: *See* Summary of financial ratios, Appendix E.

Raw materials: Basic commodities or natural resources that will be used in the production of goods.

Replacement cost: The estimated cost of acquiring new and substantially equivalent property at current prices.

Reported income: The net income published in financial statements.

Retained earnings: The sum of every dollar a company has earned since its inception, less any payments made to shareholders in the form of cash or stock dividends.

Return on assets: *See* Return on investment.

Return on equity: *See* Summary of financial ratios, Appendix E.

Return on investment: Measures overall efficiency of firm in managing assets and generating profits.

Revenue: The inflow of assets resulting from the sale of goods or services.

Sales allowance: A deduction from the original sales invoice price.

Sales return: A cancellation of a sale.

Salvage value: The amount of an asset estimated to be recoverable at the conclusion of the asset's service life.

Segment: A component of a business enterprise that sells primarily to outside markets and for which information about revenue and profit is accumulated.

Segment operating expenses: Expenses relating to unaffiliated customers and segment revenue; expenses not directly traceable to segments are allocated to segments on a reasonable basis.

Segment operating profit/loss: Segment revenue less all operating expenses.

Segment revenue: Sales of products and services to unaffiliated customers and intersegment sales, with company transfer prices used to determine sales between segments.

Selling and administrative expenses: Costs relating to the sale of products or services and to the management function of the firm.

Short-term: Generally indicates maturity of less than a year.

Single-step format: A format for presenting the income statement under which all items of revenue are grouped together and then all items of expense are deducted to arrive at net income.

Stated value: The floor price below which stock cannot be sold initially; *see also* par value.

Statement of cash flows: The financial statement that provides information about the cash inflows and outflows from operating, financing, and investing activities during an accounting period.

Statement of retained earnings: The financial statement that presents the details of the transactions affecting the retained earnings account during an accounting period.

Statement of shareholders' equity: A financial statement that summarizes changes in the shareholders' equity section of the balance sheet during an accounting period.

Stock dividends: The issuance of additional shares of stock to existing shareholders in proportion to current ownership.

Stock options: A contract that conveys the right to purchase shares of stock at a specified price within a specified time period.

Stockholders' equity: Claims against assets by the owners of the business; represents the amount owners have invested including income retained in the business since inception.

Straight-line depreciation: An accounting procedure under which equal amounts of expense are apportioned to each year of an asset's life.

Structural analysis: Analysis looking at the internal structure of a business.

Summary of financial ratios: *See* Appendix E.

Tangible: Having physical substance.

Taxable income: The net income figure used to determine taxes payable to governments.

Temporary differences: Differences between pre-tax accounting income and taxable income caused by reporting items of revenue or expense in one period for accounting purposes and in an earlier or later period for income tax purposes.

Times interest earned: *See* Summary of financial ratios, Appendix E.

Total asset turnover: *See* Summary of financial ratios, Appendix E.

Treasury stock: Shares of a company's stock that are repurchased by the company and not retired.

Trend analysis: Evaluation of financial data over several accounting periods.

Units-of-production method: An accounting method under which depreciation expense is based on actual usage.

Unqualified opinion: An opinion rendered by an independent auditor of financial statements stating that the financial statements have been presented fairly in accordance with generally accepted accounting principles.

Unrealized gains (losses) on marketable equity securities: The gains (losses) disclosed in the equity section resulting from the accounting rule that requires investments in marketable equity securities to be carried at the lower of cost or market value.

Warrant: A certificate issued by a corporation that conveys the right to buy a stated number of shares of stock at a specified price on or before a predetermined date.

Work-in-process: Products for which the manufacturing process is only partially completed.

Working capital: The amount by which current assets exceed current liabilities.

INDEX